GCSE AQA
Spanish

It's time to say 'Bienvenido' to this brilliant all-in-one guide for GCSE AQA Spanish.

We've covered every topic on the course, including all the vocab and grammar you'll need. Plus, there are exam-style questions, full practice papers and even some handy exam advice to help you prepare.

This book also includes online revision in the CGP RevisionHub. You'll find quick quizzes, summary tests, audio, Q&A videos and more in the Hub — all matched to your book! You can't say we don't treat you well...

Unlock CGP RevisionHub

Just scan a QR code in the book to access the CGP RevisionHub.
Or go to **cgpbooks.co.uk/revise** and enter this code!

0101 3494 7758 3982

By the way, this code only works for one person. If somebody else has used this book before you, they might have already claimed the code.

Complete
Revision & Practice
with new CGP RevisionHub

Published by CGP

Editors:
Siân Butler
Daniel Chapero-Hall
Becca Clifford
Elliott Garraway
Brooke McCreight
Hannah Roscoe
Matt Topping

Contributors:
Matthew Parkinson
Jacqui Richards

With thanks to Encarna Aparicio-Dominguez, Rebecca Greaves, Rose Jones, Gail Partington, Sabrina Robinson, Suzanne Rose
and Rebecca Russell for the proofreading.
With thanks to Alice Dent for the copyright research.

Acknowledgements:
Audio produced by Voice Talent Online.

AQA material is reproduced by permission of AQA.
The worked solutions to questions and commentaries on questions and possible answers
in this book have neither been provided by nor approved by AQA.

iPad is a trademark of Apple Inc., registered in the U.S. and other countries.

ISBN: 978 1 83774 126 7
Printed by W&G Baird Ltd, Antrim.
Clipart from Corel®

Based on the classic CGP style created by Richard Parsons.

Contents

Contents

Theme 3: Communication and the world around us

Contents

Grammar

How to Use this Book

This isn't a book. Or rather, this isn't *just* a book. It's full of online resources designed to help you get top marks. To learn how it all works, read these pages or scan the QR code for a walkthrough.

This book follows the AQA specification

1) The content for AQA GCSE Spanish is divided into <u>nine topics</u>.
   Each topic falls under one of <u>three themes</u>:

People and lifestyle	Popular culture	Communication and the world around us

2) In this book, there is usually <u>one</u> section for each topic. However, some topics have been <u>split into two sections</u> to make things more manageable.

3) There are also three <u>grammar sections</u> that cover the grammar you need to know.

4) The resources on the <u>CGP RevisionHub</u> are split up in the same way as the book.

There's also a 'General Stuff' topic in the book and online with content that's useful across the course.

The CGP RevisionHub is full of resources

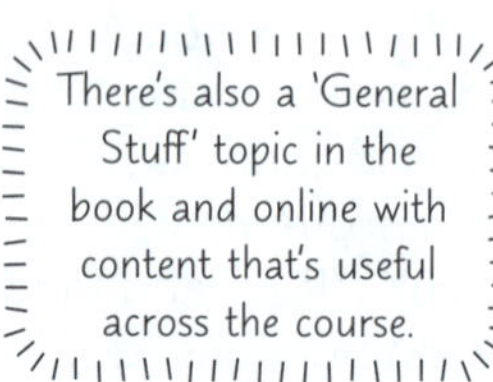

- You can use the online resources on the CGP RevisionHub <u>alongside this book</u> as you're revising.

- There's <u>audio</u>, <u>quick quizzes</u> and <u>summary tests</u>, as well as printable <u>vocab lists</u>, <u>transcripts</u> and <u>practice papers</u>.

There are resources for Foundation tier <u>and</u> Higher tier on the CGP RevisionHub. The Hub is automatically set to Higher, but you can <u>switch to Foundation</u> to only see Foundation content.

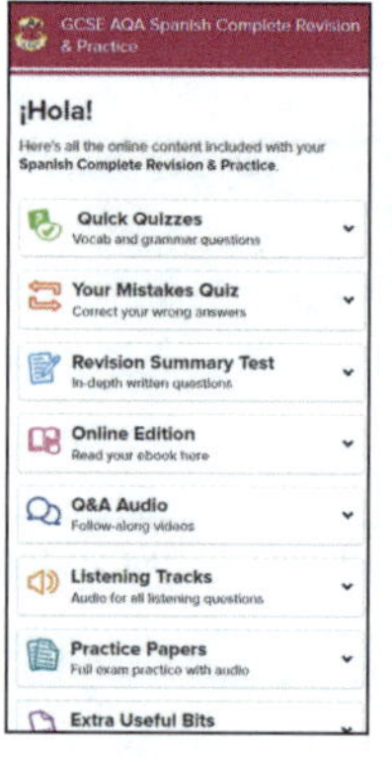

Scan this QR code to access the CGP RevisionHub, or if you're on a computer, go to www.cgpbooks.co.uk/Madrid.

Get exam-style practice

1) In your exams, you can sit <u>Foundation-tier</u> or <u>Higher-tier</u> papers.

2) In each tier, there are <u>four</u> papers: <u>Listening</u>, <u>Speaking</u>, <u>Reading</u> and <u>Writing</u>. You have to choose the <u>same tier</u> for all four papers.

For more about the exams, see p.198-201.

- In <u>Foundation tier</u>, there's <u>less vocabulary</u> and <u>less grammar</u> to learn and the questions are slightly easier. In this tier, you can earn up to <u>Grade 5</u>.

- In <u>Higher tier</u>, you can achieve <u>Grades 4-9</u>, but you'll need to learn <u>more vocab</u> and <u>more complex grammar</u>.

3) Throughout this book, there's practice for all the <u>question types</u> in the exam. Plus, there are full <u>Higher-tier practice papers</u> on pages 202-233. These can also be found on the CGP RevisionHub alongside <u>Foundation-tier practice papers</u>.

4) Most of this book is <u>helpful for both tiers</u>, but some vocab and questions have been <u>marked with a bracket</u> if they only apply to one tier.

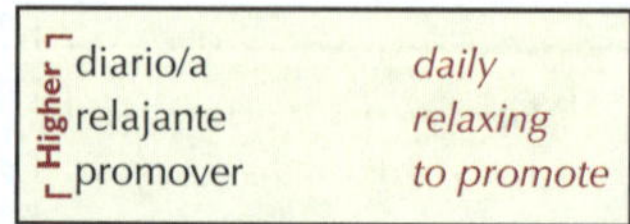

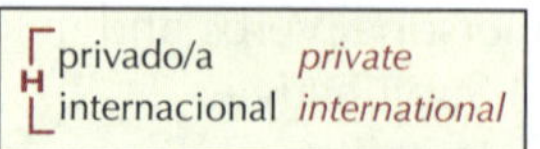

5) If you aren't sure <u>which tier</u> to take, trying out the questions should help <u>you and your teacher</u> make a <u>decision</u>.

Learn the set vocabulary

- The AQA specification contains a <u>list</u> of words you could be tested on in your <u>Listening</u> and <u>Reading</u> papers, depending on your tier.
- This vocab will also help you in your <u>Speaking</u> and <u>Writing</u> papers. In these two papers, you can use non-specification vocab, too.
- The <u>key vocab</u> is on the main pages of each section. At the end of each section, there's a <u>list</u> of all the vocab relevant to the topic. Every word on the specification is on <u>at least one</u> of these lists.
- There are <u>printable versions</u> of these lists on the CGP RevisionHub.

Practise your listening skills

1) In this book, you'll find <u>questions and example answers</u>:

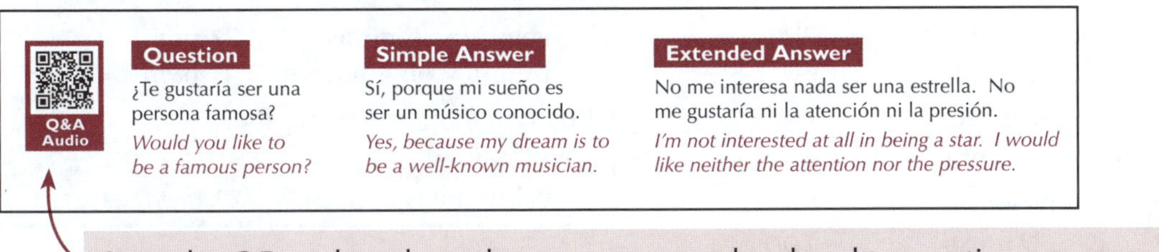

Scan the QR code to hear the sentences out loud and to practise your pronunciation.

2) There are also QR codes that take you to <u>Listening Tracks</u>. Each track <u>comes with questions</u> that test you on what you've heard.

Test your knowledge

Quick Quizzes

- The <u>QR codes</u> at the top of the page take you to a <u>quick quiz</u>.
- These <u>quizzes</u> test you on the <u>vocab</u> (or the <u>grammar</u> in Sections 13-15) on that page.
- They're a great way to keep your knowledge <u>fresh</u>.
- You can easily revisit questions that you answer incorrectly by doing the '<u>Your Mistakes</u>' quiz.

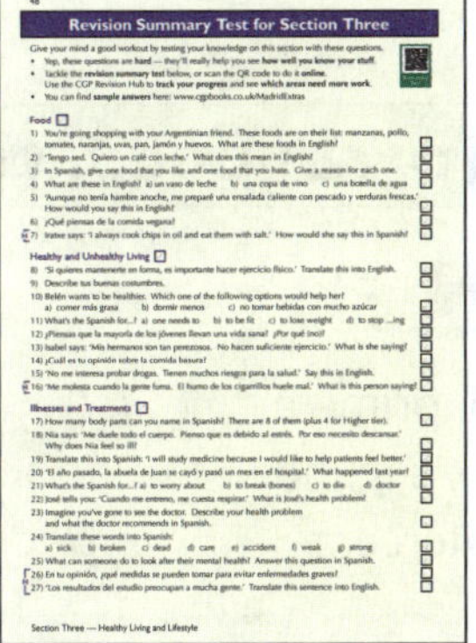

Revision Summary Tests

- For more of a challenge, try a <u>revision summary test</u>. These are found at the end of each section.
- These tests cover the <u>most important information</u> in a topic and are a good way to see <u>how much</u> you can <u>remember</u>.
- You can do these tests on <u>paper</u> or you can complete them <u>online</u>. Online, you can find <u>sample answers</u>, <u>assess your progress</u>, and look at <u>previous topics</u> to see the areas you need to work on.

Fun fact — if you rearrange the letters of 'RevisionHub', you get...

...'SnoivierUbh', which makes no sense. But do you know what *does* make sense? Using the RevisionHub alongside this book — it'll help you to get the most out of your revision and impress all those examiners.

Numbers and Times

Knowing how to say and spell your Spanish numbers is very important.

Uno, dos, tres — One, two, three

Vocabulary

cero	0	veinte, veinti-	20
uno	1	veintiuno	21
dos	2	veintidós	22
tres	3	veintitrés	23
cuatro	4	treinta	30
cinco	5	treinta y uno	31
seis	6	cuarenta	40
siete	7	cincuenta	50
ocho	8	sesenta	60
nueve	9	setenta	70
diez	10	ochenta	80
once	11	noventa	90
doce	12	cien(to)	100
trece	13	ciento uno	101
catorce	14	doscientos	200
quince	15	quinientos	500
dieciséis	16	setecientos	700
diecisiete	17	novecientos	900
dieciocho	18	mil	1000
diecinueve	19	un millón	1 000 000

All twenty-something numbers are rolled into one — like 'veintiuno' (twenty-one). After 30, numbers are joined by 'y' (and), but written separately — like 'treinta y uno' (thirty-one).

Grammar — using 'one' with masculine nouns

When you put '<u>one</u>' in front of a <u>masculine</u> word, uno becomes 'un'.

veintiún alumnos   *21 pupils*
treinta y <u>un</u> alumnos   *31 pupils*

Before a <u>feminine</u> word, the '<u>o</u>' changes to '<u>a</u>':

veintiun<u>a</u> naranjas   *21 oranges*

See p.151 for more on masculine and feminine nouns.

'Cien' becomes 'ciento' when used in front of another number (except 'mil').

mil ochocientos veintiséis	1826
mil novecientos ochenta y cuatro	1984
dos mil once	2011

Quiero cinco manzanas, por favor.	*I want five apples, please.*
Tenemos treinta y tres bolígrafos.	*We have 33 pens.*
Hay ciento veintiún alumnos.	*There are 121 students.*
Nací en dos mil diez.	*I was born in 2010.*

Primero, segundo, tercero — First, second, third

Vocabulary

primero, primera	*1st*
segundo, segunda	*2nd*
tercero, tercera	*3rd*

Grammar — 'primero', 'tercero' + masculine nouns

You can <u>drop</u> the 'o' at the end of '<u>primero</u>' or '<u>tercero</u>' when they appear in front of a masculine word.

el <u>primer</u> baile   *the <u>first</u> dance*
el <u>tercer</u> cantante   *the <u>third</u> singer*

Vivo en la primera planta del edificio.	*I live on the first floor of the building.*
Mi hermano terminó en el tercer lugar.	*My brother finished in third place.*

¿Qué hora es? — What time is it?

Vocabulary

Es la...	*It's...*
Son las...	*It's...*
el cuarto	*quarter (used in time expressions)*
medio/a	*half*
el segundo	*second*
el minuto	*minute*
la hora	*hour, time (specific)*

Grammar — at / it's X o'clock

To say '<u>at X o'clock</u>', you need '<u>a</u>':

a la una	at **one o'clock**
a las ocho	at **eight o'clock**

'La' changes to 'las' for anything other than 'one o'clock'.

To say '<u>it's X o'clock</u>', use '<u>es</u>' or '<u>son</u>':

es la una	**it's** one o'clock
son las ocho	**it's** eight o'clock

'Es' changes to 'son' for anything other than 'one o'clock'.

Es la una y media.	*It's half past one.*
Es la una menos veinte.	*It's twenty to one.*
Son las ocho y cinco.	*It's five past eight.*
Son las cinco y cuarto.	*It's quarter past five.*

five to — menos cinco

quarter to — menos cuarto

Instead of saying 'to' when telling the time in Spanish, you use 'menos' ('less' or 'minus'). So 'Son las cinco menos diez' literally means 'It's five o'clock minus ten'.

The 24-hour clock

The <u>24-hour clock</u> is also used in many Spanish-speaking countries, so make sure you can tell the time <u>both</u> ways.

(Son) <u>las veintiuna horas</u> treinta minutos.	(It's) <u>21</u>.**30**.
(Son) <u>las tres horas</u> catorce minutos.	(It's) <u>03</u>.**14**.
(Son) <u>las diecinueve horas</u> cincuenta y cinco minutos.	(It's) <u>19</u>.**55**.

The only time Max cares about is nap time.

Practice Questions

Q1 Read the text and answer the questions in English.

> Laia tiene veintidós años. Su hermana solo tiene diecisiete años, pero su abuelo tiene ochenta y ocho años. Laia vive muy cerca — en la segunda calle a la derecha.

e.g. *How old is Laia?*   She is 22.

a) How old is Laia's sister?   *[1 mark]*

b) How old is Laia's grandad?   *[1 mark]*

c) On which street does Laia live?   *[1 mark]*

Q2 Ignacio is talking about his routine. What does he normally do?
Write A if only statement A is correct. Write B if only statement B is correct.
Write A + B if both statements A and B are correct.

Listening Track 01

a) Ignacio normally wakes up...

    A. at half past seven.   **B.** at nine o'clock.   *[1 mark]*

b) At quarter to ten, Ignacio...

    A. reads his book.   **B.** gets out of bed.   *[1 mark]*

c) Ignacio prefers to...

    A. have a wash before breakfast.   **B.** eat breakfast at half past ten.   *[1 mark]*

Higher

First things first — learn your numbers...

They might be a basic topic, but numbers are very important. Once you've mastered them, you'll be able to do things like tell the time, give your birthday and ask for different quantities of things when you go shopping.

Times and Dates

Time to learn some really useful phrases which are sure to get you good marks in your Spanish GCSE.

Los momentos del día — Times of the day

Vocabulary

la mañana	*morning*	mañana	*tomorrow*
la tarde	*afternoon, evening*	ayer	*yesterday*
la noche	*night, evening*	anoche	*last night*
por la mañana	*in the morning*	pasado/a	*past, last*
por la tarde	*in the afternoon / evening*	siguiente	*following, next*
por la noche	*at night, in the evening*	a veces	*sometimes*
esta noche	*tonight*	antes	*before, beforehand*
hoy	*today*	después	*after, afterwards*

You need to add 'de' after 'antes' or 'después' if you want to say before or after something. E.g. say 'después de la fiesta', not just 'después la fiesta'.

Iré a España mañana por la mañana.	*I will go to Spain tomorrow morning.*
Esta mañana fui al castillo.	*This morning I went to the castle.*
Perdió su mochila la semana pasada.	*He lost his rucksack last week.*
Juego al fútbol por la mañana.	*I play football in the morning.*

next week — la semana que viene
the following week — la semana siguiente
in the afternoon — por la tarde

Question

¿Qué haces el fin de semana?
What do you do at the weekend?

Simple Answer

Me gusta salir con mis amigos el fin de semana.
I like to go out with my friends at the weekend.

Extended Answer

A veces me gusta salir con mis amigos el fin de semana, pero prefiero descansar o leer si estoy cansada.
Sometimes I like to go out with my friends at the weekend, but I prefer to relax or read if I am tired.

Los días de la semana — The days of the week

Days of the week are always masculine and lower case.

Vocabulary

la fecha	*date (in calendar), day*	lunes	*Monday*	viernes	*Friday*
el día	*day*	martes	*Tuesday*	sábado	*Saturday*
la semana	*week*	miércoles	*Wednesday*	domingo	*Sunday*
el fin de semana	*(at the) weekend*	jueves	*Thursday*		

Voy al centro comercial los sábados para ir de compras con mis amigos.	*I go to the shopping centre on Saturdays to go shopping with my friends.*
Intento salir todos los días. Paseo al perro después del colegio.	*I try to go out every day. I walk the dog after school.*
Fui a la biblioteca ayer porque tengo un examen de inglés el miércoles.	*I went to the library yesterday because I have an English exam on Wednesday.*
Suelo descansar los domingos.	*I tend to relax on Sundays.*

You don't translate 'at' here — you just say 'the weekend'.

at the weekend — el fin de semana

on Friday afternoons — los viernes por la tarde

Los meses del año — The months of the year

Vocabulary

enero	*January*	abril	*April*	julio	*July*	octubre	*October*
febrero	*February*	mayo	*May*	agosto	*August*	noviembre	*November*
marzo	*March*	junio	*June*	septiembre	*September*	diciembre	*December*

Voy a la playa todos los años en agosto.	*I go to the beach every year in August.*
En enero, iremos de vacaciones.	*In January, we will go on holiday.*
Mi hermano menor nació en abril.	*My younger brother was born in April.*

¿Qué fecha es? — What's the date?

In English, you say 'the third of May' or 'the twentieth of December'. In Spanish, you can say either 'el primero de' or 'el uno de' for the first of the month, but for all the other dates, you say 'the three of May' or 'the twenty of December'...

el tres de mayo	*(on) the third of May*
el veinte de diciembre	*(on) the twentieth of December*
Es el uno de / el primero de febrero.	*It's the first of February.*
Es el dos de octubre de dos mil veinticuatro.	*It's the second of October 2024.*

Practice Questions

Q1 *Read aloud the following text in Spanish.* [5 marks]

SPEAKING

Mi cumpleaños es lunes el quince de agosto. Quiero tener una fiesta grande con mis amigos. Siempre me gusta pasar tiempo con ellos. Mañana a las seis, tengo que llamar a mi restaurante favorito. Quiero reservar una mesa que está al lado de la cocina.

Answer the following questions in Spanish.

a) ¿Cuándo es tu cumpleaños?
b) Describe tu fiesta perfecta.
c) ¿Qué te gusta hacer con tus amigos?
d) ¿Qué vas a hacer mañana? [10 marks]

Q2 *Listen to what Carlos, Anabel and Julia have to say, and then answer the questions in English.*

e.g. *How often does Carlos go to the gym?* *Every day.*
a) When was Anabel's birthday meal? *[1 mark]*
b) Where did Anabel go last week? *[1 mark]*
c) When is Julia going to the theatre? *[1 mark]*

Remember — Spanish days and months **don't** need capitals...

It might be tempting to put capital letters everywhere you'd expect to see them in English, but it's best avoided. Lots of Spanish words don't actually need them — even the word 'Spanish' (write 'español', not 'Español').

Questions

Knowing about questions will come in handy in your speaking test — you'll have to understand what you're being asked in the role-play and in the reading aloud task. Best to be prepared.

Question marks and tone of voice

To turn a statement into a question, put an <u>upside down question mark</u> at the <u>beginning</u> and a <u>normal one</u> at the <u>end</u>.

When speaking, <u>raise your voice</u> at the <u>end</u> of the sentence to show you're asking a question.

Literally: 'Your dress is blue?'

¿Tu vestido es azul?	*Is your dress blue?*

¿Tienes un coche?	*Do you have a car?*

Literally: 'You have a car?'

¿Qué... — What...?

If your question starts with '<u>What...</u>', you normally need to start it with '<u>¿Qué...</u>' in Spanish.

¿Qué comes por la mañana?	*What do you eat in the morning?*

¿Qué quieres hacer el fin de semana?	*What do you want to do at the weekend?*

Go back to p.6-7 for more time phrases.

¿Cuál... — Which one..? What...?

1) '<u>¿Cuál...</u>' normally means '<u>Which...</u>' or '<u>Which one...</u>':

¿Cuál quieres?	*Which (one) do you want?*

2) However, sometimes you might need to use '<u>¿Cuál...</u>' even if you'd use '<u>What...</u>' in English. This is usually when you use the verb '<u>ser</u>' and you're asking for a <u>piece of information</u>, rather than a definition.

¿Cuál es tu problema?	*What is your problem?*

¿Cuál es tu dirección?	*What is your address?*

¿Cuándo? ¿Por qué? ¿Dónde? — When? Why? Where?

There are <u>lots of other words</u> you can use to <u>begin a question</u> — get them <u>all</u> learnt.

Vocabulary

¿Cuándo?	*When?*	¿Dónde?	*Where?*	¿Cuánto/a?	*How much?*	¿Quién(es)?	*Who?*
¿Por qué?	*Why?*	¿Cómo?	*How?*	¿Cuántos/as?	*How many?*	¿Cuál(es)?	*Which?*

¿Cuántos/as tienes?	*How many do you have?*
¿Por qué haces eso?	*Why are you doing that?*
¿De dónde eres?	*Where are you from?*
¿Cuál prefieres?	*Which do you prefer?*

Remember that question words need accents.

Question words like this are known as interrogatives. See p.157.

Tengo una pregunta — I have a question

Here are some of the <u>most common ways</u> you can use the <u>question words</u>.

¿**Cuándo** es tu cumpleaños? *When is your birthday?*

¿**Cuántos** años tienes? *How old are you?*

¿**Cuánto** cuesta(n)? *How much does it (do they) cost?*

Q&A Audio

Question

¿Cuánto cuesta ir al cine?
How much does it cost to go to the cinema?

Simple Answer

Cuesta diecisiete euros.
It costs seventeen euros.

Extended Answer

Cuesta diecisiete euros, cincuenta céntimos. Es muy caro, por eso prefiero ver las películas en casa.
It costs seventeen euros, fifty cents. It's very expensive, so I prefer to watch films at home.

Grammar (Higher only) — prepositions in questions

If you need to include a <u>preposition</u> (see p.158) in your question, it should come before the question word. Prepositions should never go at the end of a question in Spanish.

¿**Con** quién hablas? *Who are you talking <u>to</u>? (literally 'With whom are you talking?')*

¿**Para** qué te entrenas? *What are you training <u>for</u>? (literally 'For what are you training?')*

Practice Questions

Q1 *Read Carla and Olaya's role-play. Then, use the instructions on the role-play card to prepare your own role-play. You should address your friend as 'tú'. Aim to speak for about one and a half minutes.*

SPEAKING

Olaya:	¿Cuántas veces haces deporte a la semana?
Carla:	Juego al fútbol dos veces a la semana. Y tú, ¿qué deportes haces?
Olaya:	Me gusta nadar y voy a la piscina cada semana. ¿Qué piensas de la televisión?
Carla:	Me gusta la tele porque me ayuda a descansar.
Olaya:	Ahora, háblame de los libros que te gustan.
Carla:	Me gusta leer libros románticos. Me hacen feliz.
Olaya:	¿Hay alguna actividad que te gustaría probar?
Carla:	Me gustaría aprender a tocar la guitarra.

You are talking to your Spanish friend.

1. *Say how often you play sports.*
2. **?** *Ask what sports they do.*
3. *Say what you think about TV.*
4. *Say what sort of books you like.*
5. *Say an activity you would like to try in your free time.*

When you see '?', you need to ask a question.

[10 marks]

Q2 *Translate these sentences into Spanish.*

WRITING

a) *Which laptop should I buy?*

b) *Who were you dancing with?*

c) *How many TV channels are there?*

d) *What are you talking about?*

[8 marks]

Higher

To learn Spanish or not to learn Spanish, that is the question...

Learning the Spanish question words is really important, and not just for in your speaking exam — they'll also help you get out of tricky situations, such as getting lost, when using your Spanish out in the real world.

Being Polite

Being polite is an important part of the speaking test — so mind your manners with these tips.

Tú y usted — Informal and formal 'you'

Grammar — 'tú' and 'usted'

In Spanish, there are <u>four</u> different ways of saying '<u>you</u>' depending on how formal you want to be.

Tú	Vosotros/as	Usted	Ustedes
Informal singular 'you'. For <u>one person</u> who's your <u>friend</u>, a <u>family member</u> or of a <u>similar age</u>.	Informal plural 'you'. For a group of <u>two or more people</u> that you <u>know</u>. Only use 'vosotras' if everyone you're talking to is <u>female</u>.	Formal singular 'you'. For <u>one person</u> that is <u>older than you</u> or someone you <u>don't know</u>.	Formal plural 'you'. For a group of <u>two or more people</u> that you <u>don't know</u>.

Ewe better learn these...

So, there are <u>four different ways</u> to ask a question like 'Where are <u>you</u> from?':

Tú	Vosotros/as	Usted	Ustedes
¿De dónde eres?	¿De dónde sois?	¿De dónde es?	¿De dónde son?

You need to use the 'he/she/it' part of the verb for 'usted' (see p.175-195). For 'ustedes', use the 'they' part of the verb.

Hola y adiós — Hello and goodbye

You can also say '¿Cómo estás?' (informal) or '¿Cómo está?' (formal) to ask how someone is.

Vocabulary

hola	*hello, hi*	¿Qué tal?	*How are you? (informal)*	mal	*badly*
buenos días	*good morning*	bien	*well*	adiós	*goodbye*

Question
¿Qué tal?
How are you?

Simple Answer
Bien, gracias.
Well, thanks.

Extended Answer
Me siento fatal. Tengo dolor de cabeza.
I feel terrible. I've got a headache.

See p.40 for more illnesses.

Le presento a... — May I introduce...?

You need to know two things in order to introduce someone: the verb '<u>presentar</u>' and an indirect object pronoun — usually '<u>te</u>' (informal) or '<u>le</u>' (formal).

'Este/Esta es...' ('This is...') is another way to introduce someone.

Shula:	Hola Señora Valls. ¿Cómo está?	*Hello Señora Valls. How are you?*
Señora Valls:	Muy bien, gracias.	*Very well, thank you.*
Shula:	Le presento a mi novio, Arturo.	*May I introduce my boyfriend Arturo?*
Señora Valls:	Encantada.	*Pleased to meet you.*
Arturo:	Encantado.	*Pleased to meet you.*
Señora Valls:	Lo siento, tengo que irme. ¡Hasta luego!	*I'm sorry, I have to go. See you soon!*
Shula & Arturo:	¡Adiós!	*Goodbye!*

Shula is using the 'usted' form because Señora Valls is older than her.

Señora Valls says 'Encantad<u>a</u>' because she is female.

Arturo says 'Encantad<u>o</u>' because he is male.

See you on Monday! — ¡Hasta el lunes!
See you tomorrow! — ¡Hasta mañana!

Por favor y gracias — Please and thank you

Vocabulary

por favor	*please*	vale	*OK*	lo siento	*I'm sorry, I apologise*
gracias	*thanks, thank you*	claro	*of course*	¡Perdón!	*Sorry!*

¿Me puedes ayudar, por favor?	*Can you help me, please?*
Sí, claro.	*Yes, of course.*
¡Perfecto! ¡Muchas gracias!	*Perfect! Thank you very much!*
¡No te preocupes!	*No worries!*

'Perdone' is the formal version of 'Perdón' — it's used to get someone's attention, e.g. when asking someone the way. 'Con permiso' is used if you want to get past someone.

You're welcome! — ¡De nada!

Quisiera... — I would like...

1) Don't just say 'I want to...' — make sure you <u>ask</u> what you would like to do <u>politely</u> using '<u>quisiera</u>' and an <u>infinitive</u>.

Quisiera hablar.	*I would like to talk.*

2) You can also ask for a specific <u>object</u> if you put a noun <u>after</u> 'quisiera'.

Quisiera un café.	*I would like a coffee.*

3) Or you can phrase what you would like to do as a question using '<u>puedo</u>' and an infinitive.

¿Puedo sentarme?	*May I sit down?*

go to the toilet — ir al baño
eat here — comer aquí

Practice Question

Q1 *Andrés is introducing his two friends Mateo and Sakura to each other.*

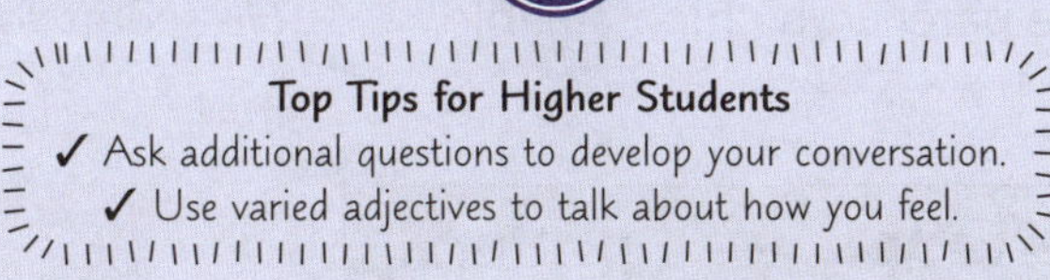

Andrés:	¡Buenos días, Mateo! ¿Qué tal?
Mateo:	Muy bien, gracias, ¿y tú?
Andrés:	Sí, bien. Esta es mi amiga, Sakura.
Mateo:	¡Hola Sakura! Encantado.
Sakura:	Encantada.
Mateo:	¿Cómo estás, Sakura?
Sakura:	No muy bien. Estoy enferma.
Mateo:	Ay, ¡qué lástima!*
Sakura:	Sí, es una pena.
Andrés:	Pues*, hasta luego, Mateo.
Mateo:	¡Adiós!

*Ay, ¡qué lástima — Oh, what a shame!
*Pues — Well

Top Tips for Higher Students
✓ Ask additional questions to develop your conversation.
✓ Use varied adjectives to talk about how you feel.

Now have a go yourself:
Write a conversation between you and your friend Diego. Write approximately 50 words in Spanish.
You should:
- *say how you both feel.*
- *introduce another friend to Diego.*
- *say what you and Diego are going to do.*

[10 marks]

Tú, vosotros, usted, ustedes — check you know them all...

If you're unsure which form to use, it's better to start with 'usted(es)' as it's politer. If whoever you're speaking to thinks 'usted' is too formal, they might say that you can 'tutear', which just means you can use the 'tú' form.

Opinions

Having opinions stops you sounding dull — but more importantly, it helps you get lots of marks.

Las opiniones — Opinions

Vocabulary

gustar	*to like, please, be pleasing (to)*	interesar	*to interest*	pensar	*to think*
		acordar	*to agree on*	parecer	*to seem*
encantar	*to love, delight, be delightful to*	de acuerdo	*in agreement*	sentir	*to feel, sense*
		odiar	*to hate*	imaginar	*to imagine*
encontrar	*to find*	creer	*to believe, think*	indicar	*to point (out)*

Grammar — 'gustar' and 'encantar'

Use '<u>me gusta</u>' and '<u>me encanta</u>' when you want to say you like or love a <u>singular</u> thing.

If you want to say you like or love a <u>plural</u> thing, <u>add</u> an '<u>n</u>' to the end.

Me gusta<u>n</u> las uvas.   **I like grapes.**   **Me encanta<u>n</u> las películas.**   **I love films.**

To say you <u>like doing an activity</u>, use an <u>infinitive</u> (see p.175) after the correct form of 'gustar' or 'encantar'.

Me gusta <u>bailar</u>.   **I like <u>dancing</u>.**   **Me encanta <u>dormir</u>.**   **I love <u>sleeping</u>.**

(No) me gustan las verduras.	*I (don't) like vegetables.*
Los idiomas (no) me interesan.	*Languages (don't) interest me.*
Encuentro la paella deliciosa.	*I find paella delicious.*
Me encantan los perros.	*I love dogs.*
¿Qué piensas de mi amigo?	*What do you think of my friend?*
Pienso que es muy simpático.	*I think he's very friendly.*
Estoy de acuerdo contigo.	*I am in agreement with you.*
Me parece un chico amable.	*He seems to me like a kind boy.*

You need an indirect object pronoun with verbs like 'gustar' because you're literally saying 'it pleases me'. See p.155 for more information.

What's your opinion of...? — ¿Cuál es tu opinión de...?

I am not in agreement — No estoy de acuerdo

shy — tímido

Prefiero... — I prefer...

If you <u>dislike</u> something, try to say what you <u>prefer</u>:

Me gusta el té, pero prefiero el café.	*I like tea, but I prefer coffee.*
No me gusta pintar — prefiero correr.	*I don't like painting — I prefer running.*

Grammar — 'preferir' is a stem-changing verb

'<u>Preferir</u>' (*to prefer*) is a <u>stem-changing verb</u> (see p.176). The second '<u>e</u>' changes to '<u>ie</u>' in the present tense:

pref**ie**ro	*I prefer*
pref**ie**res	*you prefer*
pref**ie**re	*he/she/it prefers*
pref**ie**ren	*they prefer*

The stem doesn't change for the 'we' form ('preferimos'), nor does it change for the 'you inf., pl.' form ('preferís').

Porque — Because

To start justifying your opinion, you need '<u>porque</u>' (because).

Look out, though — '<u>porque</u>' and '<u>¿por qué?</u>' <u>sound very similar</u>, but they're <u>written differently</u> and <u>mean different things</u>.

¿Por qué te gusta cocinar?	*Why do you like cooking?*
Me gusta cocinar porque...	*I like cooking because...*

(No) me gusta porque es... — I (don't) like it because it's...

Vocabulary

bueno/a	*good*	perfecto/a	*perfect*	aburrido/a	*boring*
estupendo/a	*wonderful, marvellous*	agradable	*pleasant, nice*	horrible	*horrible*
		increíble	*incredible*	malo/a	*bad*
excelente	*excellent*	bonito/a	*pretty, nice, beautiful*	maravilloso/a	*wonderful, marvellous*
genial	*great*	interesante	*interesting*		
guay	*cool*	divertido/a	*fun, enjoyable*	precioso/a	*beautiful*
emocionante	*exciting*	raro/a	*strange*	decepcionante	*disappointing*

(maravilloso/a, precioso/a and decepcionante are marked Higher)

Grammar — nouns and adjectives agree

The <u>ending</u> of the <u>adjective</u> must <u>agree</u> with the <u>noun</u> (p.165).

El libro es bueno.	***The book is good.***	'el libro' is <u>masculine</u> so 'bueno' must end in '<u>o</u>'.
La película es buena.	***The film is good.***	'la película' is <u>feminine</u> so the adjective ends in '<u>a</u>'.

Question

¿Cuál es tu opinión de esta revista?

What is your opinion of this magazine?

Simple Answer

Me gusta mucho esta revista.

I really like this magazine.

Extended Answer

Me gusta mucho esta revista porque es muy interesante. ←

I really like this magazine because it's very interesting.

If an adjective doesn't end in an 'o', it usually stays the same for both masculine and feminine nouns.

Practice Questions

Q1 *Dike and Elena are discussing the cinema. Read the dialogue and answer the questions in English.* (READING)

> **Dike**: ¿Te gusta ir al cine, Elena?
>
> **Elena**: Sí, ir al cine es muy divertido. Me gustan las películas de acción. ¿Y tú qué piensas?
>
> **Dike**: No me gusta ir al cine. Prefiero ver las películas en casa. Me encantan las comedias pero odio las películas románticas porque me parecen aburridas. ¿Qué piensas, Elena?
>
> **Elena**: Sí, estoy de acuerdo. A veces son tontas.

e.g. *Why does Elena like going to the cinema?*   Because it's fun.

a) Does Dike prefer going to the cinema or watching films at home?   *[1 mark]*

b) What is Dike's opinion of romantic films?   *[1 mark]*

c) What does Elena think of romantic films?   *[1 mark]*

Q2 *Carolina and Antonio are talking about what they do at the weekend. What are their opinions? Write P for a positive one, N for a negative one, or P+N for a positive and negative one.* (Higher)

e.g. *Carolina — swimming*   **P**

a) i) Carolina — reading   *[1 mark]*

ii) Carolina — listening to music   *[1 mark]*

b) i) Antonio — listening to music   *[1 mark]*

ii) Antonio — going out with friends   *[1 mark]*

Listening Track 03

(LISTENING)

Don't keep your opinions to yourself — share them...

Whenever you give an opinion about something, try to make sure you develop it by explaining why you like or dislike something — this will help you score better marks in both your speaking and writing exams.

Listening Questions

Having a go at some exam-style questions is a great way to make sure you're ready for the real exams.
The next four pages give you plenty of practice for the sorts of things you'll have to do in your GCSE.

1 Listen to Luisa being asked about various foods and drinks.
What is her opinion of these foods and drinks?
Write **P** for a **positive** opinion.
   N for a **negative** opinion.
   P+N for a **positive** and a **negative** opinion.

Listening Track 04

1 a Coffee

[1 mark]

1 b Eggs

[1 mark]

1 c Fish

[1 mark]

1 d Oranges

[1 mark]

1 e Sweets

[1 mark]

2 Sebastian is trying to get home to Madrid. Listen to his conversation
with the travel advice clerk, then answer the questions in **English**.

Listening Track 05

2 a Why does Sebastian want to go to Madrid?

.... *[1 mark]*

2 b Why does Sebastian have to change his travel plans?

....

.... *[1 mark]*

2 c What time will Sebastian arrive in Madrid?

.... *[1 mark]*

2 d How much money does Sebastian spend on his travel plans?

.... *[1 mark]*

Higher

Speaking Questions

Candidate's Material

- When your teacher asks you, read aloud the following text **in Spanish**.

Foundation

Hoy es el cumpleaños de mi amiga y tiene dieciséis años.

Este año, celebrará su cumpleaños el sábado.

Vamos a ir al parque temático para celebrar una fiesta.

Ha invitado a todos nuestros compañeros de clase.

Quiero comprar a mi amiga un regalo que le va a encantar.

Higher

Mi amigo siempre quiere que su cumpleaños sea una ocasión para recordar.

Acaba de reservar una mesa en un restaurante argentino para sus amigos.

Después de comer, mi amigo quiere ir a su casa para preparar una fiesta grande.

Mis amigos y yo deberíamos comprar un regalo especial para él.

A él le gustan los libros y podríamos comprarle una novela.

El año pasado, le di su juguete infantil favorito y lo agradeció mucho.

- You will then be asked four questions **in Spanish** that relate to the topic of **Free-time activities**.

- In order to score the highest marks, **answer all four questions as fully as you can**.

Teacher's Material

- Start by asking the candidate to read the text by saying *Lee el texto*.

- Allow the candidate to read the text aloud, then ask the following four questions for their tier.

- Allow the student to develop their answers as much as possible.

Foundation

- ¿Cuándo es tu cumpleaños?

- ¿Te gusta ir a las fiestas?

- ¿Cómo pasas tu cumpleaños normalmente?

- ¿Qué recibiste para tu cumpleaños el año pasado?

Higher

- Describe tu cumpleaños perfecto.

- ¿Qué piensas de las fiestas?

- ¿Cuál es el mejor regalo que has recibido?

- ¿Por qué algunas personas prefieren dar regalos en lugar de recibirlos?

Reading Questions

1   Omar has written a blog post about the seasons.

> Prefiero viajar a climas tropicales cuando hace frío en el invierno. En el verano, mi padre y yo jugamos al baloncesto todos los domingos. Mi estación favorita es el otoño porque me gusta andar debajo de los árboles bonitos. Es divertido pasar tiempo en el jardín en primavera también.

Complete the sentences. Write the letter for the correct option in each box.

1 a   In the summer, Omar and his father play...

A	basketball.
B	football.
C	computer games.

[1 mark]

1 b   In which of the following seasons does Omar **not** mention spending time outside?

A	autumn
B	winter
C	spring

[1 mark]

1 c   Why is autumn Omar's favourite season?

A	He likes walking under the trees.
B	He likes it when the weather gets cold.
C	He enjoys spending time in the garden.

[1 mark]

2   Read these texts about David and Alba's classes.

David	La semana pasada, nuestro profesor de geografía nos dijo que tiene cuarenta y ocho años. En mi instituto, el aula de geografía está en la segunda planta.
Alba	Prefiero las clases que tienen pocos alumnos. Creo que menos gente es mejor porque es más fácil escuchar al profesor. En mi clase ideal habría diez personas en lugar de veinticinco como hay en realidad.

Answer the following questions in **English**.

2 a   Where is the geography classroom in David's school?

....   *[1 mark]*

2 b   Why does Alba think classes with fewer students are better?

....   *[1 mark]*

Writing Questions

1 Using your knowledge of grammar, complete the following sentences in **Spanish**. Choose the correct Spanish word from the three options. Write the correct **word** in the space.

1 a Voy al colegio a las siete y ....

medio	mitad	media

[1 mark]

1 b Según mi reloj .... la una menos cuarto.

es	está	son

[1 mark]

2 Translate the following sentences into **Spanish**.

2 a They need to buy the food for the party.

.... *[2 marks]*

2 b She must respond to my mother today.

.... *[2 marks]*

2 c At what time should we leave for the party?

.... *[2 marks]*

2 d I have just organised an event for the 12th December.

....

.... *[2 marks]*

3 You are writing an article about free-time activities.

Write approximately **90** words in **Spanish**.

You must write something about each bullet point.

Mention:

• what you think of a book you read recently

• why you do or don't like sports

• an activity that you'd like to start doing in the future. *[15 marks]*

General Stuff — Vocabulary

That was a lot of information, but don't worry — we've summarised all the words you need across the next four pages.

Numbers

el número	number	veintiuno	twenty-one	segundo/a	second (pre- and post-noun)
cero	zero	veintidós	twenty-two		
uno	one	veintitrés	twenty-three	tercer	third (pre-noun, m only)
dos	two	treinta	thirty		
tres	three	treinta y uno	thirty-one	tercero/a	third
cuatro	four	cuarenta	forty	varios/as	several, various
cinco	five	cincuenta	fifty		
seis	six	sesenta	sixty	la mayoría	majority
siete	seven	setenta	seventy	la mitad	half, middle
ocho	eight	ochenta	eighty	el resto	rest, remainder
nueve	nine	noventa	ninety	total	total, entire
diez	ten	cien(to)	one hundred (and...)	entero/a	entire, whole
once	eleven	ciento uno	one hundred and one	junto/a	together
doce	twelve	doscientos	two hundred (and...)	máximo/a	maximum
trece	thirteen	quinientos	five hundred (and...)	mínimo/a	minimum
catorce	fourteen	setecientos	seven hundred (and...)	numeroso/a	numerous, large, big
quince	fifteen	novecientos	nine hundred (and...)		
dieciséis	sixteen	mil	thousand		
diecisiete	seventeen	un millón	one million		
dieciocho	eighteen	dos millones	two million		
diecinueve	nineteen	primer	first (pre-noun, m only)		
veinte, veinti-	twenty	primero/a	first		

(máximo/a, mínimo/a and related words marked "Higher")

Time

el tiempo	time (general)	por la mañana	in the morning
Es la...	It's...	por la tarde	in the afternoon / evening
Son las...	It's...	por la noche	at night, in the evening
el cuarto	quarter (used in time expressions)	esta noche	tonight
		hoy	today, nowadays
medio/a	half	mañana	tomorrow
el segundo	second	ayer	yesterday
el minuto	minute	anoche	last night
la hora	hour, time (specific)	reciente	recent
ahora	now, these days	tarde	late
de momento	at the moment	pasado/a	past, last
luego	then, later	último/a	last, past
el principio	beginning, start	siguiente	following, next
el fin	end	a veces	sometimes
el final	end, ending	antes	before, beforehand
el momento	moment	después	after, afterwards
el rato	moment, while, time	finalmente	finally, at last
el pasado	past	el comienzo	start, beginning
la vez	time (specific occurrence)	la frecuencia	frequency
la mañana	morning	ocurrir	to happen, occur
la tarde	afternoon, evening		
la noche	night, evening		

(el comienzo, la frecuencia and ocurrir marked "H")

For more information about words related to telling the time, head to p.5. For other time words, see p.6.

Dates

la fecha	date (in calendar), day
el día	day
la semana	week
el fin de semana	(at the) weekend
el puente	long weekend
lunes	Monday
martes	Tuesday
miércoles	Wednesday
jueves	Thursday
viernes	Friday
sábado	Saturday
domingo	Sunday
el mes	month
el año	year
la estación	season (of the year)
la primavera	spring
el verano	summer
el otoño	autumn
el invierno	winter

enero	January
febrero	February
marzo	March
abril	April
mayo	May
junio	June
julio	July
agosto	August
septiembre	September
octubre	October
noviembre	November
diciembre	December
hace X años	X years ago
anterior	previous, preceding
la época	time, age, period

If you want to say 'on Mondays', you shouldn't use 'en'. Instead, just add 'los' before 'lunes' or any other day of the week. E.g. 'I swim on Mondays' would be 'Nado los lunes'.

Questions

¿Qué?	What?
¿Cuál(es)?	Which?
¿Cuándo?	When?
¿Por qué?	Why?
¿Dónde?	Where?
¿Cómo?	How?
¿Cuánto/a?	How much?
¿Cuántos/as?	How many?
¿Quién(es)?	Who?
sí	yes
no	no
la pregunta	question
responder	to reply, respond, answer

When writing questions in Spanish, don't forget to add an upside down question mark at the start of your question. If you're asking a question out loud, remember to raise your voice at the end of the sentence.

For more on interrogative pronouns, see p.157.

Quick, they're looking! Let's pretend I've said something really witty and inspiring.

Being Polite

hola	hello, hi
buenos días	good morning
¿Qué tal?	How are you? (informal), How is...? (someone or something)
bien	well
mal	badly
adiós	goodbye
presentar	to introduce, present
por favor	please, excuse me
el favor	favour
gracias	thanks, thank you
vale	OK
de acuerdo	OK
claro	of course, clearly

lo siento	I'm sorry, I apologise
¡Perdón!	Sorry!
quisiera	(I) would like (to), would love (formal)
¡Vamos!	Come on!, Let's go!
¿Cómo es?	What is it like?
el señor	Mr., man, Sir, gentleman
la señora	Mrs., lady
introducir	to introduce, bring in
el permiso	permission

General Stuff — Vocabulary

Opinions

la opinión	*opinion, view*
gustar	*to like, please, be pleasing (to)*
me/te/le gustaría	*(I, you, he, she, it, you (sing. form) would like (informal)*
encantar	*to love, delight, be delightful to*
encontrar	*to find*
interesar	*to interest*
acordar	*to agree on, remind*
de acuerdo	*in agreement*
la razón	*reason*
la decisión	*decision*
la idea	*idea*
el lado	*side*
el ejemplo	*example*
el detalle	*detail*
odiar	*to hate*
creer	*to believe, think*
pensar	*to think*
la verdad	*truth*
la mentira	*lie*
parecer	*to seem*
sentir	*to feel, sense*
preferir	*to prefer*
aparte (de)	*besides, apart (from)*
completamente	*completely*
bueno/a	*good*

estupendo/a	*brilliant, great, marvellous, wonderful*
excelente	*excellent*
genial	*great*
guay	*cool*
emocionante	*exciting*
perfecto/a	*perfect*
ideal	*ideal*
agradable	*pleasant, nice*
increíble	*incredible*
bonito/a	*pretty, nice, beautiful*
interesante	*interesting*
divertido/a	*fun, enjoyable*
cierto/a	*certain, sure, true*
correcto/a	*correct, suitable*
exacto/a	*exact, true*
raro/a	*strange, rare*
aburrido/a	*bored, boring*
horrible	*horrible*
malo/a	*bad*
falso/a	*false*
general	*general*
semejante	*similar*
típico/a	*typical*
común	*common*
diferente	*different*
imposible	*impossible*
posible	*possible*
probable	*probable, likely*

Higher

el punto	*point, full stop, dot*
imaginar	*to imagine*
significar	*to mean*
sugerir	*to suggest*
proponer	*to propose, suggest*
considerar	*to consider*
mencionar	*to mention*
referir	*to refer*
incluir	*to include*
indicar	*to point (out), indicate*
destacar	*to emphasise, stand out, highlight*
insistir	*to insist*
vale la pena	*it's worth it*
maravilloso/a	*wonderful, marvellous*
precioso/a	*beautiful, precious*
preferible	*preferable*
evidente	*evident, obvious*
verdadero/a	*true, real*
decepcionante	*disappointing*
distinto/a	*distinct, different*
la posibilidad	*possibility*
la duda	*doubt*

Useful Nouns

la caja	*box*
las ganas	*desire*
el miedo	*fear*
la pena	*sadness, shame, pity, trouble*
el recuerdo	*memory*
(un) montón	*(a) lot of, heap, pile*
la variedad	*variety*
el plan	*plan*
la intención	*intention*
la letra	*letter*
la cosa	*thing*
la situación	*situation*
el tipo	*type, kind*
la clase	*kind, type*
el sentido	*sense, meaning*

Higher

la línea	*course*
la calidad	*quality*
la creación	*creation*
la sensación	*feeling, sensation*
la emoción	*emotion, excitement*
la impresión	*impression*
la expresión	*expression*
la manera	*way, manner*
la forma	*form, shape, way*
la parte	*part*
el objeto	*object, thing*
el caso	*case, occasion*
el deseo	*desire, wish*
el fondo	*bottom, back, end (of area), back, background*

When you learn a new noun, make sure you learn its article too. That way, you'll know how to make any adjectives agree with it.

Useful Adjectives & Adverbs

corto/a	*brief*
lento/a	*slow*
libre	*free, vacant*
vacío/a	*empty, vacant*
lleno/a	*full*
completo/a	*full, complete*
medio/a	*half, middle, average*
real	*real*
final	*final*
normal	*normal, usual*
listo/a	*ready (after estar)*
seguro/a	*sure*

como	*like*
encima	*on top*
rápidamente	*quickly*

Higher

dispuesto/a	*ready, willing, prepared*
ocupado/a	*busy, taken, occupied*
oscuro/a	*dark, obscure*
vivo/a	*bright*
pesado/a	*heavy, boring*
ligero/a	*light (in weight)*
suave	*soft, gentle, mild*
inútil	*useless*
despacio	*slow*

Remember — Spanish adjectives need to agree in gender and number with the noun they describe. However, adverbs don't need to agree.

Colours

el color	*colour*
amarillo/a	*yellow*
azul	*blue*

blanco/a	*white*
gris	*grey*
marrón	*brown*

negro/a	*black*
rojo/a	*red*
verde	*green*

Mercè believed in a 'more is more' approach.

Useful Verbs

abrir	*to open, unwrap*
abrirse	*to open up*
acercarse	*to come closer*
acordarse	*to remember*
afectar	*to affect*
afectarse	*to be moved*
bajar	*to lower*
cambiar	*to change*
convertirse	*to become, transform*
crear	*to create*
decidir	*to decide*
dejar	*to let, leave*
depender	*to depend*
diseñar	*to design*
empujar	*to push*
entrar	*to enter, go in*
escoger	*to choose*
esperar	*to wait (for), hope (for), expect*
hablar	*to speak, talk*
intentar	*to try, attempt (to)*
mirar	*to look, watch*
mostrar	*to show*
necesitar	*to need*
oír	*to hear*
ponerse	*to get, become (+ adjective)*
quedar	*to arrange to meet, remain, be left*
quitar	*to remove, take away*
recordar	*to remember, recall, remind*
repetir	*to repeat*
volver a	*to do again*
romper	*to break (object)*
separar	*to separate*

acompañar	*to go with, accompany*
agradecer	*to be grateful for*
añadir	*to add*
alcanzar	*to reach, catch up with*
aparecer	*to turn up, appear*
apreciar	*to appreciate*
arreglar	*to repair, fix, tidy*
arreglarse	*to get ready*
asegurar	*to assure*
asegurarse (de que)	*to ensure (that), make sure (that)*
atreverse	*to dare*
¡Basta!	*(that's) enough!*
consistir (en)	*to consist (of)*
contar	*to tell, count*
controlar	*to control*

Higher

cubrir	*to cover*
dedicar	*to devote, dedicate*
descargar	*to unload*
despedirse (de)	*to say goodbye (to)*
escapar	*to escape*
esconder	*to hide*
exigir	*to demand*
formar	*to form, set up*
identificar	*to identify*
impedir	*to prevent*
meter	*to put, place*
mezclar	*to mix*
mover	*to move*
notar	*to notice*
obtener	*to obtain, get*
¡Ojalá!	*I hope so!, I wish!*
tratar de	*to try to*

Revision Summary Test for Section One

Have a go at these summary questions to check off what you need to know for this section.

- These questions are **hard**, but they'll really help you see **how well you know your stuff**.
- Tackle the **revision summary test** below, or scan the QR code to do it **online**.
  You can **track your progress** online and see **which areas need more work**.
- There are **sample answers** for the test here: www.cgpbooks.co.uk/MadridExtras

Numbers and Times

1) Count out loud from 0 to 20 in Spanish.
2) How do you say these numbers in Spanish? a) 25   b) 37   c) 60   d) 104   e) 2003
3) 'Hay mil setecientas cuarenta y nueve razones.' What does this mean in English?
4) Say the following phrases in Spanish: a) the first example   b) the second day   c) the third detail
5) Describe your daily routine using at least three different times.
H 6) 'The maximum number of points you could obtain is five hundred.' Translate this into Spanish.

Times and Dates

7) Say all 7 days of the week and all 12 months of the year in Spanish.
8) ¿Cuándo es tu cumpleaños?
9) Say these words and phrases in English: a) hoy   b) el fin de semana   c) anoche   d) ayer
10) Your Chilean friend says: 'Decidiré mañana por la mañana.' What does this mean in English?
11) Describe what you like to do on long weekends.
H L 12) Paloma says: 'El futuro es el comienzo de una época de posibilidad. Es un deseo mío crear millones de recuerdos bonitos llenos de emoción.' What is she saying?

Questions

13) What is the difference between '¿Qué...?' and '¿Cuál...?'?
14) '¿Cuánto cuesta el reloj blanco? El precio no está en la caja.' What is this person asking?
15) Write a question for each of the following question words:
    a) ¿Quién...?   b) ¿Cuántos/as...?   c) ¿Dónde...?   d) ¿Cómo...?   e) ¿Por qué...?

Being Polite

16) What are the differences between 'tú', 'vosotros/as', 'usted' and 'ustedes'?
17) How do you say these in English?
    a) hola   b) ¿Qué tal?   c) bien   d) mal   e) adiós   f) por favor   g) gracias   h) lo siento
18) Imagine you're introducing a friend to your headteacher. Write out 2 sentences for each person.
19) How would you ask someone politely to repeat their idea in Spanish?

Opinions

20) How would you say that you love to design objects that don't seem real in Spanish?
21) Pepe says: 'Me gusta jugar al baloncesto porque es emocionante.' What's he saying?
22) 'I find this situation strange and boring.' How would you say this in Spanish?
23) Gonzalo asks: '¿Estás de acuerdo con mi opinión?' What does he want to know?
24) a) Explain why you dislike your least favourite school subject in Spanish.
    b) Say a subject that you like using the word 'prefiero'. Give a reason why you like it.
H 25) Give a review of a book that you have recently read or a film that you have recently watched.

About Yourself

Talking about yourself is really important — you can't get by without it. Feel free to make up the odd detail about yourself to show off all the fab Spanish vocab you've learnt.

Head to the CGP RevisionHub for all your online content: www.cgpbooks.co.uk/Madrid

Preséntate — Introduce yourself

Vocabulary

el nombre	*name*	nacer	*to be born*	gay	*gay*
el apellido	*surname*	inglés(a)	*English*	hetero(sexual)	*straight*
llamarse	*to be called*	español(a)	*Spanish*	la religión	*religion*
la edad	*age*	europeo/a	*European*	religioso/a	*religious*
el año	*year*	transgénero	*transgender*	la nacionalidad	*nationality*
el cumpleaños	*birthday*	bi(sexual)	*bi(sexual)*	el género	*gender*

¡Hola! Me llamo Riku y tengo quince años.

Hello! I'm called Riku and I'm 15 years old.

Mi cumpleaños es el dos de abril. Nací en dos mil doce.

My birthday is the 2nd of April. I was born in 2012.

Vivo en España, pero soy francesa.

I live in Spain, but I am French.

Mi familia es religiosa.

My family is religious.

Varios aspectos forman mi identidad, como la edad y el género.

Various aspects form my identity, like age and gender.

My name is... — Mi nombre es...
I'm... — Soy...

Check p.7 for a reminder of how to say dates.

Scottish — escocés / escocesa
Irish — irlandés / irlandesa
Welsh — galés / galesa

See p.34 for more nationalities and religions.

Grammar — saying your age

In Spanish, you 'have' an age, so you need 'tener' to say how old you are. 'Tener' is a stem-changing verb — see p.176.

Tengo 16 años. *I'm 16 years old.*

Grammar — nationalities

Nationalities are adjectives. Some have an accent in the masculine singular form, but drop the accent and add 'a' in the feminine form.

inglés (m., sing.) — **inglesa** (f., sing.)
ingleses (m., pl.) — **inglesas** (f., pl.)

The accent is dropped in the plural forms too.

Practice Question

Q1 Read the following text out loud.   [5 marks]

SPEAKING

¡Hola! Me llamo Estefanía y soy de Venezuela. Vivo en el norte del país, cerca de la ciudad de Caracas. Mi cumpleaños es el veinticuatro de julio. Nací en el año dos mil diez.

Now answer the questions about yourself below in Spanish.

a) ¿Cómo te llamas?
b) ¿Dónde vives?
c) ¿Cuántos años tienes?
d) ¿Cuándo es tu cumpleaños?   [10 marks]

Top Tip for Higher Students
✓ Try to give more than one detail for your answers, e.g. say the year you were born in.

Talking about myself — where to begin...

When you introduce yourself in Spanish, give the same information as you would in English, like your name, age, and where you're from. You could show off your Spanish numbers by saying your birthday too.

My Family and Friends

It's not all about you though — it's very useful to be able to talk about family and friends too.
Best to be prepared for questions about them from the examiners — they're a nosy bunch...

Mi familia — My family

Vocabulary

el miembro	*member*	los hijos	*children*	el perro	*dog*	
los padres	*parents*	el hijo	*son, child (m)*	el gato	*cat*	
el padre	*father*	la hija	*daughter, child (f)*	el caballo	*horse*	
la madre	*mother*	el hermano	*brother*	el pájaro	*bird*	
el padrastro	*stepfather*	la hermana	*sister*	el papá	*dad*	
la madrastra	*stepmother*	el tío	*uncle*	la mamá	*mum*	
los abuelos	*grandparents*	la tía	*aunt*	el familiar	*relative*	Higher
el abuelo	*grandfather*	el primo	*cousin (m)*	familiar	*of the family*	
la abuela	*grandmother*	la prima	*cousin (f)*	la mascota	*pet*	

Háblame de tu familia — Tell me about your family

Grammar — saying 'my' and 'your'

Possessive adjectives like 'my' and 'your' have to agree with the noun they come before
(see p.167). Remember — 'su(s)' could also mean 'your' if you're being formal.

mi padre	*my father*	**tu** hermana	*your sister*	**su** tía	*his / her / their aunt*
mis padres	*my parents*	**tus** hermanas	*your sisters*	**sus** tías	*his / her / their aunts*

Tengo una hermana mayor.
Se llama Ramona.

I have an older sister.
She is called Ramona.

a younger sister — una hermana menor
a bird — un pájaro

Hay cinco personas en
mi familia: mi madre, mi
padrastro, mis dos hermanos
menores y yo. Mis hermanos
se llaman Waisea y Gabriel.

There are five people in
my family: my mother, my
stepfather, my two younger
brothers and me. My brothers
are called Waisea and Gabriel.

older brothers — hermanos mayores

Soy hijo único, pero
me gustaría tener hermanos.

I'm an only child (m),
but I'd like to have siblings.

an only child (f) — hija única
the oldest — el/la mayor
the youngest — el/la menor

Para mí, mi perro Joey
es parte de la familia también.

For me, my dog Joey
is part of the family too.

I like not having siblings —
me gusta no tener hermanos

Question

¿Cómo es tu familia?
What's your family like?

Simple Answer

Soy hijo único, pero tengo muchos primos.
I'm an only child, but I have a lot of cousins.

Extended Answer

Soy hijo único, pero mi padre tiene cinco hermanos, entonces en realidad, tengo
muchos familiares. Mis primos viven cerca de aquí y siempre lo pasamos bien juntos.

I'm an only child, but my father has five siblings, so really, I have lots of relatives.
My cousins live near here and we always have a good time together.

Mis amigos — My friends

Vocabulary

la amistad	*friendship*	conocer	*to know (person, place), meet (for the first time)*
el amigo	*friend (m)*		
la amiga	*friend (f)*		
mejor	*better, best*	pasar	*to spend (time)*

Grammar — prenominal adjectives

'Bueno' becomes 'buen' <u>before</u> masculine singular nouns. 'Buen' is a <u>prenominal</u> adjective (see p.166).

Eres un <u>buen</u> amigo. *You're a good friend.*

The other forms don't need to change.

Eres una buena amiga. *You're a good friend.*
Sois buenos amigos. *You're good friends.*

Para mí, es bastante fácil hacer amigos. Pero a veces puede ser difícil.

Tengo muchas amigas pero no tengo una mejor amiga.

Mis amigos y yo somos muy similares.

La amistad es muy importante. Soy feliz porque tengo buenos amigos.

Mi buen amigo Benicio es argentino. Me gusta cuando pasamos tiempo juntos porque le conozco muy bien.

For me, it's quite easy to make friends. But sometimes it can be difficult.

I have lots of friends but I don't have a best friend.

My friends and I are very similar.

Friendship is very important. I am happy because I have good friends.

My good friend Benicio is Argentinian. I like it when we spend time together because I know him really well.

to meet new people — conocer a nueva gente

Mexican — mexicano
Chilean — chileno
Colombian — colombiano

'Conozco' (I know) is the only irregular bit of the verb 'conocer' in the present tense.

Practice Questions

Q1 *Describe your family and friends.*
You should write about 50 words in Spanish. Mention:

- *who's in your family*
- *whether you have a best friend*
- *whether you have any pets.* [10 marks]

WRITING

Top Tip for Higher Students
✓ Use possessive pronouns to talk about your family, e.g. 'Tu amigo es mayor que el mío.'

Q2 *Qori has written about her family.*
Read her comments and then answer the questions below in English.

READING

Vivo con mi mamá, mi hermana mayor y mis dos hermanas menores. Paso mucho tiempo con ellas porque disfrutamos de las mismas actividades. Los fines de semana, visito a mi padre, su mujer italiana y mi hermanastro, que se llama Marco. Tenemos la misma edad y el mismo cumpleaños. Sí, ¡nació el mismo día que yo! Me gustaría pasar más tiempo allí con ellos porque es muy divertido.*

*hermanastro — stepbrother

Higher

a) How many sisters does Qori have? [1 mark]
b) Why does Qori spend lots of time with them? [1 mark]
c) Who does Qori visit on the weekend? [1 mark]
d) What coincidence does Qori mention? [1 mark]

The vocab boxes are your friends — give them lots of attention...

No matter who makes up your own family, you could be tested on any of the main vocab from this topic. The same goes for talking about your friends, so learn all the words from these pages to help you in the exam.

Quick Quiz

Describing People

You need to use adjectives to describe people — lucky for you there are plenty on these pages.

¿Cómo eres? — What are you like?

You'll need the verbs 'tener' (to have) and 'ser' (to be) for this page. They're irregular, so check p.177-178 to see how they work.

Vocabulary

guapo/a	*good-looking*	las gafas	*glasses*	moreno/a	*brown (hair), dark (skin)*
feo/a	*ugly*	el ojo	*eye*	el tatuaje	*tattoo*
alto/a	*tall*	marrón	*brown*	el adulto	*adult*
bajo/a	*short*	verde	*green*	el anciano	*elderly person*
gordo/a	*fat*	azul	*blue*	la altura	*height*
delgado/a	*thin, slim*	gris	*grey*	la cara	*face*
pequeño/a	*little, small, young*	el pelo	*hair*	oscuro/a	*dark*
joven	*young*	corto/a	*short (hair)*	precioso/a	*beautiful, precious*
viejo/a	*old, elderly*	largo/a	*long*	infantil	*of children, children's*
describir	*to describe*	rubio/a	*blond, fair (hair)*		
parecerse a	*to look like*	negro/a	*black*		

'Marrón' loses its accent in the plural form.

Higher: el adulto, el anciano, la altura, la cara, oscuro/a, precioso/a, infantil

Tengo... — I have...

Q&A Audio

Question

¿Cómo eres?

What are you like?

Simple Answer

Soy alta. Tengo los ojos azules y tengo el pelo moreno.

I'm tall. I have blue eyes and I have brown hair.

Extended Answer

Soy de altura media — no soy ni alta ni baja. Tengo los ojos azules y llevo gafas. Tengo una cara pequeña y tengo el pelo corto.

I am average height — I'm neither tall nor short. I have blue eyes and I wear glasses. I have a small face and I have short hair.

Soy muy bajo como mis padres. Sin embargo, mi hermano es mucho más alto que yo. Tengo el pelo rubio y tengo los ojos verdes.

I'm very short like my parents. However, my brother is much taller than me. I have blond hair and I have green eyes.

Grammar — adjectives agree

Adjectives must agree with the noun they describe.
'Los ojos' are masculine plural, so adjectives like 'blue' must be in the masculine plural form — 'azules'.
'El pelo' is masculine singular, so adjectives like 'short' need to be in the masculine singular form — 'corto' — even if you're a girl.

No soy ni gorda ni delgada. Tengo los ojos marrones y el pelo negro.

I'm neither fat nor slim. I have brown eyes and black hair.

Creo que te pareces a tu padre, pero él es más bajo y tiene el pelo gris.

I think that you look like your father, but he is shorter and has grey hair.

Mis abuelos son viejos pero mi abuelo todavía se considera joven.

My grandparents are old but my grandfather still considers himself young.

Tiene el pelo rubio y largo. Es altísima. Lleva gafas y tiene los ojos azules.

She has long, blond hair. She's really tall. She wears glasses and she has blue eyes.

Es un chico guapísimo con los ojos verdes. Tiene una sonrisa preciosa.

He's a very good-looking boy with green eyes. He has a beautiful smile.

dark skin — la piel morena
dark hair — el pelo oscuro
he's red-haired — es pelirrojo
really short — bajísima
face — cara

Mi carácter — My personality

Vocabulary

simpático/a	*nice, friendly*	trabajador(a)	*hardworking*	fiel	*faithful, loyal*
alegre	*cheerful*	perezoso/a	*lazy*	sensible	*sensitive*
gracioso/a	*funny*	serio/a	*serious*	tolerante	*tolerant*
animado/a	*lively*	tranquilo/a	*calm, relaxed*	ambicioso/a	*ambitious*
tonto/a	*silly*	nervioso/a	*nervous, uptight*	orgulloso/a	*proud*
optimista	*optimistic*	contento/a	*happy, content*	vago/a	*lazy*

(**Higher**: fiel, sensible, tolerante, ambicioso/a, orgulloso/a, vago/a)

Grammar — making adjectives agree

Adjectives must agree with the nouns they describe — see p.165.

Some adjectives don't follow the normal rules:

1) '-or' endings, e.g. '**trabajador**' — add an 'a' on the end for the feminine form and then 'es' and 'as' for the masculine and feminine plurals.

2) '-ísta/-ista' endings, e.g. '**optimista**' — stay the same in the singular and add an 's' for both the masculine and feminine plurals.

Grammar — 'ser' vs 'estar'

Both 'ser' and 'estar' mean 'to be'.

To describe someone's personality use 'ser', but to describe how they feel at a given moment, use 'estar' — see p.178.

Está tranquilo. *He is feeling calm.*

Es tranquilo. *He is calm. (a calm person)*

Mi mejor amigo es sensible. Es optimista también. Sin embargo, hoy está triste.

My best friend is sensitive. He is optimistic too. However, today he is feeling sad.

Mis padres son estrictos pero divertidos al mismo tiempo. Mi madre es muy deportista pero mi padre es más artístico.

My parents are strict but fun at the same time. My mother is very sporty but my father is more artistic.

Mis profesoras son listas y simpáticas.

My teachers are intelligent and friendly.

He has a good sense of humour — Tiene un buen sentido del humor

understanding — comprensivas

Practice Questions

Q1 Ana and Pablo are describing these four people.
Write the correct order in which they are mentioned.

A 
B 
C 
D 

[4 marks]

Q2 You're writing an introduction about you and your best friend for your new blog.
Write about 90 words in Spanish. You must write something about each bullet point. Mention:

- your appearance and personality
- your best friend's appearance and personality
- why they are your best friend.

Top Tip for Higher Students
✓ Use additional tenses, e.g. to talk about when you first met your friend.

[15 marks]

Use the adjectives on this page to describe your classmates...

Just remember to make sure each adjective agrees with the noun it describes. Also, try to avoid describing everyone the same way — the examiner wants to see that you know how to use lots of different adjectives.

Quick Quiz

Relationships and Partnerships

Talking about your relationships is a great way of showing you can use irregular and reflexive verbs. It's also a great opportunity to complain about an annoying family member — a sibling, perhaps...

Las relaciones — Relationships

You need the personal 'a' with verbs like 'aguantar'. Have a look at p.160 for more information.

Vocabulary

aguantar	*to put up with, stand*	escuchar	*to listen (to)*
discutir	*to argue, discuss*	respetar	*to respect*
molestar	*to bother, annoy*	ayudar	*to help*
pelearse	*to fight*	apoyar	*to support*
llevarse (con)	*to get on (with)*	comprender	*to understand*
entenderse	*to get on*	confiar	*to trust, confide*
entender	*to understand*	animar	*to cheer up*

Higher: comprender, confiar, animar

Willow could always lean on her friends for support.

Grammar — reflexive verbs

'Pelearse', 'entenderse', 'llevarse' and 'enamorarse' are reflexive verbs. Take off the 'se' and add the correct ending to the stem like a normal verb (see p.175). Then choose the right pronoun (see p.185) and put it in front of the verb.

¿Te entiendes con ella? — *Do you get on with her?*

Nos peleamos mucho. — *We fight a lot.*

Me llevo bien con mi hermana. — *I get on well with my sister.*

Grammar (Higher only) — 'confiar'

'Confiar' is an irregular verb. In the present tense, the 'i' has an accent on it in every form except the 'we' and 'you inf., plural' forms.

Confío en él.
I trust him. — To say you trust someone, you need to use 'en'.

¿Te llevas bien con ellos? — Do you get on well with them?

Mis padres tienen una buena relación pero yo no me llevo bien con ellos.

My parents have a good relationship but I don't get on with them.

— *I don't get on very well with them* — no me relaciono muy bien con ellos

Me llevo mejor con mi hermana porque me ayuda mucho. La encuentro muy graciosa.

I get on better with my sister because she helps me a lot. I find her very funny.

— *I don't like to argue with my sister* — No me gusta discutir con mi hermana

Mi hermano y yo nos peleamos mucho porque me molesta.

My brother and I fight a lot because he annoys me.

— *I can't stand my brother* — No aguanto a mi hermano

Un buen amigo siempre te escucha y te apoya.

A good friend always listens to you and supports you.

— *helps you and cheers you up* — te ayuda y te anima

El amor — Love

Vocabulary

el novio	*boyfriend, groom*	el matrimonio	*marriage*	divorciarse	*to get divorced*
la novia	*girlfriend, bride*	casado/a	*married*	soltero/a	*single, unmarried*
la pareja	*couple, partner*	casarse	*to get married*	el estado civil	*marital status*
la boda	*wedding*	besar	*to kiss*	prometerse	*to get engaged*
el marido	*husband*	cuidar	*to take care of*	enamorarse (de)	*to fall in love (with)*
la mujer	*wife*	separarse	*to separate*	abrazar	*to hug*

Higher: el estado civil, prometerse, enamorarse (de), abrazar

En el futuro... — In the future...

Question

¿Te gustaría casarte y
tener hijos en el futuro?
*Would you like to get married
and have children in the future?*

Simple Answer

No sé si quiero casarme, pero
me gustaría tener hijos.
*I don't know if I want to get
married, but I'd like to have children.*

Grammar (Higher only)
— When I'm X years old...

To say '<u>when I'm 30</u>' (or
to say 'when' with a future
event), use the <u>subjunctive</u>.
See p.190.

Cuando <u>tenga</u> 60 años...
When <u>I'm</u> 60 years old...

Extended Answer

Quiero casarme porque me importa mucho. Me gustaría tener hijos
cuando tenga treinta años, pero no sé cuántos hijos quiero tener.

*I want to get married because it's very important to me. I'd like to have
children when I'm 30, but I don't know how many children I want to have.*

¿Qué piensas del matrimonio? — What do you think about marriage?

Las bodas son muy románticas.
Me gustaría enamorarme y casarme
porque parece emocionante.

*Weddings are very romantic. I
would like to fall in love and get
married because it seems exciting.*

Debo decir que preferiría no
casarme, porque una boda
puede costar mucho dinero.

*I must say that I would prefer
not to get married, because a
wedding can cost a lot of money.*

*I never want to get married
— no quiero casarme nunca
I'd prefer to buy myself a house
— preferiría comprarme una casa*

En mi opinión, no es necesario
casarse antes de tener hijos,
pero todavía me gustaría hacerlo.

*In my opinion, it's not necessary
to get married before having
children, but I'd still like to do it.*

*marriage can give you
security — el matrimonio
te puede dar seguridad*

Practice Questions

Q1 *Read Chea's message about her boyfriend and choose the correct options below.*

> Conocí a mi novio en una fiesta de cumpleaños cuando tenía quince años.
> Me llevo muy bien con él porque los dos tenemos el mismo sentido del humor.
> Aunque discutimos muy poco, no quiero casarme con él ahora porque somos
> muy jóvenes. Quizás en unos años ¡si me aguanta y yo le aguanto!

a) *Where did Chea meet her boyfriend?*

A. A party **C.** At school

B. A cafe **D.** Online *[1 mark]*

b) *When does she want to get married?*

A. In 15 years **C.** Never

B. She's not sure **D.** Now *[1 mark]*

Q2 *Miguel is talking about his relationships. Choose the correct
statement from each list below to complete the sentences in English.*

a) Miguel used to fight with...
A. his mum.
B. his dad.
C. his brother. *[1 mark]*

b) Miguel's boyfriend says that Miguel...
A. is happy.
B. is lazy.
C. isn't very tolerant. *[1 mark]*

(Higher)

Don't forget to back up your opinions with reasons...

It might feel a bit weird talking about your relationships and future plans... Even so, have a think about
who you do or don't get on with (and why) so you're ready for whatever the examiners might throw at you.

Listening Questions

Here's another opportunity to sharpen up your skills. Don't be tempted to miss these pages out — the time you spend getting used to the sorts of questions you'll get will be worth it in the end.

Foundation

1   Three young people are describing what they look like.

Each of them has one of the following features.

A	Black hair		D	Green eyes
B	Long hair		E	Brown hair
C	Glasses		F	Short (height)

Write the correct letter in each box.

1 a   Lola

[1 mark]

1 b   Omar

[1 mark]

1 c   Pilar

[1 mark]

2   Julia is talking to Raúl about his wedding.

What details did Raúl mention and what are Julia's thoughts about marriage?

Write **A** if only statement **A** is correct.

       B if only statement **B** is correct.

       A + B if both statements **A** and **B** are correct.

2 a   Raúl said...

A	the wedding will be on the 22nd of July.
B	he is not feeling happy.

[1 mark]

Higher

2 b   He is...

A	not sure whether he trusts his family.
B	sure that Ana will look beautiful.

[1 mark]

2 c   Julia thinks that...

A	nothing is more important than marriage.
B	weddings are romantic.

[1 mark]

Speaking Questions

Candidate's Material

- You are talking to your Spanish friend.

- Your teacher will play the part of your friend and will speak first.

- You should address your friend as *tú*.

- When you see this – **?** – you will have to ask a question.

> **In order to score full marks, you must include a verb in your response to each task.**
>
> **1.** Describe the physical appearance of one of your family members. (Give **one** detail.)
>
> **2.** Describe the personality of one of your family members. (Give **one** detail.)
>
> **?** **3.** Ask your friend about an activity they like to do with friends.
>
> **4.** Describe your best friend. (Give **one** detail.)
>
> **5.** Say if you get on better with your friends or your family. (Give **one** reason.)
>
> **6.** Say whether family is important to you. (Give **two** details.)
>
> **7.** Say whether you would like to get married in the future and why.
>   (Give **one** opinion and **one** reason.)

(Higher: questions 6–7)

Teacher's Material

- You begin the role-play.

- You should address the candidate as *tú*.

- You must read out the teacher's role shown below **without any changes**.

- You must begin the role-play by using the introductory text below.

Introductory text: *Estás hablando con tu amigo español/tu amiga española.*
Yo soy tu amigo/tu amiga.

> **1.** Describe a un miembro de tu familia físicamente.
>
> **2.** Describe la personalidad de un miembro de tu familia.
>
> **?** **3.** Allow the candidate to ask you a question about what you do with friends.
>   Give an appropriate response.
>
> **4.** ¿Cómo es tu mejor amigo o amiga?
>
> **5.** ¿Te llevas mejor con tus amigos o con tu familia?
>
> **H** **6.** ¿Para ti, es importante la familia? ¿Por qué?
>
> **7.** ¿Te gustaría casarte en el futuro? ¿Por qué?

Reading Questions

1   You read a blog about Spanish teenagers and their relationships with friends and family.

> **Dani**
> Tengo catorce años y tengo una hermana mayor que tiene cuatro años más que yo.
> Tengo una buena relación con mi familia pero no me entiendo muy bien con gente de mi edad.
>
> **Alejandro**
> Tengo una familia católica. Mis padres dicen que es importante llevarse bien con la familia y
> con los amigos, pero ellos discuten mucho. Yo me llevo bien con todos porque soy alegre.

Answer the questions below in **English**.

1 a   How old is Dani's sister?

.... *[1 mark]*

1 b   Who thinks they get along well with everyone?

.... *[1 mark]*

1 c   According to Alejandro, who argues a lot?

.... *[1 mark]*

2   Translate these sentences into **English**.

2 a   Luisa es guapísima. Tiene los ojos azules.

.... *[2 marks]*

2 b   Me llevo mejor con mi hermano menor que con mi hermana mayor.

.... *[2 marks]*

2 c   Estaremos felices si nuestros padres nos permiten tener una mascota.

.... *[2 marks]*

2 d   Antes de casarse, mis abuelos no vivían juntos.

.... *[2 marks]*

2 e   Cuando sea adulto, seré tolerante y comprensivo.

.... *[2 marks]*

Writing Questions

1 Using your knowledge of grammar, complete the following sentences in **Spanish**. Choose the correct Spanish word from the three options in the grid. Write the correct **word** in the space.

1 a Su cumpleaños .... el veintitrés de julio.

es	son	está

[1 mark]

1 b Mis padres son muy ....

serias	seria	serios

[1 mark]

2 You are writing a blog post about weddings.

Write approximately **90** words in **Spanish**.

You must write something about each bullet point.

Mention:

- your opinion on weddings

- a wedding you went to recently

- the qualities you would like your future partner to have.

[15 marks]

3 Translate the following sentences into **Spanish**.

3 a She has two brothers and one sister.

.... *[2 marks]*

3 b I have an English grandfather and a French grandmother.

.... *[2 marks]*

3 c My friends and I encourage and support each other.

.... *[2 marks]*

3 d He will always feel proud to be transgender.

.... *[2 marks]*

3 e We used to practise Spanish with our Argentinian relatives.

.... *[2 marks]*

Identity and Relationships with Others — Vocabulary

No need to be nervous — this friendly vocab list is here to help you learn all the words and phrases from this section.

About Yourself

el nombre	name
el apellido	surname
presentar	to introduce, present
llamar	to call, name
llamarse	to be called
la edad	age
el año	year
tener ... años	to be ... years old
el cumpleaños	birthday
nacer	to be born
la identidad	identity
británico/a	British
inglés(a)	English
español(a)	Spanish
francés(a)	French
alemán(a)	German
italiano/a	Italian
europeo/a	European
mexicano/a	Mexican
cubano/a	Cuban
chileno/a	Chilean
colombiano/a	Colombian
argentino/a	Argentinian
chino/a	Chinese
el sexo	sex
transgénero	transgender
bi(sexual)	bi(sexual)
gay	gay
hetero(sexual)	straight, heterosexual
la religión	religion
religioso/a	religious
católico/a	Catholic
cristiano/a	Christian
musulmán(a)	Muslim
judío/a	Jewish

Higher:

el nacimiento	birth, origin
la nacionalidad	nationality
latino/a	Latin, Latin American
el género	gender

My Family and Friends

la familia	family
el miembro	member
los padres	parents
el padre	father
la madre	mother
el padrastro	stepfather
la madrastra	stepmother
los abuelos	grandparents
el abuelo	grandfather
la abuela	grandmother
los hijos	children
el hijo	son, child (m)
la hija	daughter, child (f)
el hermano	brother
la hermana	sister
menor	younger
mayor	older
el tío	uncle
la tía	aunt
el primo	cousin (m)
la prima	cousin (f)
el niño	child (m), little boy
la niña	child (f), young girl
el bebé	baby
el perro	dog
el gato	cat
el caballo	horse
el pájaro	bird
la amistad	friendship
el amigo	friend (m)
la amiga	friend (f)
mejor	better, best
viejo/a	old, long-standing (pre-noun)
conocer	to know (person, place), to meet (for the first time)
pasar	to spend (time)

Higher:

el papá	dad
la mamá	mum
familiar	of/relating to the family
el familiar	relative, family member
el/la menor	the youngest
el/la mayor	the oldest
la generación	generation
la mascota	pet
la cola	tail

Describing People — Appearances

guapo/a	good-looking
hermoso/a	handsome
feo/a	ugly
alto/a	tall
bajo/a	short
gordo/a	fat
delgado/a	thin, slim
pequeño/a	little, small, young
joven	young
viejo/a	old, elderly (post-noun)
describir	to describe
parecerse a	to look like
sonreír	to smile
la sonrisa	smile
llevar	to wear
las gafas	glasses
el ojo	eye
marrón	brown
verde	green
azul	blue
gris	grey
rojo/a	red
el pelo	hair
corto/a	short (hair)
largo/a	long
rubio/a	blond, fair (hair)
negro/a	black
moreno/a	brown (hair), dark (skin)
pintarse	to put on makeup
el tatuaje	tattoo
la persona	person
el chico	boy
la chica	girl
la mujer	woman
el hombre	man
la gente	people

Higher:

precioso/a	beautiful, precious
oscuro/a	dark
infantil	of children, children's
la cara	face
la altura	height
el adulto	adult
el anciano	elderly person

Describing People — Personalities and Emotions

el carácter	*personality, character*
la personalidad	*personality*
simpático/a	*nice, friendly*
alegre	*cheerful, happy, lively*
contento/a	*happy, content, pleased*
feliz	*happy, glad, content*
gracioso/a	*funny*
el humor	*humour, mood*
animado/a	*lively*
tonto/a	*silly*
(ser) listo/a	*(to be) clever, intelligent*
trabajador(a)	*hardworking*
perezoso/a	*lazy*
deportivo/a	*sporty*
artístico/a	*artistic*
duro/a	*resilient*
optimista	*optimistic*
serio/a	*serious*
independiente	*independent*
tranquilo/a	*calm, relaxed*

nervioso/a	*nervous, uptight*
triste	*sad, unhappy, upset*
enojado/a	*angry*
comprensivo/a	*understanding*
fiel	*faithful, loyal*
sensible	*sensitive*
tolerante	*tolerant*
estricto/a	*strict*
loco/a	*crazy, insane*
ambicioso/a	*ambitious*
orgulloso/a	*proud*
vago/a	*lazy*

Higher (comprensivo/a through vago/a)

'listo/a' changes its meaning depending on whether you use it with 'ser' or 'estar'. Use 'ser' if you want to say that someone is clever, e.g. 'Es un hombre listo.' Use 'estar' if you want to say that someone is ready, e.g. 'La mujer está lista.'

Relationships and Partnerships

la relación	*relationship*
aguantar	*to put up with, stand*
discutir	*to argue, discuss*
molestar	*to bother, annoy, upset, disturb*
pelearse	*to fight (physically)*
llevarse (con)	*to get on (with)*
entenderse	*to get on*
entender	*to understand*
escuchar	*to listen (to)*
respetar	*to respect*
ayudar	*to help*
apoyar	*to support*
el sentimiento	*feeling, sentiment*
el amor	*love*
la pareja	*couple, partner*
el/la compañero/a	*companion*
el novio	*boyfriend, groom*
la novia	*girlfriend, bride*
la boda	*wedding*
el marido	*husband*
la mujer	*wife*
el matrimonio	*marriage*
civil	*civil*
casado/a	*married*
casarse	*to get married*
besar	*to kiss*
cuidar	*to take care of*
separarse	*to separate (of a couple)*
divorciarse	*to get divorced*
soltero/a	*single, unmarried*

relacionarse con	*to relate to, get on with*
comprender	*to understand*
confiar	*to trust, confide*
el secreto	*secret*
perdonar	*to forgive, excuse*
animar	*to encourage, cheer up*
alegrar	*to make happy, cheer up*
la cita	*(romantic) date*
romántico/a	*romantic*
enamorarse (de)	*to fall in love (with)*
el cariño	*affection, love*
el estado civil	*marital status*
la independencia	*independence*
prometer	*to promise*
prometerse	*to get engaged*
llorar	*to cry*
abrazar	*to hug*
reírse	*to laugh*

Higher (relacionarse con through reírse)

Malai loved her personal space. Berto also loved Malai's personal space...

Revision Summary Test for Section Two

Try the questions on this page so you're all set to talk about yourself, your family and your friends.

- These questions are **really tricky**, but they'll help you see **how well you know your stuff**.
- Tackle the **revision summary test** below, or scan the QR code to do it **online**.
  You can **keep track of your progress** online and see **which areas need more work**.
- There are **sample answers** here: www.cgpbooks.co.uk/MadridExtras

About Yourself ☑

1) Preséntate en español. Da tu nombre, apellido, edad y cumpleaños.

2) How many words related to religion, gender and sexuality can you list in Spanish?
   There are 11 in this section (plus 1 for Higher tier).

3) 'Nací en Sudamérica y esto es una parte importante de mi identidad.' Translate this into English.

4) List the 13 Spanish words from this section (plus 2 for Higher tier) that describe where you're from.

[H][L] 5) Pablo says: 'Te presento a mi amigo. Se llama Carlos y su lugar de nacimiento es Barcelona.'
   Translate his sentences into English.

My Family and Friends ☑

6) How many words related to family members can you name in Spanish?
   There are at least 19 you need to know (plus 3 for Higher tier).

7) In Spanish, write about why you like your friends. Give at least two details.

8) 'I met my best friend for the first time when I was a baby. She is a special person in my life
   and her friendship is really important to me.' Translate this sentence into Spanish.

9) Would you like to have any pets? Why (or why not)? Answer in Spanish.

[H][L] 10) 'De los niños en mi familia, Diego es el menor y Leya es la mayor. Esa niña es de una generación
   completamente diferente a la mía.' Translate these sentences into English.

Describing People ☑

11) How would you say the following words in Spanish?
   a) tall b) short c) fat d) thin e) old f) young g) ugly h) good-looking i) small

12) 'Tiene el pelo largo y rubio, los ojos azules y lleva gafas rojas.' Translate this description into English.

13) ¿Cómo te describirías físicamente y cómo describirías tu carácter?

14) 'La chica que está allí con el pelo negro y los ojos marrones se parece a la mujer de la película
   que vimos ayer.' Translate this sentence into English.

15) How many adjectives can you think of to describe someone's personality or emotions in Spanish?
   There are 20 you need to know in this section (plus 9 for Higher tier).

[H][L] 16) 'La anciana tenía una sonrisa preciosa y el pelo oscuro y corto. También tenía tatuajes y
   se pintaba la cara de un estilo tradicional.' Translate these sentences into English.

Relationships and Partnerships ☑

17) What is your relationship like with your family and friends? Answer in Spanish.

18) How would you say the following words in Spanish?
   a) girlfriend b) husband c) wife d) married e) single f) to separate g) to divorce

19) 'My parents don't understand my feelings. It annoys me a lot.' Translate this into Spanish.

20) Write down the English for the following verbs: a) besar b) ayudar c) pelearse d) cuidar

21) 'No aguanto a mi hermano mayor. El hombre no me respeta y discutimos.' Translate this into English.

22) In Spanish, write about the qualities you think are most important in a relationship or marriage.

Higher 23) 'Me enamoré con mi novio en la primera cita. Es muy romántico y creo que nos prometeremos
   en el futuro.' Translate these sentences into English.

Food

Quick Quiz

There's a lot of vocab on this page, but don't panic — just learn a few chunks at a time.

La comida — Food

Don't forget you can access your online content here: www.cgpbooks.co.uk/Madrid

Vocabulary

la fruta	*fruit*	el jamón	*ham*
la manzana	*apple*	el pollo	*chicken*
la naranja	*orange*	el pescado	*fish*
la uva	*grape*	la paella	*paella (dish usually of rice and seafood)*
la verdura	*vegetable*		
la ensalada	*salad*	el caramelo	*sweet*
el tomate	*tomato*	vegetariano/a	*vegetarian*
las patatas fritas	*chips, fries*	vegano/a	*vegan*
la hamburguesa	*burger*	la bebida	*drink*
la comida rápida	*fast food*	el agua (f)	*water*
la comida basura	*junk food*	la leche	*milk*
el bocadillo	*sandwich*	el café	*coffee*
el huevo	*egg*	el alimento	*food, nourishment*
el pan	*bread*	el arroz	*rice*
la carne	*meat*	el aceite	*oil*

[Higher] (el alimento, el arroz, el aceite)

I said paella — not pie, Ella...

¿Qué comes? — What do you eat?

Suelo comer una ensalada de frutas para el desayuno.

I usually eat a fruit salad for breakfast.

'Soler' (*to usually do something*) is a stem-changing verb ('o' to 'ue'). See p.176.

Mi padre es vegano. Por eso nunca prepara comida con productos animales.

My dad is vegan. Therefore, he never prepares food with animal products.

cheese — queso
cream — nata

Para la comida, me gusta comer un bocadillo de pollo.

For lunch, I like to eat a chicken sandwich.

'el almuerzo' is another way to say lunch.

Grammar — meal times

These are the nouns for Spanish meals:

el desayuno	*breakfast*
la comida	*lunch*
la cena	*dinner, evening meal*

'comida' also means 'food' or 'meal'.

These nouns can be made into verbs:

desayunar	*to have breakfast*
comer	*to have lunch*
cenar	*to have dinner, tea (evening meal)*

This also means 'to eat'.

Practice Question

Q1 *Three friends are talking about food. Answer the questions in English.*

e.g. What did Joaquín eat a lot of when he was younger? sweets

a) Joaquín avoids foods that are high in two things. Name one. *[1 mark]*

b) What does Alejandra say she needs to eat more of? *[1 mark]*

c) What does Raquel find difficult as a vegetarian? *[1 mark]*

LISTENING

Listening Track 10

Take a moment to digest this page before moving on...

Food — my favourite subject. If you're struggling to remember the words for some foods, you could give them a label in the kitchen. Then every time you see or eat them, you can repeat the word in Spanish.

Healthy and Unhealthy Living

Time for two pages about healthy living, complete with reflexive verbs. Pass the biscuits, then.

Una vida sana — A healthy life

'la dieta' means your general diet, e.g. what you eat or drink normally. 'el régimen' means a specific diet, e.g. for weight loss or medical conditions.

Vocabulary

la vida	*life*	la dieta	*diet (general)*
la salud	*health*	equilibrado/a	*balanced*
sano/a	*healthy, wholesome*	la costumbre	*habit*
suficiente	*sufficient, enough*	el sueño	*sleep*
la importancia	*importance*	dormir	*to sleep*
activo/a	*active*	dormirse	*to fall asleep*
físico/a	*physical*	descansar	*to rest, relax*
el ejercicio	*exercise*	diario/a	*daily*
estar en forma	*to be fit*	relajante	*relaxing*
entrenarse	*to train, go training*	promover	*to promote*

Higher: diario/a, relajante, promover

Question

¿Crees que es importante estar en forma?

Do you believe it's important to be fit?

Simple Answer

Sí, pienso que es importante entrenarse y comer bien.

Yes, I think it's important to train and to eat well.

Grammar — reflexive verbs

'entrenarse' is a reflexive verb (see p.185).

Me entreno todos los días.
I train every day.

Extended Answer

Diría que es importante entrenarse, pero no tengo tiempo para hacerlo todos los días. Voy al gimnasio dos veces a la semana y siempre elijo comida sana.

I would say that it's important to train, but I don't have time to do it every day. I go to the gym twice a week and I always choose healthy food.

Las buenas costumbres — Good habits

Es importante intentar comer una dieta equilibrada todos los días.

It's important to try to eat a balanced diet every day.

to avoid junk food — evitar la comida basura

Hago ejercicio los fines de semana porque no tengo mucho tiempo libre durante la semana.

I do exercise at weekends because I don't have much free time during the week.

I prefer to rest after school — prefiero descansar después del colegio

Vale la pena tener buenas costumbres como beber dos litros de agua todos los días.

It's worth having good habits like drinking two litres of water every day.

getting enough sleep — dormir lo suficiente

Es importante cuidar la salud mental también.

It's important to take care of your mental health too.

En mi opinión, la mente y el cuerpo son igualmente importantes. Por eso siempre dedico tiempo a hacer actividades relajantes.

In my opinion, the mind and the body are equally important. Therefore, I always devote time to doing relaxing activities.

daily life causes a lot of stress — la vida diaria causa mucho estrés

Las malas costumbres — Bad habits

Vocabulary

perezoso/a	*lazy*	la cantidad	*quantity, amount*
el peso	*weight*	el consumo	*consumption*
perder	*to lose*	el sobrepeso	*obesity, excess weight*
el riesgo	*risk*	el cigarrillo	*cigarette*
la droga	*drug*	el humo	*smoke, fumes*
fumar	*to smoke*	el alcohol	*alcohol*

Higher (el consumo ... el alcohol)

Soy una persona muy perezosa. Me encanta echarme en el sofá y ver la televisión durante horas.

I'm a very lazy person. I love to lie down on the sofa and watch TV for hours.

Los cigarrillos tienen muchos riesgos. El humo afecta la salud y puede causar enfermedades graves.

Cigarettes have lots of risks. The smoke affects your health and it can cause serious illnesses.

No quiero probar las drogas porque son peligrosas.

I don't want to try drugs because they are dangerous.

Una vez, bebí alcohol con mis amigos. No me gustó.

Once, I drank alcohol with my friends. I didn't like it.

Grammar — to stop ...ing

To say 'to stop ...ing', use 'dejar de' followed by the infinitive.

Quiero dejar de fumar.
I want to stop smoking.

to smoke because it smells horrible — fumar porque huele horrible

'Oler' *(to smell)* is an irregular verb.

Practice Questions

Q1 *Write an article for a magazine about healthy living. You should write about 90 words in Spanish. Mention:*

- *whether you exercise or not*
- *if you have a balanced diet*
- *two things you could do to lead a healthier life* [15 marks]

WRITING

Top Tips for Higher Students
✓ Give plenty of details about what makes your diet balanced.
✓ Use impersonal phrases like 'vale la pena' to say what is worth doing.

Q2 *Read Karima's thoughts on alcohol and drugs. Answer the questions in English.*

READING

Para mí, beber alcohol es tan peligroso como tomar drogas. Los jóvenes piensan que no importa si toman unas copas con los amigos, pero no prestan atención a las consecuencias. A veces, no saben ni dónde están ni cuánto han bebido. El año pasado, mi amigo bebió demasiado y tuvo que ir al hospital. Era muy irresponsable.

a) What is Karima's opinion on drinking alcohol? [1 mark]
b) What two consequences of drinking alcohol does Karima mention? [2 marks]
c) What happened to Karima's friend? [1 mark]

(Higher)

Some of this vocab is pretty tricky — so keep testing yourself...

All the biscuits seem to have disappeared... It's not all about physical health — practise talking about mental health too. Once you've tackled the healthy side of things, you can deal with unhealthy living.

Illnesses and Treatments

They might not be the cheeriest of topics, but you do need to know about illness and treatments.

Las enfermedades — Illnesses

Vocabulary

sentirse	*to feel (+ adjective)*	el cuerpo	*body*	el dolor	*pain, ache*
enfermo/a	*ill, sick*	la cabeza	*head*	la herida	*wound, injury*
cansado/a	*tired, tiring*	el ojo	*eye*	el cáncer	*cancer*
preocuparse por	*to worry about*	la lengua	*tongue*	la sangre	*blood*
respirar	*to breathe*	el diente	*tooth*	la pierna	*leg*
romperse	*to break (bones)*	la mano	*hand*	el brazo	*arm*
roto/a	*broken*	el pie	*foot*	la boca	*mouth*
doler	*to hurt, be painful*	la piel	*skin*	el cerebro	*brain*
caerse	*to fall over*	el corazón	*heart*	la mente	*mind*

(Higher: el dolor, la herida, el cáncer, la sangre, la pierna, el brazo, la boca, el cerebro, la mente)

Me siento... — I feel...

Question

¿Cómo te sientes?
How do you feel?

Simple Answer

Me duele la mano.
My hand hurts.

Extended Answer

Me duelen el pie y la pierna.
Tengo dolor de cabeza también.

My foot and leg hurt. I have a headache too.

> The verb 'romper' means 'to break', but you need the reflexive verb (see p.185) 'romperse' to talk about broken bones.

Grammar — 'doler' — to hurt

'Doler' works in a similar way to 'gustar' — to say what's hurting you, you need to use an indirect object pronoun (see p.155) before the verb. You also need to add an 'n' in the plural.

Me duele la pierna.	*My leg hurts.* ← Literally, 'the leg hurts me'.
Me duelen los pies.	*My feet hurt.*
Le duelen el brazo y la mano.	*His / her arm and hand hurt.*

You also need to remember that 'doler' is a stem-changing verb. See p.176.

Ayer me caí mientras corría y me rompí el brazo.

Yesterday I fell over while I was running and I broke my arm.

El año pasado, un familiar mío sufría una enfermedad grave. Me preocupé mucho por él.

Last year, a relative of mine was suffering from a serious illness. I worried a lot about him.

Lucho contra el sobrepeso. Estoy tratando de perder peso, pero es más difícil de lo que pensaba.

I struggle with excess weight. I'm trying to lose weight, but it's more difficult than I thought.

Siempre me siento enferma. Es muy duro porque me impide hacer actividades físicas.

I always feel ill. It's very hard because it stops me doing physical activities.

Mucha gente se preocupa por su peso y su apariencia.

Lots of people worry about their weight and their appearance.

I broke my wrist — me rompí la muñeca
I twisted my ankle — me torcí el tobillo

> In Spanish, you need to use the definite article ('the') instead of 'my' when you talk about body parts that you've hurt.

I get tired quickly — me canso rápidamente

have recurring health problems — tienen problemas de salud recurrentes

Necesito ir al médico — I need to go to the doctor

Vocabulary

el cuidado	*care, carefulness*	el/la médico/a	*doctor*	mental	*mental*
el accidente	*accident*	el/la paciente	*patient*	la cita	*appointment*
el hospital	*hospital*	la medicina	*medicine*	superar	*to overcome*

(Higher: mental, la cita, superar)

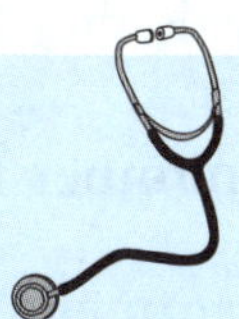

Tengo una cita con el médico porque me duele una herida en la mano.

I have an appointment with the doctor because a wound on my hand hurts.

I have a pain in my back — tengo un dolor en la espalda

Cuando era niño, tenía que tomar medicina para poder respirar mejor. Ahora ya no la necesito.

When I was a child, I had to take medicine to be able to breathe better. Now I no longer need it.

Superar las enfermedades mentales puede ser muy difícil. Es importante hablar con alguien si tienes problemas.

Overcoming mental illnesses can be very difficult. It's important to speak to someone if you have problems.

Alguna gente se siente nerviosa antes de visitar al médico.

Some people feel nervous before visiting the doctor.

appropriate treatments — tratamientos apropiados

Los médicos pueden ofrecer a los pacientes tanto apoyo como sea posible.

Doctors can offer patients as much support as possible.

lots of useful advice — muchos consejos útiles

Practice Questions

Q1 *Read this passage about an accident.*

SPEAKING

> El mes pasado, mi hermano tuvo un accidente en el parque. Se cayó del equipo de patio y le dolía mucho la cabeza. Mi madre quería llevarle al hospital para preguntar a los médicos si había algún problema. Sin embargo, mi hermano tenía miedo de ir al hospital entonces quería quedarse en casa.

Top Tip for Higher Students
✓ Use relative pronouns to add more detailed clauses to your sentences, e.g. 'Me rompí el brazo, lo que me dolió mucho.'

Now it's your turn. Talk about an accident you or a family member had in the past and what was done about it. Aim to talk for about two minutes. **[10 marks]**

Q2 *Listen to the conversation between Aitor and the doctor, then answer the questions below.*

LISTENING

Listening Track 11

a) What caused Aitor to start feeling unwell? **[1 mark]**

b) What does the doctor ask Aitor? **[1 mark]**

c) Why is Aitor having trouble falling asleep? **[1 mark]**

d) Write down two pieces of advice that the doctor gives Aitor. **[2 marks]**

(Higher)

'Doler' works in a similar way to 'gustar'...

No one likes feeling unwell, but it's important that you know how to talk about illness in Spanish. It's rather handy to learn the vocab for visiting a doctor too, so make sure you give those words a good going over.

Listening Questions

If you know what to expect in the exams, life will seem a whole lot easier and more pleasant. With that in mind, here's another batch of realistic questions for you to have a go at.

1 A reporter is interviewing two teenagers about their health problems. What health problem does each person mention and how do they treat it?

Write the correct **letter** for the problem and the correct **number** for the treatment.

Listening
Track 12

	Problem			**Treatment**
A	dry skin		1	goes to hospital regularly
B	eye problems		2	does exercise in the swimming pool
C	damage to their foot		3	takes medicine each night
D	a broken tooth		4	eats a special diet

1 a Sasha: problem [ ]   treatment [ ]

[2 marks]

1 b Jalil: problem [ ]   treatment [ ]

[2 marks]

2 Listen to this interview with Rosalía in a podcast about healthy eating. Write the correct letter in each box.

Listening
Track 13

2 a Rosalía became interested in breakfast to help...

A	her oldest daughter.
B	her youngest daughter.
C	herself.

[ ]

[1 mark]

2 b The majority of scientists think that breakfast is...

A	compulsory.
B	healthy.
C	important.

[ ]

[1 mark]

2 c Rosalía recommends that people...

A	only eat fruit for breakfast.
B	eat a balanced breakfast.
C	avoid eggs at breakfast.

[ ]

[1 mark]

(Higher)

Speaking Questions

Candidate's Material

- Spend a few minutes looking at the two photos. Make notes on them to use during the test.

- Your teacher will ask you to talk about the content of the photos. You should talk for approximately **one minute** at Foundation tier and **one and a half minutes** at Higher tier. **You must say at least one thing about each photo**.

- After you have spoken about the content of the photos, your teacher will then ask you some questions related to any of the topics within the topic of **Healthy Living and Lifestyle**.

Teacher's Material

- Candidates should talk about the photos above for approximately **one minute** at Foundation tier or **one and a half minutes** at Higher tier. They may use any notes they have made during the preparation time. Begin by asking the candidate to tell you about the photos:

  - Háblame de las fotos.

- When the candidate has finished talking about the photos, ask them the following unprepared conversation questions on the topic of **Healthy Living and Lifestyle**:

  - ¿Piensas que tienes una dieta equilibrada? ¿Por qué?

  - Háblame de una actividad física que haces.

  - ¿Cuál es tu opinión sobre las drogas?

  - ¿Qué consejo darías a un amigo para ayudarle a mejorar su salud?

  - ¿Qué piensas del alcohol? ¿Por qué?

  - Describe la última vez que fuiste al médico. ¿Qué pasó?

Reading Questions

1 Some friends are writing about food.

Which food does each person mention? Write the correct letter in each box.

A	fish
B	salad
C	chips

D	burgers
E	sandwiches
F	grapes

Foundation

1 a

Me gusta
la ensalada.

1 b

Odio las
patatas fritas.

1 c

Me encantan
los bocadillos.

[3 marks]

2 You read this news article about a recent report on unhealthy lifestyles.

> *Un estudio reciente ha descubierto que una cantidad enorme de gente lucha contra el sobrepeso. Los expertos han identificado tres factores cruciales que parecen contribuir al problema: el consumo de alcohol, una falta de conocimiento sobre la comida sana y una tendencia a hacer poco ejercicio. El científico que dirigió la investigación espera animar al gobierno a tomar medidas suficientes para ayudar a la gente a cambiar las malas costumbres.*

Answer the following questions in **English**.

Higher

2 a What has the study discovered?

.... *[1 mark]*

2 b Give **two** factors mentioned in the article that seem to contribute to obesity.

1. ....

2. .... *[2 marks]*

2 c What does the scientist who led the investigation hope to do?

.... *[1 mark]*

Writing Questions

1   Write an article about healthy and unhealthy living.

Write approximately **50** words in **Spanish**.

You must write something about each bullet point. Mention:

- food
- drink
- exercise
- smoking
- drugs.

[10 marks]

2   Translate the following sentences into **Spanish**.

2 a   I want to be a vegetarian in the future.

....   *[2 marks]*

2 b   She prepares a sandwich with ham and tomato.

....   *[2 marks]*

2 c   My friends say that exercise is relaxing.

....   *[2 marks]*

2 d   When my father was ill, he lost a lot of weight.

....

....   *[2 marks]*

2 e   I would never take drugs because there are too many risks.

....

....   *[2 marks]*

3   You are writing a blog post about health issues.

Write approximately **150** words in **Spanish**.

You must write something about each bullet point.

Mention:

- a health issue that you or someone you know recently had
- what could be done to avoid a similar problem in the future.

[25 marks]

Healthy Living and Lifestyle — Vocabulary

It's time for a recap of all the vocab from this section before you hop, skip and jump to the next topic.

Food

la fruta	fruit
la manzana	apple
la naranja	orange
la uva	grape
la verdura	vegetable
la ensalada	salad
el tomate	tomato
las patatas fritas	chips, fries
la hamburguesa	burger
la comida rápida	fast food
la comida basura	junk food
el bocadillo	sandwich
el huevo	egg
el pan	bread
la carne	meat
el jamón	ham
el pollo	chicken
el pescado	fish
la paella	paella (dish usually of rice and seafood)
el caramelo	sweet
vegetariano/a	vegetarian
vegano/a	vegan
la bebida	drink
el agua (f)	water
la leche	milk
el café	coffee
el vino	wine
el desayuno	breakfast

la comida	food, meal, lunch
la cena	dinner, evening meal
cenar	to have dinner, tea (evening meal)
preparar	to prepare
comer	to eat
beber	to drink
probar	to try, taste
gustar	to please, be pleasing to
odiar	to hate
el hambre (f)	hunger
la sed	thirst
dulce	sweet
rico/a	tasty
fresco/a	fresh
caliente	hot (temperature), warm
la sal	salt
la grasa	fat, grease
el azúcar	sugar
la botella	bottle
la copa	cup, (wine) glass
el vaso	(drinking) glass
el alimento	food, nourishment
el arroz	rice
el aceite	oil
cocinar	to cook
saludable	healthy
asqueroso/a	disgusting, revolting

Higher (brackets el alimento through asqueroso/a)

Healthy Living

la vida	life
la salud	health
sano/a	healthy, wholesome
suficiente	sufficient, enough
la importancia	importance
se necesita	you need (to) (general), one needs (to)
llevar	to lead
evitar	to avoid, prevent
activo/a	active
físico/a	physical
el ejercicio	exercise
estar en forma	to be fit
mantenerse	to keep oneself
entrenarse	to train, go training
entrenar	to train
la dieta	diet (general)
equilibrado/a	balanced

el paso	step
la costumbre	habit
el sueño	sleep
dormir	to sleep
dormirse	to fall asleep
descansar	to rest, relax
diario/a	daily
relajante	relaxing
relajar(se)	to relax
acostarse	to go to bed
pasear	to take for a walk, go for a walk
promover	to promote

Higher (brackets diario/a through promover)

'Entrenar' means 'to train someone else', whereas 'entrenarse' means 'to train yourself'.

Unhealthy Living

demasiado(s)/a(s)	*too much (many) + noun, too much, too + adjective*
perezoso/a	*lazy*
el peso	*weight*
el régimen	*diet (for weight loss or medical conditions)*
perder	*to lose*
el riesgo	*risk*
la droga	*drug*
fumar	*to smoke*
dejar de (+ infinitive)	*to stop (+ ing)*
probar	*to try*

Higher

la cantidad	*quantity, amount*
el consumo	*consumption*
el sobrepeso	*obesity, excess weight*
el cigarrillo	*cigarette*
el humo	*smoke, fumes*
huele (a)	*it smells (of)*
el alcohol	*alcohol*
la consecuencia	*consequence*

Illnesses and Treatments

la enfermedad	*illness, disease*
grave	*serious*
sentirse	*to feel (+ adjective)*
sentir	*to feel, sense*
enfermo/a	*ill, sick*
cansado/a	*tired, tiring*
preocupar	*to (be a) worry*
preocuparse por	*to worry about*
el estrés	*stress*
respirar	*to breathe*
romperse	*to break (bones)*
roto/a	*broken*
doler	*to hurt, be painful*
morir	*to die*
muerto/a	*dead*
caer	*to fall*
caerse	*to fall over*
el cuerpo	*body*
la cabeza	*head (body part)*
el ojo	*eye*
la vista	*sight*
la lengua	*tongue*
el diente	*tooth*
la mano	*hand*
el pie	*foot*
débil	*weak*
fuerte	*strong*
la piel	*skin*
el corazón	*heart*
el cuidado	*care, carefulness*
el accidente	*accident*
el hospital	*hospital*
el/la médico/a	*doctor*
ayudar	*to help*
apoyar	*to support*
el apoyo	*support*

Use 'sentirse' when you want to talk about how you feel physically or mentally, e.g. 'Me siento mal'. Use 'sentir' when you want to talk about general feelings, emotions or sensations, e.g. 'Siento frío'.

el/la paciente	*patient*
la medicina	*medicine*
tomar	*to take, have, drink*
el resultado	*result*

Higher

luchar	*to fight, struggle*
sufrir	*to suffer*
el dolor	*pain, ache*
la herida	*wound, injury*
el cáncer	*cancer*
vivo/a	*alive*
la muerte	*death*
la sangre	*blood*
la pierna	*leg*
el brazo	*arm*
la boca	*mouth*
el cerebro	*brain*
la mente	*mind*
mental	*mental*
la cita	*appointment*
echarse	*to lie down*
la tasa	*rate*
la medida	*measure*
tratar	*to treat*
superar	*to get over, overcome*
resultar	*to be, to turn out (+ adjective)*

Revision Summary Test for Section Three

Give your mind a good workout by testing your knowledge on this section with these questions.

- Yep, these questions are **hard** — they'll really help you see **how well you know your stuff**.
- Tackle the **revision summary test** below, or scan the QR code to do it **online**.
  Use the CGP RevisionHub to **track your progress** and see **which areas need more work**.
- You can find **sample answers** here: www.cgpbooks.co.uk/MadridExtras

Food ☑

1) You're going shopping with your Argentinian friend. These foods are on their list: manzanas, pollo, tomates, naranjas, uvas, pan, jamón y huevos. What are these foods in English?

2) 'Tengo sed. Quiero un café con leche.' What does this mean in English?

3) In Spanish, give one food that you like and one food that you hate. Give a reason for each one.

4) What are these in English? a) un vaso de leche   b) una copa de vino   c) una botella de agua

5) 'Aunque no tenía hambre anoche, me preparé una ensalada caliente con pescado y verduras frescas.' How would you say this in English?

6) ¿Qué piensas de la comida vegana?

H 7) Iratxe says: 'I always cook chips in oil and eat them with salt.' How would she say this in Spanish?

Healthy and Unhealthy Living ☑

8) 'Si quieres mantenerte en forma, es importante hacer ejercicio físico.' Translate this into English.

9) Describe tus buenas costumbres.

10) Belén wants to be healthier. Which one of the following options would help her?
    a) comer más grasa   b) dormir menos   c) no tomar bebidas con mucho azúcar

11) What's the Spanish for...? a) one needs to   b) to be fit   c) to lose weight   d) to stop ...ing

12) ¿Piensas que la mayoría de los jóvenes llevan una vida sana? ¿Por qué (no)?

13) Isabel says: 'Mis hermanos son tan perezosos. No hacen suficiente ejercicio.' What is she saying?

14) ¿Cuál es tu opinión sobre la comida basura?

15) 'No me interesa probar drogas. Tienen muchos riesgos para la salud.' Say this in English.

H 16) 'Me molesta cuando la gente fuma. El humo de los cigarrillos huele mal.' What is this person saying?

Illnesses and Treatments ☑

17) How many body parts can you name in Spanish? There are 8 of them (plus 4 for Higher tier).

18) Nia says: 'Me duele todo el cuerpo. Pienso que es debido al estrés. Por eso necesito descansar.' Why does Nia feel so ill?

19) Translate this into Spanish: 'I will study medicine because I would like to help patients feel better.'

20) 'El año pasado, la abuela de Juan se cayó y pasó un mes en el hospital.' What happened last year?

21) What's the Spanish for...? a) to worry about   b) to break (bones)   c) to die   d) doctor

22) José tells you: 'Cuando me entreno, me cuesta respirar.' What is José's health problem?

23) Imagine you've gone to see the doctor. Describe your health problem and what the doctor recommends in Spanish.

24) Translate these words into Spanish:
    a) sick   b) broken   c) dead   d) care   e) accident   f) weak   g) strong

25) What can someone do to look after their mental health? Answer this question in Spanish.

H 26) En tu opinión, ¿qué medidas se pueden tomar para evitar enfermedades graves?

27) 'Los resultados del estudio preocupan a mucha gente.' Translate this sentence into English.

School Subjects

Quick Quiz

School subjects — as if you don't get enough of them at school. However, it's important to learn what they are in Spanish and to be able to say what you think about them.

Remember there's also lots of online content here: www.cgpbooks.co.uk/Madrid

Las asignaturas — School subjects

Vocabulary

el inglés	*English*	las matemáticas	*maths*	la cocina	*food technology*
el español	*Spanish*	las ciencias	*science(s)*	la educación física	*physical education (PE)*
el francés	*French*	la geografía	*geography*		
el italiano	*Italian*	la historia	*history*	el dibujo	*art*
el alemán	*German*	la religión	*religion (RE)*	el teatro	*drama*
el chino	*Chinese*	la informática	*ICT*	la música	*music*

Mi asignatura favorita es... — My favourite subject is...

Q&A Audio

Question

¿Cuál es tu asignatura favorita?
What's your favourite subject?

Simple Answer

Mi asignatura favorita es la música. Me encanta tocar la guitarra.
My favourite subject is music. I love to play the guitar.

Extended Answer

El español es mi asignatura favorita ya que es muy interesante.
Será útil también porque espero ir a España el verano que viene.

Spanish is my favourite subject as it's very interesting. It will be useful too because I hope to go to Spain next summer.

Me gusta la historia. Es interesante aprender sobre el pasado.

I like history. It's interesting to learn about the past.

→ *still relevant* — todavía relevante

Gonzalo odia las ciencias pero los idiomas son más fáciles para él.

Gonzalo hates science but languages are easier for him.

biology — la biología
chemistry — la química
physics — la física

Nos encantan las matemáticas aunque para otros son una asignatura dura.

We love maths even though for others it's a hard subject.

difficult — difícil
complicated — complicado/a

Practice Question

Q1 *You are writing a blog post about your school subjects.*
You should write about 50-90 words in Spanish.
Write about:

- *which subject(s) you dislike*
- *which subject(s) you find hard or easy*
- *what your favourite subject is.*   [15 marks]

Top Tip for Higher Students
✓ Use the superlatives 'el/la mejor' or 'el/la peor' to say which subjects are the best or worst.

Subject yourself to learning all the asignaturas...

Remember — each school subject has its own gender. Many are masculine and singular, while some are feminine and/or plural, e.g. 'las ciencias'. Make sure you know the correct spelling and gender for each one.

School Life

Same old routine, day in, day out. At least that'll make it easier to talk about it in the exam.
Maybe you'll also get a chance to mention all the things you love (or hate) about school...

Mi horario — My timetable

Vocabulary

el día	*day*	comenzar	*to start, begin*
la lista	*list, register*	empezar	*to start, begin*
la clase	*class, lesson*	terminar	*to finish, end*
el recreo	*break*	durar	*to last*

Grammar — telling the time

If you're saying what time something is at, remember to put '<u>a</u>' first.

La hora de comer es <u>a la una</u>.
Lunchtime is <u>at one o'clock</u>.

For more about time, see p.5.

Mi colegio empieza a las nueve y el profesor pasa la lista a las nueve y cinco.

My school starts at nine o'clock and the teacher reads the register at five past nine.

at twenty to nine
— a las nueve menos veinte

we go to the assembly room
— vamos al salón de actos

Tengo cinco clases al día y cada clase dura cuarenta minutos.

I have five lessons a day and each lesson lasts forty minutes.

A las tres y media vuelvo a casa.

At half past three I return home.

the school day finishes
— el día escolar termina

Question

¿Qué haces durante el recreo?

What do you do during break?

Simple Answer

Durante el recreo, juego al fútbol con mis amigas.

During break, I play football with my friends.

Extended Answer

Prefiero leer durante el recreo porque mis amigos van al club de tenis, que a mí no me gusta.

I prefer to read during my break because my friends go to the tennis club, which I don't like.

En clase — In class

Vocabulary

la pantalla	*screen*	el papel	*paper*
la puerta	*door*	la regla	*ruler*
la mesa	*table*	el bolígrafo	*pen*
la silla	*chair*	la mochila	*school bag*
olvidar (+ noun)	*to forget*	el aula (f)	*classroom*
llevar	*to take, carry, wear*	prestar	*to lend*
el libro	*book*	el diario	*diary, journal*

Higher (el aula, prestar, el diario)

Grammar — el aula

'Aula' is <u>feminine</u>, but it uses '<u>el</u>' when it's <u>singular</u>. Any <u>adjectives</u> must be in the <u>feminine</u> form.

<u>El</u> aula está <u>llena</u>.
The classroom is <u>full</u>.

¿Me puedes prestar un bolígrafo para la prueba de geografía?

Can you lend me a pen for the geography test?

a pencil — un lápiz

Ayer, puse un estuche y varios libros en mi mochila.

Yesterday, I put a pencil case and several books in my school bag.

an exercise book — un cuaderno

Me he olvidado de traer mi regla.

I have forgotten to bring my ruler.

'Olvidar' is usually followed by a noun, whereas 'olvidarse de' is usually followed by a verb.

¿Cómo es tu colegio? — What's your school like?

Vocabulary

el instituto	*secondary school*	el uniforme	*uniform*	el gimnasio	*gym*
la escuela	*(primary) school*	la instalación	*facility*	los servicios	*toilets*
público/a	*public*	el patio	*playground*	la biblioteca	*library*
religioso/a	*religious*	el campo	*pitch, field (sport)*	privado/a	*private*
moderno/a	*modern*	la piscina	*swimming pool*	internacional	*international*

Hay quinientos alumnos en mi instituto y llevamos uniforme.

There are 500 students at my school and we wear a uniform.

we don't have to wear a uniform — no tenemos que llevar uniforme

Soy alumna aquí desde hace tres años. Me gusta este colegio y me llevo bien con los profesores.

I've been a student here for three years. I like this school and I get on well with the teachers.

the teachers are very nice — los profesores son muy simpáticos

La escuela de mi hermano tiene un campo de deportes grande donde pueden jugar al hockey.

My brother's school has a big sports field where they can play hockey.

a small gym where they can keep fit — un gimnasio pequeño donde pueden mantenerse en forma

En mi colegio, las aulas no tienen suficientes sillas.

In my school, the classrooms don't have enough chairs.

the computers don't work well — los ordenadores no funcionan bien

Practice Questions

Q1 *Juan and Marta are talking about their timetables. Choose the correct option from the times below to complete the sentences in English.*

Listening Track 14

a) On Mondays, Juan and Marta have English at...
  A. 8:30   **B.** 9:45   **C.** 9:20   *[1 mark]*

b) Then they go to their history class at...
  A. 10:15   **B.** 10:30   **C.** 11:15   *[1 mark]*

c) Juan prefers Wednesdays, when they have music at...
  A. 11:45   **B.** 12:15   **C.** 13:30   *[1 mark]*

Higher

Q2 *Read this message from Daraja about her school and answer the questions below in English.*

¡Hola! Soy Daraja. Voy a un colegio privado y hay ochocientos alumnos. En general, me encantan las instalaciones. Lo mejor es la biblioteca — hay muchos libros y estoy segura de que podrías encontrar todo lo que necesitas. Además, tenemos una piscina enorme y un campo deportivo. Lo malo es el gimnasio porque está muy sucio.

a) How many people go to Daraja's school?   *[1 mark]*
b) Why does she think the library is the best facility?   *[1 mark]*
c) How does Daraja describe the pool?   *[1 mark]*
d) Why does Daraja dislike the gym?   *[1 mark]*

You might want to schedule break time after this...

There is only so much vocabulary and grammar that you can learn in one go, so split up your revision and try to practise in manageable chunks. Having a rest from time to time will make it much easier to focus.

Quick Quiz

School Pressures and Difficulties

Now is your chance to vent your frustrations and find some solutions to those school difficulties...

Las reglas — The rules

Vocabulary

necesario/a	*necessary, required*	pedir	*to ask for*
hay que	*you must (general)*	permitir	*to allow, permit*
tener que	*to have to, must*	prohibir	*to prohibit, forbid*
deber	*to have to, must*	⌈obligatorio/a	*compulsory*
poder	*to be able to, can*	H⌊el permiso	*permission*

Ernie wasn't very impressed with the new uniform rules...

No deberías **gritar la respuesta** en clase.

You should not shout the answer in class.

→ *arrive late* — llegar tarde

Hay que **levantar la mano** antes de contestar.

You must raise your hand before answering.

→ *write in blue or black ink* — escribir en tinta azul o negra

Es obligatorio **llevar camisa blanca y zapatos negros.**

It's compulsory to wear a white shirt and black shoes.

→ *to wear a tie* — llevar corbata

Está prohibido **usar el móvil** en clase.

It's forbidden to use your mobile phone in class.

→ *to run in the corridors* — correr en los pasillos
to eat chewing gum — comer chicle

Las presiones del colegio — School pressures

Vocabulary

aprender	*to learn*	el examen	*exam*	⌈lograr	*to achieve, manage to (+ verb)*
estudiar	*to study*	aprobar	*to pass*	conseguir	*to get, obtain*
repasar	*to revise*	la nota	*grade*	Higher suspender	*to fail*
el estrés	*stress*	los deberes	*homework*	⌊equivocarse	*to be wrong, make a mistake*

Los exámenes causan **mucho estrés** cuando **necesitas aprobar.**

Exams cause lots of stress when you need to pass.

→ *you don't have enough support* — no tienes suficiente apoyo

Sienten presión de sus padres **para conseguir buenas notas.**

They feel pressure from their parents to get good grades.

El acoso **es un problema grave** en mi colegio. Creo que más gente debería **pensar en el efecto que pueden tener sus palabras.**

Bullying is a serious problem in my school. I think more people should think about the effect their words can have.

→ *exists in many forms* — existe en muchas formas

Tengo miedo de equivocarme en los exámenes y **suspenderlos.**

I'm afraid of making mistakes in the exams and failing them.

→ *not being able to study the Baccalaureate* — no poder estudiar el Bachillerato

La presión de grupo **es difícil.** Me gustaría hacer felices a mis amigos, pero **no quiero romper las reglas.**

Peer pressure is difficult. I would like to make my friends happy, but I don't want to break the rules.

Evitar problemas — Preventing problems

Tengo suerte porque mis amigos me apoyan mucho.

I'm lucky because my friends support me a lot.

my parents help me to study — mis padres me ayudan a estudiar

Para reducir el estrés, intenta repasar poco a poco.

To reduce stress, try to revise little by little.

to do sport or something fun — hacer deporte o algo divertido

Es importante respetar a todos tus compañeros.

It's important to respect all your classmates.

other students — otros alumnos

Necesito confiar en mi profesora para contarle mis problemas.

I need to trust in my teacher in order to tell her my problems.

not suffer in silence — no sufrir en silencio

Q&A Audio

Question

¿Cómo puedes reducir el estrés del colegio?

How can you reduce stress from school?

Simple Answer

Para reducir el estrés, es importante hablar con alguien.

To reduce stress, it's important to talk with someone.

Extended Answer

En mi opinión, charlar con mis amigos es la mejor manera de reducir el estrés. Me ayudan mucho a pensar en soluciones prácticas.

In my opinion, chatting with my friends is the best way to reduce stress. They help me a lot to think of practical solutions.

Practice Questions

Q1 *Look at the two photos below. Talk in Spanish about what is in the photos. You should talk for about a minute and say something about each photo.*

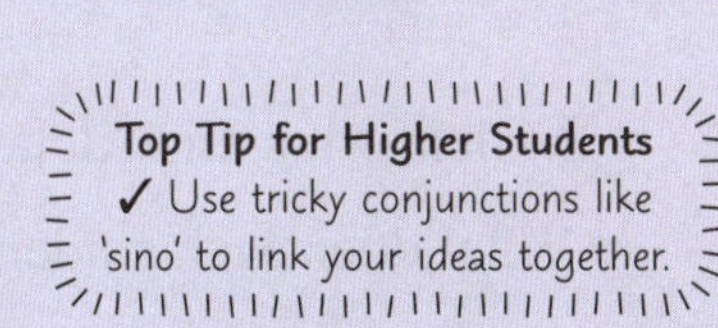

[5 marks]

Q2 *Listen to Omar talking about causes of stress at school. There are two correct statements in each list below. Choose the correct options from each list.*

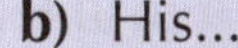

a) Omar...
- **A.** has to do homework on Mondays.
- **B.** gets more homework than others.
- **C.** says exams stress him the most.
- **D.** leaves it late to do his homework.

[2 marks]

b) His...
- **A.** parents tell him to relax.
- **B.** friends aren't as stressed.
- **C.** parents support him a lot.
- **D.** friends compete with him.

[2 marks]

Make revision less stressful by varying your study techniques...

There are lots of different ways to recap and revise the content of these pages. For example, try making a list of the main rules at your school or a mind map of the different causes of stress — in Spanish of course...

Listening Questions

You'll soon be ready to deal with whatever the examiners throw at you. Don't forget there's a practice exam at the back of the book, so you can try questions on different topics under time pressure.

1   You will hear 4 short sentences. Listen carefully and, using your knowledge of Spanish sounds, write down in **Spanish** exactly what you hear for each sentence.

   You will hear each sentence **three** times: the first time as a full sentence, the second time in short sections and the third time again as a full sentence.

   Use your knowledge of Spanish sounds and grammar to make sure that what you have written makes sense. Check carefully that your spelling is accurate.

Listening Track 16

1 a   Sentence 1

....   *[2 marks]*

1 b   Sentence 2

....   *[2 marks]*

1 c   Sentence 3

....   *[2 marks]*

1 d   Sentence 4

....   *[2 marks]*

2   Malek, Alba and Alejandro are talking about different issues at school.

   What does each student think is not a problem at their school?

   What does each student believe needs to improve at their school?

Listening Track 17

A	Exams	C	Peer pressure	E	School rules
B	Homework	D	Behaviour	F	Teachers

Write the correct letter in each box.

	Not a problem	**Needs to improve**
2 a Malek		

[2 marks]

| **2 b**   Alba | | |

[2 marks]

| **2 c**   Alejandro | | |

[2 marks]

Speaking Questions

Candidate's Material

- When your teacher asks you, read aloud the following text **in Spanish**.

Foundation

Llego al instituto a las ocho y diez.

En mi mochila llevo muchos bolígrafos para mi clase de dibujo.

Mis asignaturas favoritas son la religión y la geografía.

También me encanta la educación física.

El gimnasio es muy grande y bastante moderno.

Higher

A mí no me gustan las matemáticas porque me resultan complicadas.

Entonces, debería estudiar más para mejorar mis notas.

No sería capaz de repasar bien sin los libros de mi hermano.

Suspendo el francés desde hace meses pero no es la culpa de la profesora.

Es difícil escuchar a la profesora porque siempre hay mucho ruido en la clase.

Es necesario que mi clase tenga menos estudiantes.

- You will then be asked four questions **in Spanish** that relate to the topic of **Education**.

- In order to score the highest marks, **answer all four questions as fully as you can**.

Teacher's Material

- Start by asking the candidate to read the text by saying *Lee el texto*.

- Allow the candidate to read the text aloud, then ask the following four questions for their tier.

- Allow the student to develop their answers as much as possible.

Foundation

- ¿Cómo es tu colegio?

- ¿Qué uniforme tienes que llevar?

- ¿Cómo son tus profesores?

- Describe el mejor día de la semana en tu colegio.

Higher

- Háblame de tu asignatura favorita.

- Describe a tus compañeros.

- ¿Qué hiciste durante el recreo ayer?

- ¿Cómo sería tu instituto ideal?

Reading Questions

1 Read Leya's email to a pen pal about her school, then answer the questions below. Write the correct letters in the boxes.

> Las clases empiezan a las nueve menos diez pero prefiero estar en el colegio un poco antes para hablar con mis amigos. Tenemos seis clases cada día y tenemos una hora para comer. Casi siempre tenemos una asignatura dura por la tarde, como matemáticas o alemán, entonces normalmente salgo del colegio cansada. Creo que sería mejor tener menos tiempo para comer y una vuelta a casa más temprana, pero claro, ¡no puedo cambiar el horario!

1 a Classes start at...

A	ten to nine.
B	nine o'clock.
C	ten past nine.

[1 mark]

1 b Leya thinks that maths is...

A	more useful than German.
B	better in the afternoon.
C	a difficult subject.

[1 mark]

1 c Leya wishes that she could...

A	have shorter lunch breaks.
B	start school earlier.
C	go home for lunch.

[1 mark]

2 What do these people think about school?   Write **P** for a **positive** opinion, **N** for a **negative** opinion or **P + N** for a **positive** and **negative** opinion.

2 a
> **Manuel**: Todas mis asignaturas son demasiado sencillas. Por eso, encuentro mi instituto muy aburrido.

[1 mark]

2 b
> **Monika**: El día empieza a una hora temprana. Aunque me hace cansada, estoy contenta en clase porque me encanta aprender.

[1 mark]

2 c
> **Toni**: Para mis amigos el colegio es genial, pero yo no lo veo así. Hay tantas restricciones con las cuales no estoy de acuerdo.

[1 mark]

2 d
> **Jorge**: Encuentro algunas asignaturas verdaderamente complicadas. En cambio, creo que otras son muy útiles y educativas.

[1 mark]

Writing Questions

1   You are writing an email to your Cuban friend about what you study.

Write approximately **50** words in **Spanish**.

You must write something about each bullet point.

Mention:

- maths
- science
- languages
- your teachers
- your classmates.

[10 marks]

2   Translate the following sentences into **Spanish**.

2 a   The headteacher was very serious.

....   *[2 marks]*

2 b   We revise in the library.

....   *[2 marks]*

2 c   I must study English because it is compulsory.

....   *[2 marks]*

2 d   My friend is going to study at a private secondary school.

....   *[2 marks]*

2 e   I used to study lots of different languages.

....   *[2 marks]*

3   You are writing an article about school life.

Write approximately **150** words in **Spanish**.

You must write something about both bullet points.

Mention:

- the positive aspects of your school
- what you would change about your school.

[25 marks]

Foundation

Higher

Education — Vocabulary

Much like your average day of school, this vocab list seems rather long — but you'll get through it in the end.

School Subjects

la asignatura	school subject		la educación física	physical education (PE)
la educación	education		el dibujo	art
el inglés	English		el teatro	drama
el español	Spanish		la música	music
el francés	French		favorito/a	favourite
el italiano	Italian		práctico/a	practical, useful
el alemán	German		útil	useful
el chino	Chinese		fácil	easy
el idioma	language		sencillo/a	simple, easy
la lengua	language		duro/a	hard
las matemáticas	maths		difícil	difficult, hard
las ciencias	science(s)		educativo/a	educational
la geografía	geography		la selección	choice, selection
la historia	history		el castellano	(Castilian) Spanish
la religión	religion	Higher	el lenguaje	language, speech
la informática	ICT		la literatura	literature
la cocina	food technology		complicado/a	difficult, complicated

School Life

el horario	timetable, schedule		el colegio	(secondary) school
el día	day		el instituto	secondary school
la lista	list, (school) register		la escuela	(primary) school
la clase	class, lesson, classroom		público/a	public
el recreo	break (at school)		religioso/a	religious
el club	club		moderno/a	modern
comenzar	to start, begin		el uniforme	uniform
empezar	to start, begin		la camisa	shirt
temprano/a	early		el pantalón	trousers
terminar	to finish, end		la falda	skirt
durar	to last		el zapato	shoe
el/la director(a)	headteacher		la instalación	facility
el/la secretario/a	secretary		el patio	yard, playground
el/la profesor(a)	teacher		el campo	pitch, field (sport)
el/la estudiante	student		la piscina	swimming pool
el/la alumno/a	student, pupil		el gimnasio	gym
el/la compañero/a	classmate, group member		los servicios	toilets
la tecnología	technology		la biblioteca	library
la pantalla	screen		el equipo	equipment
la puerta	door		el aula (f)	classroom
la mesa	table		prestar	to lend, pay (attention)
la silla	chair, seat		el diario	diary, journal
olvidar (+ noun)	to forget (something)	Higher	privado/a	private
olvidarse de (+ verb)	to forget (to do something)		internacional	international
llevar	to take, carry, wear		charlar	to chat
el libro	book		firmar	to sign
el papel	paper		desde hace + present tense	to have been + -ing + for + time
la regla	ruler			
el bolígrafo	pen			
la mochila	school bag, rucksack			

School Pressures and Difficulties

la regla	*rule*
necesario/a	*necessary, required*
hay que	*you must (general), one must*
tener que	*to have to, must*
deber	*to have to, must*
poder	*to be able to, can*
pedir	*to ask for*
mandar	*to order*
permitir	*to allow, permit*
permitirse	*to afford*
prohibir	*to prohibit, forbid*
gritar	*to shout*
callarse	*to be quiet, quieten down*
levantar	*to raise*
preguntar	*to ask (a question)*
contestar	*to answer, reply, respond*
explicar	*to explain*
saber	*to know (how to)*
conocer	*to know (person, place)*
responsable	*responsible*
independiente	*independent*
escribir	*to write*
enseñar	*to teach, show*
aprender	*to learn*
estudiar	*to study*
el estudio	*study, learning*
repasar	*to revise, review*
preparar(se)	*to prepare (oneself)*
mejorar	*to improve, make better*
la presión	*pressure*
el estrés	*stress*
el examen	*exam*
la prueba	*test*
aprobar	*to pass (test)*
sacar	*to get, obtain*
la nota	*grade, note, mark*
el resultado	*result*
el error	*error, mistake*
la falta	*mistake*
costar	*to be hard*
el éxito	*success*
la suerte	*luck, fortune*
los deberes	*homework*
la tarea	*task, homework*
el proyecto	*project*
el trabajo	*work, effort*
trabajar	*to work*
trabajador(a)	*hardworking*
cansado/a	*tired, tiring*
el esfuerzo	*effort*
la confianza	*confidence, trust*

la palabra	*word*
la frase	*phrase, sentence*
el consejo	*(piece of) advice*
el apoyo	*support*
apoyar	*to support*
respetar	*to respect*
la discusión	*discussion, argument*
el acoso	*bullying*
la violencia	*violence*
el comportamiento	*behaviour*
causar	*to cause*
continuar	*to continue*
obligatorio/a	*compulsory*
el permiso	*permission*
lograr	*to achieve, manage to (+ verb)*
conseguir	*to get, obtain*
suspender	*to fail*
equivocarse	*to be wrong, make a mistake*
sentarse	*to sit (down)*
la respuesta	*answer, reply*
el nivel	*level*
pegar	*to hit, stick (on)*
castigar	*to punish*
estricto/a	*strict*
capaz	*capable, able*
consciente	*conscious, aware*
reflejar	*to reflect*
entregar	*to deliver, hand in*
confiar	*to trust, confide*
expresar	*to express*
ordenar	*to tidy, organise*
el orden	*order*
la enseñanza	*education, teaching*
la inteligencia	*intelligence*
la imaginación	*imagination*
el conocimiento	*knowledge*
el silencio	*silence*
la responsabilidad	*responsibility*
la independencia	*independence*

(Higher)

Elfa loved revising for food technology — it was a piece of cake...

Revision Summary Test for Section Four

This section has been all about school and learning... Try this test to see how much you've learned.

- These questions are **hard**, but they'll really help you see **how well you know your stuff**.
- Tackle the **revision summary test** below, or scan the QR code to do it **online**.
  You can **track your progress** online and see **which areas need more work**.
- There are **sample answers** for the test here: www.cgpbooks.co.uk/MadridExtras

School Subjects ☑

1) List the school subjects covered in this section. There are 17 (plus 2 for Higher tier). ☑
2) '¿Cuál es tu asignatura favorita y por qué?' Translate this question, then answer it in Spanish. ☑
3) In Spanish, give two words that mean 'language' (plus another one for Higher tier). ☑
4) How would you say the words below in Spanish?
   a) education b) practical c) useful d) simple e) hard f) educational g) difficult ☑
H 5) 'No logro encontrar la respuesta en la selección de libros complicados.' Translate this into English. ☑

School Life ☑

6) How would you say the words and phrases below in English?
   a) una escuela moderna   b) un instituto religioso   c) olvidarse de   d) el horario ☑
7) There are two different Spanish verbs meaning 'to start' or 'to begin'. Write down both of them. ☑
8) Cruz says: 'Durante el recreo, me gusta ir al club de teatro. ¿Qué te gusta hacer?'
   Translate what they said into English, then answer their question in Spanish. ☑
9) How do you say the words below in Spanish?
   a) headteacher b) secretary c) to forget (something) d) equipment e) technology f) register ☑
10) Alex asks: '¿Qué uniforme llevas?' What is Alex's question? Answer it in Spanish. ☑
11) Translate the words below into English:
    a) la pantalla b) la mesa c) la silla d) la puerta e) terminar f) temprano/a g) público/a ☑
12) '¿Qué llevas en tu mochila?' Translate this question into English, then answer it in Spanish. ☑
13) Raúl says: 'I have been going to an international school for two years and the facilities are great.'
    Translate his sentence into Spanish, then write two sentences about your own school's facilities. ☑
14) 'La profesora ordena el aula mientras los alumnos escriben en silencio.' Translate this into English. ☑

[Higher — brackets around questions 13 and 14]

School Pressures and Difficulties ☑

15) How do you say the words below in English?
    a) gritar b) callarse c) la frase d) preguntar e) pedir f) conocer g) la palabra h) la falta ☑
16) Give a school rule starting with each phrase: a) Es necesario b) Hay que c) Tengo que d) Debo ☑
17) 'Me cuesta mucho hacer los deberes y hago muchos errores.' Translate this sentence into English. ☑
18) How do you say the words below in Spanish?
    a) to allow b) result c) explain d) to work e) hardworking f) to know (how to) g) to forbid ☑
19) Antonio says: 'Estoy cansado de preparar tareas y proyectos para el colegio.' What is he saying? ☑
20) Write at least two sentences in Spanish about bad behaviour at your school and how to improve it. ☑
21) In your opinion, what do you need to do to succeed in exams? Answer in Spanish. ☑
22) In Spanish, suggest two different things that might help with school pressures. ☑
H 23) 'No puedo permitirme suspender la prueba. Confía en mí.' Translate these sentences into English. ☑
24) What are two things that you would change about your school? Answer in Spanish. ☑

Education Post-16

Quick Quiz

You may not have thought about your future plans, but they may appear in the exam.

Remember there's also lots of online content here: www.cgpbooks.co.uk/Madrid

¿Qué harás? — What will you do?

Vocabulary

estudiar	*to study*	aprobar	*to pass (test)*	la formación (Higher)	*training, education*
el Bachillerato	*Baccalaureate (equivalent to A levels)*	la prueba	*test*	el título (Higher)	*title, (university) degree*
la universidad	*university*	el examen	*exam*	el derecho (Higher)	*law (subject of study)*
la medicina	*medicine*	la nota	*grade, mark*	la traducción (Higher)	*translation*
		la profesión	*profession*	conseguir (Higher)	*to get, obtain*
		entrenarse	*to train*	suspender (Higher)	*to fail*

See p.49 for more subjects.

Quiero hacer el Bachillerato porque espero conseguir un título en derecho en la universidad.

I want to do the Baccalaureate (A levels) because I hope to get a degree in law at university.

to train as a plumber — entrenarme como fontanero

to work with my hands — trabajar con las manos

Todo depende de mis exámenes. Si los apruebo, continuaré estudiando. Si los suspendo, haré un curso de formación profesional.

It all depends on my exams. If I pass them, I will continue studying. If I fail them, I will do a professional training course.

I will take a gap year — me tomaré un año sabático

Q&A Audio

Question

¿Cuáles son tus planes para el futuro?

What are your plans for the future?

Simple Answer

Quiero empezar a trabajar.

I want to start working.

Extended Answer

Me gustaría dejar de estudiar tan pronto como sea posible. Preferiría trabajar en una profesión para ganar experiencia laboral.

I would like to stop studying as soon as possible. I would prefer to work in a profession to gain work experience.

Grammar — conditional

To say that something could, should or would happen, use the conditional (p.183).

Me gustaría estudiar música.

I would like to study music.

'Quisiera' can also be used to say 'I would like' (p.184).

Practice Question

Q1 *Look at the two photos below. Talk in Spanish about what is in the photos. You should talk for about a minute and say something about each photo.*

SPEAKING

Top Tip for Higher Students
✓ Use the passive voice accurately, e.g. 'los estudiantes son enseñados por un experto.'

[5 marks]

Show that you can use the future tenses and the conditional...

Impress examiners by showing them that you know how to use a range of tenses correctly. Have a think of some set phrases that you can confidently slot into your writing or speaking exams, then learn them by heart.

Career Choices and Ambitions

All this revising is hard work and now you've got another job to do — learn about careers.

Los empleos — Jobs

Vocabulary

trabajar	*to work*	el/la escritor(a)	*writer*	el/la soldado/a	*soldier*	
el trabajo	*job*	el/la periodista	*journalist*	el/la empresario/a	*business person, entrepreneur*	
la carrera	*career*	el/la pintor(a)	*painter*			
el/la médico/a	*doctor*	el/la peluquero/a	*hairdresser*	el/la obrero/a	*worker, labourer*	
el/la enfermero/a	*nurse*	el/la policía	*police officer*			
el/la cuidador(a)	*carer*	la policía	*police (organisation)*	la construcción	*construction (industry)*	
el/la abogado/a	*lawyer*					
el/la ingeniero/a	*engineer*	el ejército	*army*			

(Higher: el/la soldado/a, el/la empresario/a, el/la obrero/a, la construcción)

Cuando era más pequeño, mi padre era soldado en el ejército. Viajábamos mucho.

When I was younger, my father was a soldier in the army. We used to travel a lot.

worked abroad a lot — trabajaba mucho en el extranjero

Me gustaría ser escritora de ficción porque me encanta escribir historias.

I would like to be a fiction writer because I love writing stories.

Me importa tener un trabajo bien pagado, como el de ingeniero.

It's important to me to have a well-paid job, like an engineer.

a job that would make me happy — un trabajo que me haría feliz

Question

¿Cuál sería el trabajo de tus sueños?

What would be your dream job?

Simple Answer

Quiero ser médico.

I want to be a doctor.

Extended Answer

Siempre he querido ser médico, por eso voy a estudiar medicina en la universidad. Quisiera ayudar a los demás.

I have always wanted to be a doctor, so I'm going to study medicine at university. I would like to help others.

Grammar — I'm a...

You <u>don't</u> usually use the article '<u>un(a)</u>' (p.153) when talking about jobs.

> <u>Soy</u> pintor(a).   *<u>I'm</u> a painter*.

You <u>do</u> if you use an <u>adjective</u>.

> Soy <u>un buen</u> jardinero.
> *I'm <u>a good</u> gardener*.

Quisiera solicitar... — I would like to apply for...

Vocabulary

el puesto	*post, position*	el salario	*salary*	solicitar	*to request, apply for*	
buscar	*to look for, fetch*	ganar	*to earn*	cobrar	*to earn*	
la oferta	*offer*	pagar	*to pay (for)*	rechazar	*to reject*	
aceptar	*to accept*	montar	*to set up*	despedir	*to sack, dismiss*	

(Higher: solicitar, cobrar, rechazar, despedir)

You need to use the subjunctive (see p.190) here as the sentence refers to a hypothetical job rather than a job that you know exists.

Quisiera solicitar el puesto de cuidador que encontré en su sitio web.

I would like to apply for the position of carer that I found on your website.

Busco un trabajo en la construcción que tenga un salario muy competitivo y días de vacaciones suficientes.

I am looking for a job in construction that has a very competitive salary and enough days off.

En el lugar de trabajo — In the work place...

Vocabulary

la empresa	*company, business, firm*	el/la jefe/a	*boss, manager*	el laboratorio	*laboratory*
la compañía	*company*	el/la compañero/a	*colleague*	la reunión	*meeting*
la oficina	*office*	el/la empleado/a	*employee*	atender	*to serve, look after (patient, customer)*
el/la director(a)	*director, manager*	el/la cliente	*client, customer*		

(Higher: el laboratorio, la reunión, atender)

La experiencia laboral — Work experience

Ayudo en una tienda de ropa en mi tiempo libre. Lo mejor es charlar con los clientes.

I help in a clothes shop in my free time. The best thing is chatting with customers.

No tengo empleo, pero a veces paseo al perro de mis vecinos y me pagan.

I don't have a job, but sometimes I walk my neighbours' dog and they pay me.

Trabajo en un restaurante los sábados. Me gusta el empleo, pero no gano mucho.

I work in a restaurant on Saturdays. I like the job, but I don't earn a lot.

that the employees get discounts — que los empleados reciben descuentos

a hairdresser's — una peluquería

I hope to find another job and earn more money — espero conseguir otro empleo y ganar más dinero

Practice Questions

Q1 Tao has written about his future career plans. **(WRITING)**

> Cuando era más pequeño, pensaba que me gustaría ser profesor. Mis padres son profesores y aunque encuentran el trabajo interesante, mi padre dice que causa bastante estrés. Ahora he decidido que estudiaré fotografía porque me encantaría tomar fotos de bodas.

Top Tips for Higher Students
- ✓ Use the subjunctive to say what is important in a future job.
- ✓ Use impersonal verbs like 'hace falta' to say what is necessary.

Now it's your turn. Write an article for a blog about what you want to do in the future. Mention:
- your dream job
- what you need to do to get your dream job
- what made you want your dream job.

[15 marks]

Q2 Read what Padma has written about her family and their jobs, then answer the following questions. Write **P** for Padma, **M** for madre and **H** for hermana. **(READING)**

> Mi madre quería una familia en lugar de una carrera y eso era común para las mujeres de su época. Hoy más mujeres deciden trabajar mientras su pareja cuida a los niños. Por ejemplo, mi hermana es enfermera y su marido se queda en casa con los niños. A mí, me gustaría trabajar y quiero ser policía. Sería un honor proteger mi ciudad y sentirme útil.

(Higher)

a) Who didn't want a career?   [1 mark]

b) Who works as a nurse?   [1 mark]

c) Who wants to feel useful?   [1 mark]

Think about the positives and negatives of jobs...

It's perfectly fine to not know what you want to do yet — if there are several jobs you're considering, have a think about the reasons why you may or may not like them, then figure out how to say it all in Spanish.

Listening Questions

Now it's time to see how much vocabulary you can remember from the topic of Future Study and Work. It'll be a good test to see exactly how much future studying and work you need to do for this topic...

1   Ana, Raúl, Lola and Iván are chatting about their jobs. What are their opinions?

Write **P** for a **positive** opinion.

    N for a **negative** opinion.

    P + N for a **positive** and **negative** opinion.

Listening Track 18

1 a   Ana
[1 mark]

1 b   Raúl
[1 mark]

1 c   Lola
[1 mark]

1 d   Iván
[1 mark]

2   Julia and Jorge are discussing their university plans on a Spanish podcast.

Choose the correct answer and write the letter in each box.

Listening Track 19

2 a   Julia wants to study...

A	geography.
B	business.
C	maths.

[1 mark]

2 b   When Jorge finishes his studies, he would prefer...

A	to go to university.
B	to do something practical.
C	to learn to drive.

[1 mark]

2 c   Jorge's mother thinks...

A	you'll earn a lot of money if you get a degree.
B	you can get a job you enjoy without a degree.
C	you don't need a career to earn money.

[1 mark]

Speaking Questions

Candidate's Material

- You are talking to your Argentinian friend.

- Your teacher will play the part of your friend and will speak first.

- You should address your friend as *tú*.

- When you see this — ? — you will have to ask a question.

In order to score full marks, you must include a verb in your response to each task.

1. Say if you want to go to university or not. (Give **one** detail.)

2. Describe what a family member does as a job. (Give **one** detail.)

3. Say whether or not you have any work experience. (Give **one** detail)

? **4.** Ask your friend what their dream job is.

5. Describe your dream job. (Give **one** detail.)

6. Describe a past event that made you want your dream job. (Give **two** details.)

Higher **7.** Say what is most important to you in your future job.
(Give **one** detail and **one** reason.)

Teacher's Material

- You begin the role-play.

- You should address the candidate as *tú*.

- You must read out the teacher's role shown below **without any changes**.

- You must begin the role-play by using the introductory text below.

Introductory text: *Estás hablando con tu amigo argentino/tu amiga argentina.*
Yo soy tu amigo/tu amiga.

---

1. ¿Quieres ir a la universidad?

2. Describe el empleo que hace un miembro de tu familia.

3. ¿Tienes alguna experiencia laboral?

? **4.** Allow the candidate to ask you a question about your dream job.
Give an appropriate response.

5. ¿Cuál es el trabajo de tus sueños?

6. Describe un evento pasado que te hizo querer el trabajo de tus sueños.

7. ¿Cuál es lo más importante en tu trabajo del futuro? ¿Por qué?

Reading Questions

1 You see an article in a magazine that is offering advice about future study and work.

> ¿Tienes 16 años? ¿No sabes qué quieres hacer en el futuro? Aquí tienes tres opciones posibles:
>
> 1. ESTUDIAR — Si te encanta aprender, podrías continuar tus estudios con el Bachillerato.
> 2. ENTRENAR — Si prefieres las asignaturas prácticas, podrías aprender una profesión.
>   Esta opción combinaría la experiencia laboral con el estudio de algo completamente nuevo.
> 3. TRABAJAR Y ESTUDIAR — Si no te gusta estudiar, podrías buscar un empleo. Seguirías
>   con los estudios también, pero pasarías más horas en el lugar de trabajo que en el colegio.

Answer the following questions in **English**.

1 a What could someone do if they love learning?

.... *[1 mark]*

1 b What sort of person could learn a profession?

.... *[1 mark]*

1 c Why would looking for a job benefit someone who doesn't like studying?

.... *[1 mark]*

2 You read these adverts in a newspaper.

> **A)** *Necesitamos ayuda con el diseño de nuestro sitio web. Ponte en contacto y una prueba será enviada por nuestro equipo.*

> **B)** *Buscamos un experto en lenguas. Hace falta tener un título en un idioma y cinco años de experiencia laboral.*

> **C)** *Tenemos un puesto en una empresa de lujo. Es importante que vayas a nuestra oficina para obtener más información.*

> **D)** *¿Acabas de terminar tu carrera? ¿Quieres trabajar con niños durante el verano? Entonces, ¡llámanos hoy!*

Which statement matches each job advert?

Write the correct letter in each box.

2 a You will have to work during the summer. ☐ *[1 mark]*

2 b They will send you a test to complete. ☐ *[1 mark]*

2 c You need a degree and work experience. ☐ *[1 mark]*

Higher

Writing Questions

1 You receive this photo in a message from your friend.

What is in this photo? Write **three** sentences in **Spanish**.

.... *[2 marks]*

.... *[2 marks]*

.... *[2 marks]*

2 Translate the following sentences into **Spanish**.

2 a I want to study Spanish.

.... *[2 marks]*

2 b He wore a suit to the office yesterday.

.... *[2 marks]*

2 c I would like to apply for the position of journalist.

.... *[2 marks]*

2 d My sister set up a business because she is an entrepreneur.

.... *[2 marks]*

2 e They used to help their dad in his flower shop.

.... *[2 marks]*

3 You are writing an article about your future ambitions.

Write approximately **90** words in **Spanish**.

You must write something about each bullet point. Mention:

- what you think about further study and university
- the job you wanted to do when you were younger
- a job you would like to do in the future. *[15 marks]*

Foundation

Higher

Future Study and Work — Vocabulary

Now it's time to re-educate yourself on all the vocabulary covered in this section — work through it carefully.

Education Post-16

el futuro	*future*
continuar	*to continue*
estudiar	*to study*
el estudio	*study, learning*
el Bachillerato	*Baccalaureate (equivalent to A levels)*
la universidad	*university*
la carrera	*(university) degree course*
la medicina	*medicine*
aprobar	*to pass (test)*
la prueba	*test*
el examen	*exam*
la nota	*grade, mark, note*
el resultado	*result*

la profesión	*profession*
el proyecto	*project, plan*
entrenarse	*to train*
la formación	*training, education*
el título	*title, (university) degree*
universitario/a	*university*
el derecho	*law (subject of study)*
la traducción	*translation*
la economía	*economics*
conseguir	*to get, obtain*
suspender	*to fail*

(la formación to suspender marked **Higher**)

For more vocabulary related to subjects you can study, flick back to p.49.

Career Choices and Ambitions

trabajar	*to work*
independiente	*independent, self-sufficient*
el empleo	*work, job, occupation*
el trabajo	*job*
la carrera	*career*
el/la médico/a	*doctor*
el/la enfermero/a	*nurse*
el/la cuidador(a)	*carer*
el/la abogado/a	*lawyer*
el/la ingeniero/a	*engineer*
el/la escritor(a)	*writer*
el/la periodista	*journalist*
el/la pintor(a)	*painter*
el/la peluquero/a	*hairdresser*
el/la policía	*police officer*
la policía	*police (organisation)*
el ejército	*army*
el sueño	*dream*
soñar	*to dream*
el puesto	*post, position*
buscar	*to look for, fetch*
la oportunidad	*opportunity, chance*
la oferta	*offer*
aceptar	*to accept*
el salario	*salary*
ganar	*to earn*
pagar	*to pay (for)*
montar	*to set up*
el negocio	*business*
la empresa	*company, business, firm*
la compañía	*company*
la oficina	*office*

el/la director(a)	*director, manager*
el/la jefe/a	*boss, manager, leader*
el/la compañero/a	*colleague*
el/la empleado/a	*employee*
el/la cliente	*client, customer*
el traje	*suit*
la experiencia	*experience*
laboral	*(of) work, relating to work*
próximo/a	*next*
llegar a (+ infinitive)	*to manage to (+ verb), succeed in (+ verb)*
el/la soldado/a	*soldier*
el/la empresario/a	*business person, entrepreneur*
el comercio	*commerce, trade, business*
el/la obrero/a	*worker, labourer*
la construcción	*construction (industry)*
solicitar	*to request, apply for*
cobrar	*to earn*
rechazar	*to reject*
emplear	*to employ, use*
despedir	*to sack, dismiss*
el laboratorio	*laboratory*
el/la experto/a	*expert*
profesional	*professional*
hace falta (+ infinitive)	*it's necessary (+ verb)*
la ocasión	*opportunity*
la reunión	*meeting*
la huelga	*strike*
atender	*to serve, look after (patient, customer)*

(el/la soldado/a to atender marked **Higher**)

Revision Summary Test for Section Five

Whatever it is you'd like to do after school, use this page to know how to talk about it in Spanish.

- Yep, these questions are **hard** — they'll really help you see **how well you know your stuff**.
- Tackle the **revision summary test** below, or scan the QR code to do it **online**.
  Use the CGP RevisionHub to **track your progress** and see **which areas need more work**.
- You can find **sample answers** here: www.cgpbooks.co.uk/MadridExtras

Education Post-16 ☑

1) How many university subjects can you name in Spanish?
    There's 1 in this section (plus 3 for Higher tier).

2) How would you say the sentence below in English?
    'Para ir a la universidad, tengo que aprobar una prueba y sacar buenas notas en mis exámenes.'

3) In Spanish, tell your parents that you want to continue your studies and do your A levels.

4) Carmen says: 'Preferiría estudiar una profesión en lugar de hacer una carrera en la universidad.'
    Translate what she says into English.

5) Your friend doesn't want to go to university. What could they do instead?
    Tell them in Spanish and give two details.

6) Answer the following question in Spanish: '¿Qué quieres hacer después de los exámenes?'

7) Luis says: 'Aunque suspendí mi primer proyecto universitario, conseguí un resultado
    muy bueno para mi último.' Translate what he says into English.

Career Choices and Ambitions ☑

8) How many jobs and positions can you list in Spanish? There are 12 in this section
    (plus 4 for Higher tier). Make sure you list both the feminine and masculine forms.

9) Fernando says: 'Ser jefe de una empresa es mi sueño. Quiero llevar ropa de moda en
    la oficina.' Translate what he says into English.

10) a) In Spanish, how would you ask someone if they have any work experience?
    b) What would be your answer to this question? Answer in Spanish and give at least one detail.

11) You see an advert that says the following: 'Hemos montado un negocio y buscamos empleados
    con experiencia en el puesto de director.' What is this advert saying?

12) What's the Spanish for...?
    a) self-sufficient   b) offer   c) police (organisation)   d) suit   e) to manage to

13) 'In the future, my job will pay me well and it will give me the opportunity to work with customers.'
    Say this sentence in Spanish.

14) You're talking to a friend who has recently got a new job. They say: 'Acepté el puesto en el ejército
    porque el salario es más alto que el que gano ahora.' What does this mean in English?

15) Describe what a family member or friend does for a living in Spanish.

16) Your Colombian friend asks you: '¿En qué carrera te gustaría trabajar en el futuro?'
    Answer them in Spanish and give at least one reason for your choice.

17) Aldara says: 'Hizo falta despedir a mi compañero porque siempre rechazó las reglas. Espero que
    la próxima persona que empleamos sea mejor.' Translate what she says into English.

18) Rafael says: 'No cobramos suficiente dinero, por eso no habrá nadie en la reunión. Continuaremos
    esta huelga porque la compañía debe atender a sus empleados.' Translate what he says into English.

Cinema and TV

Learn how to talk about your favourite films and TV shows on these pages.

Don't forget you can access your online content here: www.cgpbooks.co.uk/Madrid

En el cine — At the cinema

Vocabulary

el cine	*cinema*	recomendar	*to recommend*
la película	*film, movie*	preferir	*to prefer*
la escena	*scene (of film)*	pensar	*to think*
la pantalla	*screen*	el/la protagonista	*protagonist, main character*
el personaje	*character (in book, film)*	el diálogo	*dialogue*

Me gusta mucho ir al cine
porque siempre me divierto.

*I really like to go to the cinema
because I always have a good time.*

I can eat lots of popcorn — puedo comer muchas palomitas

Pienso que vale la pena ver
películas en la pantalla grande.

*I think it's worth seeing
films on the big screen.*

Me encantan las películas que
tienen personajes que me hacen reír.

*I love films that have characters
who make me laugh.*

solve a mystery — resuelven un misterio

Prefiero las películas de aventura
porque son emocionantes.

*I prefer adventure films
because they are exciting.*

they scare me less than horror films — me dan menos miedo que las películas de terror

Para mí, los protagonistas
deben contar una buena historia y
el diálogo tiene que ser divertido.

*For me, the main characters
must tell a good story and the
dialogue has to be enjoyable.*

Cada escena debería tener sentido.
Quiero creer lo que estoy viendo.

*Each scene should have meaning.
I want to believe what I'm seeing.*

excellent special effects — efectos especiales excelentes

La última película que vi... — The last film I saw...

Q&A Audio

Question

Describe la última
película que viste.

*Describe the last
film you saw.*

Simple Answer

El sábado, vi una película
de acción. Me gustó mucho.

*On Saturday, I saw an
action film. I really liked it.*

Extended Answer

El fin de semana pasado, vi una película
de acción. Se trataba de dos familias
que luchaban durante cientos de años.

*Last weekend, I saw an action film.
It was about two families who were
fighting for hundreds of years.*

Grammar — I saw...

To say '<u>I saw...</u>' you need the <u>preterite</u>
tense. Check how to form it on p.179.

El viernes, <u>vi</u> una película romántica.

On Friday, <u>I saw</u> a romantic film.

<u>Unlike</u> most verbs when they're in
the '<u>yo</u>' form of the <u>preterite</u> tense,
'<u>vi</u>' <u>doesn't</u> have an <u>accent</u>.

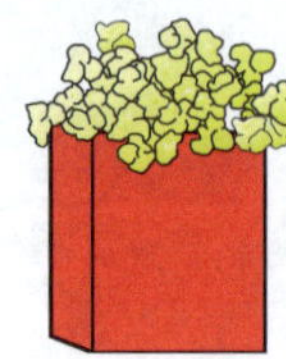

Grammar (Higher only) — 'se trata de'

Use '<u>se trata de</u>' to say what a film is about:

Se trata de unos jóvenes muy ricos.

It's about some very rich young people.

And you can use it in the <u>imperfect</u> to say
what a film <u>was</u> about:

Se trataba del amor.   *It was about love.*

Remember — 'de' + 'el' = 'del'.

¿Qué hay en la tele? — What's on TV?

Vocabulary

la tele, televisión	*TV, television*	interesar	*to interest*
la serie	*series*	encantar	*to love, delight*
el programa	*programme*	aguantar	*to put up with, stand (tolerate)*
el concurso	*quiz*		
el anuncio	*advert*	**[Higher]** el canal	*channel*
la noticia	*news*	la telenovela	*soap opera, TV serial*
actual	*current*	el documental	*documentary*

When 'la noticia' is singular, it means 'a piece of news'. The plural of 'las noticias' is used to mean 'the news' as a TV programme.

¿Qué te gusta ver? — What do you like watching?

Suelo ver la televisión en Internet porque es más fácil encontrar los programas que prefiero.

I normally watch TV on the internet because it's easier to find the programmes that I prefer.

Me gustan mucho las telenovelas porque hay risas, discusiones, relaciones... ¡Nunca son aburridas!

I really like soap operas because there are laughs, arguments, relationships... They're never boring!

A mi abuela le encantan los concursos porque puede contestar las preguntas.

My grandmother loves quizzes because she can answer the questions.

No aguanto muchos canales porque hay demasiados anuncios.

I can't stand a lot of channels because there are too many adverts.

I prefer to watch series from other countries — prefiero ver las series de otros países

cartoons — dibujos animados

Practice Questions

Q1 Translate these sentences into Spanish.

WRITING

a) *She doesn't like the cinema at all.*
b) *I recommend lots of films to my friends.*
c) *He said that the characters did silly things.*
d) *The scene at the end of the film was very sad.*

[8 marks]

[Higher]

Q2 Read Eli's email about TV and choose the correct options below.

READING

En la televisión británica, creo que hay demasiadas telenovelas. Sin embargo, no hay tantos anuncios como en España. En mi familia, preferimos ver los documentales y las noticias porque nos interesa aprender nueva información sobre el mundo.

a) Eli believes...

  A. there are too many soap operas on British TV.
  B. there are fewer adverts on Spanish TV.

b) Eli's family...

  A. prefer to avoid documentaries
  B. are interested in learning about the world.

[2 marks]

Don't just say what you watch — say why you like it too...

Whether you're watching films on the big screen or TV shows on the small screen, make sure you feel confident with the topic of cinema and TV. You never know when all this vocab will come in handy.

Quick Quiz

Music

I thought I could hear music... This topic is worth revising well — it often comes up in the exams and it's great for showing off your knowledge of tenses.

La música — Music

When you're using the 'yo' form of 'tocar' in the preterite tense (see p.179), the 'c' changes to 'qu'.

Vocabulary

escuchar	*to listen (to)*	el/la músico/a	*musician*
la canción	*song*	tocar	*to play (an instrument)*
bajar	*to download*	el instrumento	*instrument*
clásico/a	*classical*	la guitarra	*guitar*
alto/a	*loud (volume)*	en vivo	*live (e.g. performance, broadcast)*
el concierto	*concert*		
el espectáculo	*show, spectacle*	la orquesta	*orchestra*
el/la cantante	*singer*	asistir	*to attend*

Higher (en vivo, la orquesta, asistir)

'asistir' is usually followed by the preposition 'a'.

¿Te gusta la música? — Do you like music?

Toco el piano desde hace seis años. Espero ser músico cuando sea mayor.

I have been playing the piano for six years. I hope to be a musician when I'm older.

Me gusta escuchar la música clásica porque me hace sentir tranquilo.

I like to listen to classical music because it makes me feel calm.

Me encanta la música en vivo porque es una experiencia más emocionante.

I love live music because it's a more exciting experience.

Asistí a un concierto el año pasado y no me divertí. La música estaba demasiado alta y no entendí lo que cantaban las cantantes.

I went to a concert last year and I didn't enjoy myself. The music was too loud and I didn't understand what the singers were singing.

Me parece genial que puedo bajar muchos tipos de música rápidamente.

It seems great to me that I can download many types of music quickly.

the clarinet — el clarinete
the drums — la batería
rap music — la música rap
rock music — la música rock
pop music — la música pop
the lyrics — la letra
download — descargar

Practice Question

Q1 Marisol is a famous Spanish singer. Listen to the interview and then answer the questions in English.

e.g. What instrument did Marisol's grandfather teach her to play? guitar

a) What is an advantage that Marisol mentions about listening to music on the internet? [1 mark]

b) Why does Marisol like going to concerts? [1 mark]

c) What does Marisol say she'll be doing in the coming year? [1 mark]

Remember — you 'tocar' an instrument...

It doesn't matter what sort of music you're into or what instrument you play — just make sure you can talk about it in Spanish. Try to practise saying what you, your family and friends like listening to and why.

Sport

It's time to get off the sofa and get moving with a page on sport. On your marks, get set, go!

¿Practicas algún deporte? — Do you practise any sports?

Vocabulary

el deporte	*sport*	el baloncesto	*basketball*
jugar	*to play*	la temporada	*season (of sport)*
practicar	*to practise*	el partido	*(sports) match*
participar	*to participate*	el equipo	*team*
la carrera	*race*	la natación	*swimming*
bailar	*to dance*	la selección	*national sports team*
el fútbol	*football*	el torneo	*tournament*

(*Higher*: la natación, la selección, el torneo)

Question

¿Te gusta hacer deportes?
Do you like playing sports?

Simple Answer

Sí, me gusta jugar al baloncesto porque es emocionante.
Yes, I like playing basketball because it's exciting.

Extended Answer

Sí, me gusta jugar al baloncesto después del colegio porque es emocionante y me ayuda a mantenerme en forma.
Yes, I like playing basketball after school because it's exciting and it helps me keep fit.

Grammar — 'jugar' + 'a' + sport

Use 'jugar a' to say what sports you play. In Spanish, you can't say 'Juego a el fútbol'. So if the sport is a masculine noun (like 'el fútbol'), the 'a' and the article 'el' combine to form 'al'.

Juego al netball.   **I play netball.**
Juegas al rugby.   **You play rugby.**

'Jugar' is a stem-changing verb — its stem changes from 'u' to 'ue' in the present tense. See p.176.

Monto a caballo varias veces a la semana. Me gusta porque puedo hacer deporte con mis amigos.

A mí no me interesa la temporada de fútbol, pero veo la Copa Mundial porque mi país suele ganar sus partidos.

I go horse riding a few times a week. I like it because I can do sport with my friends.

The football season doesn't interest me, but I watch the World Cup because my country usually wins its matches.

I play tennis — juego al tenis

the sports centre is near my house — el polideportivo está cerca de mi casa

athletics — el atletismo

the Olympic Games — los Juegos Olímpicos

lots of medals — muchas medallas

Practice Question

Q1 Write an article for a blog about sports. You should write about 90 words in Spanish. Mention:
- *what sports you play*
- *the advantages of participating in sport*
- *what sport you'd like to try in the future.*

[15 marks]

Top Tip for Higher Students
✓ Use 'desde hace' to talk about how long you've been doing a sport.

Be a good sport and learn all the vocab on this page...

As well as learning the words for different sports, try to learn the reasons why you do or don't like them. Expressing your opinion is a great way to impress the examiner and get more marks in the exam.

Going Out and Other Hobbies

If cinema, TV, music and sport aren't your thing, you've come to the right place. Here are two whole pages about other interesting activities you might get up to in your spare time.

Salir con los amigos — Going out with friends

Vocabulary

el tiempo libre	*free time*	el camarero	*waiter*
salir	*to go out, leave*	la camarera	*waitress*
el parque temático	*theme park*	el plato	*plate, dish*
el teatro	*theatre*	la opción	*option*
la escena	*stage (theatre)*	vegetariano/a	*vegetarian*
la entrada	*admission ticket*	vegano/a	*vegan*
gratis	*free (of charge)*	las tapas	*small dishes of food*
el restaurante	*restaurant*	la obra	*play (theatre)*
la carta	*menu*	divertir	*to amuse, entertain*
la cuenta	*bill*	elegir	*to choose*

Higher — (la obra, divertir, elegir)

Question

¿Que le gustaría tomar?
What would you like?

Simple Answer

Quiero la sopa, por favor.
I want the soup, please.

Extended Answer

De primer plato, quisiera la sopa y de segundo plato, la paella.
For the starter, I'd like the soup and for main course, the paella.

Grammar — ordering politely

Use 'quisiera' to order what you'd like politely. 'Quisiera' comes from the verb 'querer' (*to want*). See p.184.

Quisiera probar el filete.
I'd like to try the steak.

Me encanta ir a restaurantes, pero a veces es difícil elegir lo que quieres comer.

I love to go to restaurants, but sometimes it's hard to choose what you want to eat.

the dishes can be disappointing — los platos pueden ser decepcionantes

El fin de semana pasado, fui al parque temático con mi hermano mayor. Las entradas costaron mucho dinero, pero nos divertimos muchísimo.

Last weekend, I went to the theme park with my older brother. The admission tickets cost a lot of money, but we had a great time.

the roller coasters were marvellous — las montañas rusas eran estupendas

Mañana mis amigas y yo vamos al teatro a ver una obra sobre un evento histórico.

Tomorrow my friends and I are going to the theatre to see a play about a historical event.

a musical about the war — un musical sobre la guerra

Las actividades — Activities

Vocabulary

cantar	*to sing*	el periódico	*newspaper*	cocinar	*to cook*
el videojuego	*computer game*	el artículo	*article*	la pintura	*painting, paint*
el arte	*art*	la ficción	*fiction*	la obra	*work, book*
el dibujo	*drawing, art*	escribir	*to write*	la lectura	*reading*
pintar	*to paint*	la novela	*novel*	el género	*genre*
leer	*to read*	la historia	*story*	el diario	*newspaper*

Higher — (cocinar, la pintura, la obra, la lectura, el género, el diario)

¿Qué haces en tu tiempo libre? — What do you do in your free time?

Hay muchas actividades que me interesan.
Prefiero cocinar y hacer pasteles.

There are lots of activities that interest me. I prefer to cook and make cakes.

I have a lot of hobbies — tengo muchos pasatiempos

Pinto cuando tengo tiempo libre porque el arte es mi actividad favorita.

I paint when I have free time because art is my favourite activity.

whenever I can — siempre que puedo

A mi hermana le encanta leer.
Lee todo los géneros, pero prefiero leer libros de ciencia ficción.

My sister loves to read. She reads all genres, but she prefers to read science fiction books.

autobiographies — autobiografías
detective stories — novelas policíacas

¿Qué piensas? — What do you think?

Vocabulary

aburrido/a	*bored, boring*	divertido/a	*fun, enjoyable*
emocionante	*exciting*	favorito/a	*favourite*
estupendo/a	*wonderful, marvellous*	horrible	*horrible*
		imposible	*impossible*
excelente	*excellent*	raro/a	*strange, rare*
increíble	*incredible*	maravilloso/a	*wonderful, marvellous*
interesante	*interesting*	decepcionante	*disappointing*
genial	*great*	fatal	*terrible, awful*
guay	*cool*	extraño/a	*strange*

Higher (maravilloso/a, decepcionante, fatal, extraño/a)

Mikolaj thinks your favourite film is really exciting. Absolutely incredible. Just marvellous. No, really.

Practice Questions

Q1 Translate these sentences into English.

READING

a) *La carta tiene mucha variedad. Quiero probar un plato chino.*

b) *Las entradas son gratis para los niños pequeños.*

c) *Leer los periódicos es aburrido y los artículos pueden ser muy raros.*

[6 marks]

Q2 Look at the two photos below. Talk in Spanish about what is in the photos. You should talk for about a minute and say something about each photo.

SPEAKING

[5 marks]

Charm waiters and examiners alike with 'quisiera'...

Don't panic if you're struggling to remember all the vocab from these two pages — just try breaking it down and learning it in smaller chunks. Then you can put it all into practice in the exam-style questions...

Listening Questions

Before you dash out to a restaurant or head to a concert, let's put your knowledge to the test with some exam-style questions. They'll help you prepare for what you're likely to see in the real exams.

---

1 Listen to this conversation between Amira, Diego and Karima.
What reason do they each give for why they like going to the cinema?

Write the correct letter in each box.

A	the food	C	the variety of films	E	meeting new people
B	it's good for families	D	offers for students	F	the big screen

Listening Track 21

1 a Amira   ☐

[1 mark]

1 b Diego   ☐

[1 mark]

1 c Karima   ☐

[1 mark]

---

2 A group of friends are discussing what they like doing in their free time.
Answer the questions in **English**.

Listening Track 22

2 a What activity did the first speaker used to like?

.... *[1 mark]*

2 b What activity does the first speaker do now?

.... *[1 mark]*

2 c What does the second speaker say about free time?

.... *[1 mark]*

2 d Why does the third speaker enjoy their hobby?

.... *[1 mark]*

2 e What activity does the third speaker want to try in the future?

.... *[1 mark]*

Higher

Speaking Questions

Candidate's Material

- Spend a few minutes looking at the two photos. Make notes on them to use during the test.

- Your teacher will ask you to talk about the content of the photos. You should talk for approximately **one minute** at Foundation tier and **one and a half minutes** at Higher tier. **You must say at least one thing about each photo**.

- After you have spoken about the content of the photos, your teacher will then ask you some questions related to any of the topics within the topic of **Free-time Activities**.

Teacher's Material

- Candidates should talk about the photos above for approximately **one minute** at Foundation tier or **one and a half minutes** at Higher tier. They may use any notes they have made during the preparation time. Begin by asking the candidate to tell you about the photos:

  - Háblame de las fotos.

- When the candidate has finished talking about the photos, ask them the following unprepared conversation questions on the topic of **Free-time Activities**:

  - ¿Qué aspectos de la música te gustan?

  - ¿Qué piensas del deporte? ¿Por qué?

  - Describe una actividad que te gusta hacer con los amigos.

  - ¿Qué prefieres hacer en tu tiempo libre en casa? ¿Por qué?

  - ¿Cuál es tu opinión sobre el teatro? ¿Por qué?

  - ¿Qué grupo musical te gustaría ver en un concierto? ¿Por qué?

Reading Questions

1   Translate the following sentences into **English**.

Foundation

1 a   No aguanto el baloncesto porque es aburrido.

....   *[2 marks]*

1 b   Algunas actividades pueden ser difíciles y peligrosas.

....   *[2 marks]*

Higher

1 c   Nuestro colegio ganó el torneo de fútbol.

....   *[2 marks]*

1 d   Tres de mis amigos van a ser parte del equipo de natación.

....   *[2 marks]*

2   You see this magazine article about a Spanish TV programme.

> *Hay un nuevo programa en la televisión que se llama 'La vida de Luis'. En una entrevista, el actor principal, un hombre que ha trabajado en esta industria por más de veinticinco años, hablaba alegremente sobre el programa que todos esperan.*
>
> *"El director quería crear un programa que sí, es de ficción, pero que muestra aspectos reales de la vida. Tendrá muchos momentos graciosos, pero también habrá temas serios como el paro. Creo que será muy interesante y original."*

Which statements are correct?

Write **A** if **only** statement **A** is correct.
Write **B** if **only** statement **B** is correct.
Write **A + B** if **both** statements are correct.

2 a

A	'La vida de Luis' is an old TV show.
B	'La vida de Luis' is a new TV show.

[1 mark]

2 b

A	The main actor has been in the business for over 25 years.
B	The director is over 25 years old.

[1 mark]

2 c

A	'La vida de Luis' will have funny moments.
B	'La vida de Luis' will have serious themes.

[1 mark]

Writing Questions

Foundation

1 Write an email to your Spanish friend about what you do in your free time.

Write approximately **50** words in **Spanish**.

You must write something about each bullet point.

Mention:
- television
- music
- sport
- going out
- hobbies.

[10 marks]

2 Translate the following sentences into **Spanish**.

2 a I love quizzes because they are entertaining.

.... *[2 marks]*

2 b He likes singing while he paints.

.... *[2 marks]*

2 c I would like to pay the bill, please.

.... *[2 marks]*

Higher

2 d In my opinion, the play was awful.

.... *[2 marks]*

2 e The national sports team will play its first match tomorrow.

.... *[2 marks]*

3 You are writing an article about the cinema.

Write approximately **150** words in **Spanish**.

You must write something about each bullet point.

Mention:
- what is enjoyable about going to the cinema.
- a film you saw recently and what you thought about it.

[25 marks]

Free-time Activities — Vocabulary

Take a moment to refresh your memory about all the vocabulary in this section with the next two pages.

Cinema

el cine	*cinema*
la película	*film, movie*
la escena	*scene (of film)*
el efecto especial	*special effect*
la acción	*action*
la ciencia ficción	*science fiction*
la pantalla	*screen*
el/la director(a)	*director*
el personaje	*character (in book, film)*
ver	*to see, watch*
recomendar	*to recommend*
preferir	*to prefer*
pensar	*to think*

Higher

el/la protagonista	*protagonist, main character*
el diálogo	*dialogue*
romántico/a	*romantic*
la aventura	*adventure*
divertirse	*to enjoy oneself, have a good time*
tratarse de	*to be about*

The low special effects budget called for some improvisation...

TV

la tele / televisión	*TV, television*
la serie	*series*
el programa	*programme*
el concurso	*quiz, competition*
la telerrealidad	*reality TV*
el anuncio	*advert*
la noticia	*news*
actual	*current*
la risa	*laugh*
gracioso/a	*funny*
interesar	*to interest*

encantar	*to love, delight, be delightful to*
aguantar	*to put up with, stand (tolerate)*

Higher

el canal	*channel*
la telenovela	*soap opera, TV serial*
el documental	*documentary*
emitir	*to broadcast*

'la noticia' means 'a piece of news'. If you want to talk about the news as a TV programme, you'll need to say 'las noticias'.

Music

escuchar	*to listen (to)*
la música	*music*
la canción	*song*
la letra	*lyrics*
bajar	*to download*
musical	*musical*
clásico/a	*classical*
alto/a	*loud (volume)*
el concierto	*concert*
el espectáculo	*show, spectacle*
el/la cantante	*singer*
la voz	*voice*
el/la músico/a	*musician*

There are two words for 'to play' in Spanish. Use 'jugar' to talk about playing sports (see p.73) and 'tocar' to talk about playing an instrument (see p.72).

tocar	*to play (an instrument), touch*
el instrumento	*instrument*
la guitarra	*guitar*

Higher

descargar	*to download*
en vivo	*live (e.g. performance, broadcast)*
el público	*audience*
la orquesta	*orchestra*
la banda	*(musical) band*
asistir	*to attend*

Sport

el deporte	*sport*
jugar	*to play*
hacer	*to do*
practicar	*to practise*
participar	*to participate*
correr	*to run*
la carrera	*race*
el paso	*pace*
nadar	*to swim*
bailar	*to dance*
dar un paseo	*to go for a walk, stroll*
el fútbol	*football*

el baloncesto	*basketball*
la temporada	*season (of sport, music)*
el partido	*(sports) match*
el equipo	*team*
deportivo/a	*sports*
Higher	
la natación	*swimming*
la selección	*national sports team*
el torneo	*tournament*
echar	*to throw, cast*
desde hace + present tense	*to have been + -ing for + time*

Going Out

el tiempo libre	*free time*
salir	*to go out, leave*
el parque temático	*theme park*
el teatro	*theatre*
la escena	*stage (theatre)*
la entrada	*entrance, admission ticket*
gratis	*free (of charge)*
el restaurante	*restaurant*
la carta	*menu*
la cuenta	*bill*
el camarero	*waiter*

la camarera	*waitress*
el plato	*plate, dish*
la opción	*option*
vegetariano/a	*vegetarian*
vegano/a	*vegan*
las tapas	*small dishes of food, bar snacks*
H	
la obra	*play (theatre)*
divertir	*to amuse, entertain*
elegir	*to choose*

Other Hobbies

la actividad	*activity*
la red	*net (fishing)*
cantar	*to sing*
el videojuego	*computer game*
el arte	*art*
el dibujo	*drawing, art*
pintar	*to paint*
leer	*to read*
el periódico	*newspaper*
el artículo	*article*
la ficción	*fiction*
escribir	*to write*
la carta	*letter*
el correo	*mail, post*
la novela	*novel*
la historia	*story*
el/la autor(a)	*writer, author*
aburrido/a	*bored, boring*
emocionante	*exciting*
estupendo/a	*brilliant, great wonderful, marvellous*
excelente	*excellent*
increíble	*incredible*
interesante	*interesting*
genial	*great*

guay	*cool*
divertido/a	*fun, enjoyable*
favorito/a	*favourite*
horrible	*horrible*
imposible	*impossible*
raro/a	*strange, rare*
cocinar	*to cook*
la pintura	*painting, paint*
colgar	*to hang (up)*
la obra	*work, book*
la lectura	*reading*
el género	*genre*
el diario	*newspaper*
el contenido	*content, contents*
Higher la sección	*section*
tratar	*to deal with*
soler	*to normally (+ verb), to tend to (+ verb), to usually (+ verb)*
emocionado/a	*excited*
maravilloso/a	*wonderful, marvellous*
decepcionante	*disappointing*
fatal	*terrible, awful*
extraño/a	*strange*

Revision Summary Test for Section Six

Before you go off to enjoy your spare time, try this quick summary test to talk about it in Spanish.

- These questions are **really tricky**, but they'll help you see **how well you know your stuff**.
- Tackle the **revision summary test** below, or scan the QR code to do it **online**. You can **keep track of your progress** online and see **which areas need more work**.
- There are **sample answers** here: www.cgpbooks.co.uk/MadridExtras

Cinema and TV ☑

1) 'No recomiendo el cine porque muestra demasiados anuncios.' What does this mean in English? ☑
2) In Spanish, say that you love films that have exciting scenes and interesting characters. ☑
3) Describe una película que has visto recientemente. ☑
4) Say this in English: 'Este director siempre hace películas graciosas. Oí muchas risas en el cine.' ☑
5) List the different types of TV programme in Spanish. There are 3 in this section (plus 2 for Higher tier). ☑
6) 'No me interesan los programas de televisión. ¡Todas las series actuales son semejantes!' How would you say this in English? ☑
7) ¿Cuál es tu opinión sobre ver la televisión en Internet? ☑
H 8) Txaro says: 'No aguanto los canales que solo emiten la telerrealidad.' What is she saying? ☑

Music ☑

9) Renata says: 'Soy cantante clásica. El mes que viene, voy a cantar una nueva canción en un espectáculo musical.' Translate what she says into English. ☑
10) Aditi asks you about your music tastes. In Spanish, tell her what you like and don't like about music. ☑
11) 'Aprendía a tocar la guitarra, pero era demasiado difícil. Quisiera intentar tocar otro instrumento.' What does this mean in English? ☑
12) Say this in English: 'No me gustaría ir a un concierto. Prefiero escuchar música sin otra gente.' ☑
H 13) ¿Qué piensas de la música en vivo? ☑

Sport ☑

14) Answer the following question in Spanish: ¿Practicas algún deporte? ☑
15) 'La temporada de fútbol termina en mayo. Cuando no hay partidos que jugar, doy un paseo todos los días.' What is this person saying? ☑
16) What's the Spanish for...? a) to run   b) pace   c) to swim   d) to dance   e) team ☑
17) Iván says: 'Participo en muchas actividades deportivas y gané mi última carrera.' What is he saying? ☑
H 18) 'When I am older, I'd like to be part of the national sports team and play in important tournaments.' Translate this sentence into Spanish. ☑

Going Out and Other Hobbies ☑

19) Say these English words in Spanish:
    a) to go out   b) menu   c) bill   d) waiter / waitress   e) dish ☑
20) 'Pido las tapas cuando voy a un restaurante. Hay tantas opciones.' What is this person saying? ☑
21) There are 13 adjectives to describe hobbies (plus 5 for Higher tier). How many can you remember? ☑
22) Galia says: '¿Quieres ir al parque temático este fin de semana?' What does this mean? ☑
23) How would you tell your Cuban friend in Spanish that you think the theatre is a type of art? ☑
24) In Spanish, describe your hobbies. ☑
Higher 25) 'Mi tío escribe artículos para la sección de consejos en un diario. Los leo en mi tiempo libre porque el contenido trata cosas útiles.' How would you say this in English? ☑
26) Describe dos actividades que quieres probar en el futuro. ☑

Celebrations

In Spain and Latin America, events like weddings and birthdays usually involve big gatherings.
Here you can learn how to talk about them and your own celebrations in Spanish.

¿Qué celebras? — What are you celebrating?

*Head to the CGP RevisionHub
for all your online content:
www.cgpbooks.co.uk/Madrid*

Vocabulary

la celebración	*celebration*	la novia	*bride*
celebrar	*to celebrate*	el novio	*groom*
el cumpleaños	*birthday*	recibir	*to receive*
¡Feliz cumpleaños!	*Happy birthday!*	el regalo	*present, gift*
¡Enhorabuena!	*Congratulations!*	la tarjeta	*written card*
el ambiente	*atmosphere*	celebrarse	*to hold (an event)*
la sorpresa	*surprise*	reunir	*to gather, bring together*
invitar	*to invite*	reunirse	*to get together*
el matrimonio	*marriage*	regalar	*to give (as a gift)*
la boda	*wedding*	ofrecer	*to offer, present*

Higher: celebrarse, reunir, reunirse, regalar, ofrecer

Jorge decided the best way to
celebrate his birthday was a
good old-fashioned siesta.

Me encanta reunirme con mis amigos.

I love getting together with my friends.

Celebré mi cumpleaños en familia. Organizaron una fiesta para mi. Fue una sorpresa. Recibí regalos y unas tarjetas.

I celebrated my birthday with family. They organised a party for me. It was a surprise. I received presents and some cards.

with my best friends
— con mis mejores amigos
on holiday
— de vacaciones

Mi prima me invitó a su boda en junio. El ambiente era muy feliz. Les regalé una pintura.

My cousin invited me to her wedding in June. The atmosphere was very happy. I gave them a painting as a gift.

was full of joy
— estaba lleno de alegría

Question

¿Celebraste algo recientemente?
Did you celebrate something recently?

Simple Answer

El mes pasado fui a una boda en la playa.
Last month I went to a wedding on the beach.

Extended Answer

El mes pasado fui a una boda en la playa. Desafortunadamente, el ambiente no era ideal porque ¡todos teníamos demasiado calor!

Last month I went to a wedding on the beach. Unfortunately, the atmosphere wasn't ideal because we were all too hot!

Practice Question

Q1 *You are writing a blog post about celebrations.*
You should write about 90 words in Spanish. Write about:

- *your favourite event to celebrate*
- *how you celebrated your birthday last year*
- *a celebration you'll be part of in the future.*   [15 marks]

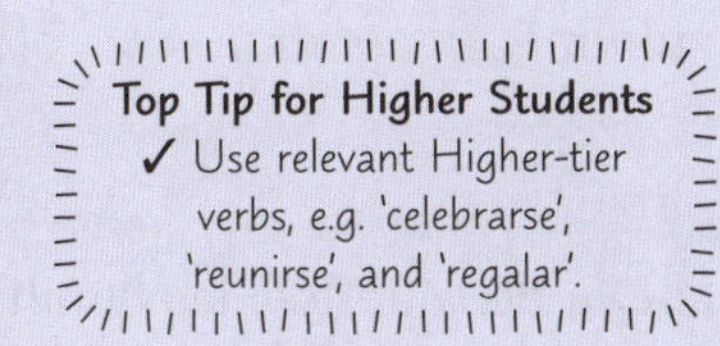

WRITING

Top Tip for Higher Students
✓ Use relevant Higher-tier verbs, e.g. 'celebrarse', 'reunirse', and 'regalar'.

You could talk about celebrations in the past, present or future...

For the exam, it's a good idea to practise talking about your birthday and other celebrations in different tenses. Try writing some Spanish sentences about your last birthday, or what you'll do for it next year.

Customs and Festivals

Read on to learn all about different customs and festivals in Spanish-speaking countries.

Los Sanfermines — The running of the bulls

One Spanish festival that can be controversial is <u>Los Sanfermines</u>, which takes place in <u>Pamplona</u> each July.

Vocabulary

la tradición	*tradition*	la costumbre	*custom*	la plaza de toros	*bullring*
tradicional	*traditional*	el toro	*bull*	la corrida	*bullfight*

Muchas personas corren por las calles estrechas con los toros peligrosos hasta la plaza de toros.

La corrida de toros es una tradición en España, pero es polémica porque alguna gente piensa que es cruel. Sin embargo, otros creen que es un arte.

Many people run through the narrow streets with the dangerous bulls to the bullring.

Bullfighting is a tradition in Spain, but it's controversial because some people think that it's cruel. However, others believe it's an art.

Las fiestas de Valencia — The festivals of Valencia

Vocabulary

la Tomatina	*Spanish tomato festival*	Las Fallas	*Valencian celebration involving*
los fuegos artificiales	*fireworks*		*burning of papier mâché models*

'La Tomatina' tiene lugar en agosto en Buñol. Los participantes se tiran tomates unos a otros.

'Las Fallas' se celebran cada marzo en Valencia. Hay cinco días de fuegos artificiales y desfiles. El último día se queman creaciones de papel maché.

'La Tomatina' takes place in August in Buñol. Participants throw tomatoes at each other.

'Las Fallas' is celebrated each March in Valencia. There are five days of fireworks and parades. On the last day, they burn papier mâché creations.

El Día de Muertos — Day of the Dead

El <u>Día de Muertos</u> is a tradition that happens in Mexico, South America and elsewhere around <u>1st November</u>.

Vocabulary

la cultura	*culture*	el disfraz	*costume*	la flor	*flower*
cultural	*cultural*	el traje	*costume*	pintarse	*to put on makeup*

La Catrina is a popular female skeleton icon.

El Día de Muertos, las familias limpian y arreglan las tumbas de sus familiares y celebran fiestas.

Alguna gente lleva un disfraz de 'la Catrina'. Respetan a los muertos con flores y música mariachi.

On the Day of the Dead, families clean and tidy the graves of their relatives and throw parties.

Some people dress up as 'la Catrina'. They respect the dead with flowers and Mexican folk music.

share stories — comparten historias

they put makeup on their faces like — se pinta la cara como

Las fiestas religiosas — Religious festivals

Vocabulary

la Semana Santa	*Easter Week*	Nochevieja	*New Year's Eve*
Nochebuena	*Christmas Eve*	el Día de Reyes	*Epiphany, 6th January*
Navidad	*Christmas*	los Reyes Magos	*the Three Kings, the Three Wise Men*

La Semana Santa es un evento serio en España. Hay desfiles con música y se llevan pasos por las calles.

Easter Week is a serious event in Spain. There are processions with music, and religious images are carried around the streets.

Muchos españoles celebran el Día de Reyes. Los Reyes Magos traen regalos a los niños.

Many Spaniards celebrate Epiphany. The Three Kings bring gifts to children.

En Navidad, nos damos regalos y comemos juntos.

At Christmas, we give each other presents and we eat together.

Grammar (Higher only) — the passive

To say that something is done <u>without</u> saying <u>who</u> does it, use '<u>se</u>' and the <u>3rd person</u> part of the verb (see p.189).

<u>Se ven</u> los desfiles.
The processions <u>are watched</u>.

During Hanukkah — Durante Janucá
For Diwali — Para Diwali

Question
¿Cuál es tu fiesta favorita?
What's your favourite festival?

Simple Answer
Mi fiesta favorita es el Eid al-Fitr. Lo celebro en familia.
My favourite festival is Eid al-Fitr. I celebrate it with family.

Extended Answer
Mi fiesta favorita es el Eid al-Fitr. Visitamos a nuestros familiares y ofrecemos regalos a los niños.
My favourite festival is Eid al-Fitr. We visit our relatives and offer gifts to the children.

Practice Questions

Q1 Read the following text out loud.   [5 marks]   SPEAKING

> Me interesan las fiestas de España y Sudamérica. Las tradiciones del Día de Muertos son hermosas. La gente celebra las vidas de los muertos. En España, se comen doce uvas a medianoche en Nochevieja. Me gusta celebrar la Nochevieja con mis amigos.

Top Tip for Higher Students
✓ Use relative pronouns like 'lo que' to add more details to your answers.

Now answer the questions below in Spanish.   [10 marks]

a) ¿Cómo celebras la Nochevieja?

b) ¿Cuál es tu opinión sobre los Sanfermines?

c) ¿Te gustaría ir a una fiesta española?

d) Describe la fiesta favorita que celebras.

Higher

Q2 In a podcast, Carmen is asking Vicente about festivals in Spain. Fill each gap in the sentences below with **one or two** words.

LISTENING

a) _______ is so popular that you need to buy a ticket before attending.
During the _______ the streets are full of people.   [2 marks]

b) Las Fallas began centuries ago to celebrate the start of _______.
The festival is celebrated with fireworks and _______.   [2 marks]

Learn the key vocabulary for a festival in case it crops up...

Test yourself on the words about festivals by coming up with a sentence to describe each one on these pages. Remember to include where and when each festival takes place, plus some details about what happens.

Listening Questions

You've guessed it — you've reached more lovely exam-style question pages. There are plenty of questions here to help you prepare for the sort of stuff you'll see in the exams.

---

1 Listen to two friends, Lin and Sara, talking about the festivals they celebrate. Write the correct letter in each box.

Listening Track 24

1 a What does Lin say about Chinese New Year celebrations?

A	he prefers them to Spanish New Year traditions.
B	he likes Chinese New Year and Spanish New Year equally.
C	he thinks the parades last too long.

[1 mark]

1 b Lin feels that the tradition of eating twelve grapes at midnight...

A	is surprisingly difficult to do.
B	is just a silly tradition.
C	seems silly, but is actually really fun.

[1 mark]

1 c What's Sara's favourite thing about celebrating Christmas?
Write your answer in **English**.

.... *[1 mark]*

2 You are in a museum in Mexico taking a guided tour about the Day of the Dead.

What does the guide tell you?

Write **A** if only statement **A** is correct.

    B if only statement **B** is correct.

    A + B if both statements **A** and **B** are correct.

Listening Track 25

2 a The guide mentions that on the wall...

| A | the oldest photos are on the left. |
| B | the most recent photos are on the right. |

[1 mark]

2 b In celebration of the Day of the Dead...

| A | many Mexicans wear fancy dress. |
| B | the shops sell special fruit dishes. |

[1 mark]

2 c The Day of the Dead...

| A | is a day of celebration. |
| B | is a serious occasion. |

[1 mark]

2 d This tradition is celebrated...

| A | at the beginning of November. |
| B | at the end of November. |

[1 mark]

Higher

Speaking Questions

Candidate's Material

- When your teacher asks you, read aloud the following text **in Spanish**.

Foundation

- Los habitantes de España celebran muchas costumbres.
- Durante la Semana Santa hay varios desfiles con música.
- Mucha gente viaja a las ciudades de España para ver los pasos.
- La Tomatina es una fiesta genial.
- En la Nochevieja se puede ver fuegos artificiales.

Higher

- El baile y la música son importantes en las culturas hispanohablantes.
- Intentaré aprender a bailar flamenco, porque me parece divertido.
- Acabo de visitar Valencia para asistir a Las Fallas.
- El domingo probé paella, un plato típico de la región.
- Vi una corrida de toros. ¡Sigo pensando que es peligrosa!
- Querría visitar España durante las celebraciones de la Navidad.

- You will then be asked four questions **in Spanish** that relate to the topic of **Customs, festivals and celebrations**.

- In order to score the highest marks, **answer all four questions as fully as you can**.

Teacher's Material

- Start by asking the candidate to read the text by saying *Lee el texto*.

- Allow the candidate to read the text aloud, then ask the following four questions for their tier.

- Allow the student to develop their answers as much as possible.

Foundation

- ¿Qué fiestas hay en tu país?
- ¿Cómo pasas la Navidad?
- ¿Prefieres pasar las fiestas con amigos o familia? ¿Por qué?
- ¿Qué te gusta hacer para celebrar tu cumpleaños?

Higher

- ¿Cómo celebraste la Nochevieja el año pasado?
- ¿Qué piensas de pasar las fiestas con amigos?
- ¿Qué platos de países hispanohablantes quieres probar?
- ¿Cuál es tu opinión sobre las tradiciones de las bodas?

Reading Questions

1   Julia is writing to her Spanish exchange partner after having spent Christmas with their family in Spain.

What is her opinion on different aspects of her trip?

Write **P** for a **positive** opinion. Write **N** for a **negative** opinion.

> *Gracias por invitarme a pasar unos días divertidos con tu familia. Lo pasé genial. En mi país tenemos una tradición diferente para dar regalos a los niños, ¡pero prefiero la tradición española con los tres Reyes Magos! Además, me encanta que España tenga* más días de fiesta para celebrar la Navidad. Es una pena decir que no me gustó la paella, aunque es un plato importante en la cultura española. En cambio, me encantó muchísimo visitar los mercados de Navidad y probar los caramelos típicos de España. ¡Espero volver a visitarte!*
>
> **tenga = has*

1 a   The Three Kings   *[1 mark]*

1 b   The length of Christmas celebrations   *[1 mark]*

1 c   Paella   *[1 mark]*

1 d   Visiting the Christmas markets   *[1 mark]*

2   Translate these sentences into **English.**

2 a   Me encantan los fuegos artificiales aunque hacen mucho ruido.

....   *[2 marks]*

2 b   Mi hermano me engaña todo el tiempo, incluso en mi cumpleaños.

....   *[2 marks]*

2 c   No invitaremos a mucha gente a nuestra boda.

....   *[2 marks]*

2 d   Los habitantes celebran esta tradición desde hace tres siglos.

....   *[2 marks]*

Writing Questions

Foundation

1   You receive this photo in a message from your friend in Pamplona, Spain.

What is in this photo? Write **three** sentences in **Spanish**.

....   *[2 marks]*

....   *[2 marks]*

....   *[2 marks]*

2   You are writing a blog about traditions in Spain and Latin America.
Write approximately **90** words in **Spanish**.
You must write something about each bullet point. Mention:

•   a custom from Spain or Latin America that you find interesting

•   a festival that you have been to in the past

•   a Spanish or Latin American tradition you'd like to experience in the future.   *[15 marks]*

Higher

3   Translate the following sentences into **Spanish**.

3 a   Who are you going to spend Christmas with?

....   *[2 marks]*

3 b   I have just seen a show at Las Fallas.

....   *[2 marks]*

3 c   Last year we spent New Year's Eve in Spain.

....   *[2 marks]*

3 d   Every December my friends come with me to a Christmas Eve event.

....   *[2 marks]*

Customs, Festivals and Celebrations — Vocabulary

Grab a party hat — it's time to get to grips with the vocab you'll need to talk about festivals and celebrations.

Celebrations

la celebración	*celebration*
celebrar	*to celebrate*
el cumpleaños	*birthday*
¡Feliz cumpleaños!	*Happy birthday!*
¡Enhorabuena!	*Congratulations!*
la alegría	*joy, happiness*
el ambiente	*atmosphere, environment*
la sorpresa	*surprise*
invitar	*to invite*
el matrimonio	*marriage*
la boda	*wedding*
la novia	*bride*
el novio	*groom*
recibir	*to receive*
el regalo	*present, gift*
la tarjeta	*written card*

Higher

celebrarse	*to hold (an event)*
sorprender	*to surprise*
reunir	*to gather, bring together*
reunirse	*to get together*
regalar	*to give (as a gift)*
ofrecer	*to offer, present*

Because what's a party without cake and silly hats?

Customs and Festivals

la tradición	*tradition*
tradicional	*traditional*
la costumbre	*custom, tradition*
la fiesta	*party, festival*
los Sanfermines	*festival in Pamplona involving running of the bulls*
el animal	*animal*
el toro	*bull*
la plaza de toros	*bullring*
la corrida	*bullfight*
el/la habitante	*local (person), inhabitant*
la Tomatina	*Spanish tomato festival*
el tomate	*tomato*
tirar	*to throw, pull*
los fuegos artificiales	*fireworks*
Las Fallas	*Valencian celebration involving burning of papier mâché models*
el espectáculo	*show, spectacle*
la cultura	*culture*
cultural	*cultural*
el Día de Muertos	*Day of the Dead (Mexican celebration)*
el disfraz	*costume, fancy dress*
el traje	*costume*
la flor	*flower*
pintarse	*to put on makeup*
el santo	*saint, saint's day*
religioso/a	*religious*
la Semana Santa	*Easter Week, Holy Week*

el desfile	*procession, parade*
el paso	*religious image carried in Holy Week processions*
el cielo	*heaven*
Nochebuena	*Christmas Eve*
Navidad	*Christmas*
Nochevieja	*New Year's Eve*
la uva	*grape*
el Día de Reyes	*Epiphany, 6th January*
los Reyes Magos	*the Three Kings, the Three Wise Men*
real	*royal*
el rey	*king*
la reina	*queen*
la cocina	*cooking*
el baile	*dance*
el flamenco	*flamenco (dance / music from the south of Spain)*
la historia	*story*
el interés	*interest*
especial	*special*
la región	*region*

Higher

la ocasión	*occasion*
el evento	*event*
nacional	*national*
el siglo	*century*
escaparse	*to run away*
el juguete	*toy*
engañar	*to trick, deceive*

Revision Summary Test for Section Seven

Try the summary questions on this page to consolidate what you know about celebrations.

- Yep, these questions are **hard** — they'll really help you see **how well you know your stuff**.
- Tackle the **revision summary test** below, or scan the QR code to do it **online**.
  Use the CGP RevisionHub to **track your progress** and see **which areas need more work**.
- You can find **sample answers** here: www.cgpbooks.co.uk/MadridExtras

Celebrations ✓

1) Monika's birthday is today. What 2 phrases could you say to congratulate her in Spanish?

2) Your friend writes: 'There was a lot of joy in the atmosphere of that celebration.'
   How could they say this in Spanish?

3) List the words in this section that relate to weddings. There are 4 you need to know.

4) '¿Qué haces para celebrar tu cumpleaños?' Translate this question into
   English, then answer it in Spanish, including as much detail as possible.

5) 'Mis padres me dieron una sorpresa. Recibí zapatos nuevos de ellos.' Translate this into English.

6) '¿Has ido a una celebración recientemente?' Translate this question into
   English, then answer it in Spanish. Give as much detail as you can.

7) Translate this sentence into Spanish:
   'My parents held a party where all the family got together to surprise my grandparents.'

Customs and Festivals ✓

8) What's the English for...?
   a) el santo   b) la Semana Santa   c) el desfile   d) el paso   e) el cielo

9) How many words for Christmas and New Year celebrations can you list in Spanish?
   There are 4 in this section.

10) a) Can you name 4 festivals from Spanish-speaking countries?
    b) Choose one of these festivals and describe it in Spanish, giving as much detail as you can.

11) 'Muchas turistas visitan la región de Valencia durante sus fiestas populares.'
    How would you say this in English?

12) 'Me encantaría visitar Chile para ver sus costumbres y probar la cocina.' Say this in English.
    Then, write about a custom from a Spanish-speaking country you'd like to experience.

13) Write these words in English, then decide which one isn't usually part of Las Fallas celebrations:
    a) las flores   b) los fuegos artificiales   c) los disfraces   d) los tomates

14) 'Day of the Dead traditions are important for many people.' How would you say this in Spanish?

15) Say 'En un baile español que se llama flamenco, se puede ver trajes hermosos.' in English.

16) How would you say these words in Spanish?
    a) inhabitant   b) cultural   c) royal   d) king   e) queen   f) story

17) Translate this question into English, then answer it in Spanish using complete sentences:
    '¿Cómo celebraste tu tradición favorita el año pasado?'

18) Translate this into Spanish: 'The Three Kings have been giving toys to children for centuries.'

19) Imagine you're in Pamplona for the Sanfermines festival. Write a description
    in Spanish of what you might see there, including as much detail as possible.

Favourite Celebrities

Roll out the red carpet — it's time to learn how to talk about celebrities.

Remember there's also lots of online content here: www.cgpbooks.co.uk/Madrid

Tu famoso favorito — Your favourite celebrity

Vocabulary

el/la famoso/a	*celebrity, famous person*	el/la cantante	*singer*	el/la influencer	*influencer*
la actriz	*actor (f), actress*	el/la músico/a	*musician*	**Higher** el/la deportista	*sportsperson*
el actor	*actor (m)*	el/la director(a)	*director*	la banda	*(musical) band*
el/la artista	*artist, performer*	el/la jugador(a)	*player*	actuar	*to act*
		el/la autor(a)	*writer, author*	el/la aficionado/a	*fan*

Mi famosa favorita es una cantante mexicana. Será emocionante verla en vivo.

My favourite celebrity is a Mexican singer. It'll be exciting to watch her live.

Uno de mis famosos favoritos es actor en películas de acción. Presenta un programa de entrevistas también.

One of my favourite celebrities is an actor in action films. He hosts a talk show too.

he manages a children's charity — dirige una organización benéfica para niños

Soy gran aficionado a un grupo de pop. Estoy aprendiendo todas sus canciones.

I'm a huge fan of a pop group. I am learning all their songs.

an indie band — una banda indie

Question

¿Qué hace tu famoso favorito?

What does your favourite celebrity do?

Simple Answer

Mi famosa favorita es autora. Escribe libros de ciencia ficción.

My favourite celebrity is an author. She writes science-fiction books.

Extended Answer

Mi famoso favorito es jugador de baloncesto y también es conocido por apoyar a su comunidad local.

My favourite celebrity is a basketball player and he's also known for supporting his local community.

Me gusta esta persona porque... — I like this person because...

Vocabulary

la estrella	*star*	seguir	*to follow*	la cara	*face, expression*
famoso/a	*famous, well-known*	la voz	*voice*	**Higher** el estilo	*style*
conocido/a	*known, well-known*	de moda	*fashionable*	el talento	*talent*
importante	*important, influential*	el carácter	*personality*	el contenido	*content*

Me gusta este famoso porque tiene una voz hermosa y unos tatuajes bonitos. Siempre lleva ropa negra.

I like this celebrity because he has a beautiful voice and some nice tattoos. He always wears black clothes.

a cool guitar — una guitarra guay

Sigo a mi estrella favorita desde hace dos años porque da buenos consejos y tiene buen estilo.

I have been following my favourite star for two years because she gives good advice and she has good style.

she communicates well with her fans — se comunica bien con sus aficionados

Mi famosa favorita es cómica. Sus chistes me hacen reír mucho.

My favourite celebrity is a stand-up comedian. Her jokes make me laugh a lot.

Tipos diferentes de famosos — Different types of celebrities

Una persona famosa que me inspira es científica. Ganó un Premio Nobel por sus contribuciones a la medicina.

One famous person who inspires me is a scientist. She won a Nobel Prize for her contributions to medicine.

Mi famoso favorito cocinaba en la televisión. Parece una persona muy simpática y me gustan las recetas que publica.

My favourite celebrity used to cook on TV. He seems like a really nice person and I like the recipes that he publishes.

Hay un influencer que viene de mi pueblo. Es conocido por jugar a videojuegos.

There's an influencer who comes from my town. He's known for playing computer games.

Sigo a una famosa que crea contenido en Internet.

I follow a celebrity who creates content on the internet.

Mi famoso favorito ha grabado muchos documentales sobre la naturaleza. Siempre son interesantes.

My favourite celebrity has recorded a lot of nature documentaries. They're always interesting.

The fame had clearly gone to Larry's head.

a content creator — un creador de contenido

shares their art on social media — comparte su arte en las redes sociales

broadcasts podcasts each week — emite podcasts cada semana

Grammar — formation of feminine nouns

In Spanish, there are <u>rules</u> for <u>changing masculine nouns</u> (particularly with jobs and positions) to their <u>feminine form</u>. See p.151.

Nouns that end in <u>-o</u> change to <u>-a</u>: **el músic<u>o</u> = <u>la</u> músic<u>a</u>**

Nouns that end in <u>-or</u> add <u>-a</u>: **el direct<u>or</u> = <u>la</u> direct<u>ora</u>**

Nouns ending in <u>-ante</u>, <u>-ente</u> or <u>-ista</u> do not change: **el art<u>ista</u> = <u>la</u> art<u>ista</u>**

When you're talking about what job someone does, you don't use the article, e.g. 'Es cocinero' — 'He's a chef'. However, you do include the article if you use an adjective, e.g. 'Es un buen cocinero' — 'He's a good chef'. See p.153.

Practice Questions

Q1 You are listening to a podcast where two people are discussing their favourite celebrities. Answer the questions in English.

Listening Track 26

    a) Why is a director Luis's favourite celebrity?   *[1 mark]*

    b) What did he learn from a magazine? Give **one** detail.   *[1 mark]*

    c) Give **one** detail of Carla's favourite celebrity's appearance.   *[1 mark]*

    d) What did her favourite celebrity do recently?   *[1 mark]*

Q2 Write about your favourite celebrity. You should write about 90 words in Spanish. Mention:

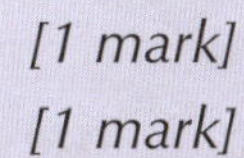

Top Tip For Higher Students
✓ Use 'desde hace' to talk about how long your favourite celebrity has been doing something.

    • *who your favourite celebrity is*

    • *what they have done in their career*

    • *why you like them.*   *[15 marks]*

You can invent a celebrity if you don't have a favourite...

Don't worry if you don't have a favourite celebrity — you can always imagine someone and describe them instead. The most important thing is that you can describe a celebrity using clear and accurate Spanish.

Celebrity Life

Fame may lead to photoshoots and swanky parties, but it has some drawbacks too...

La vida de una estrella — The life of a star

Vocabulary

la telerrealidad	*reality TV*	el público	*public*	
la entrevista	*interview*	la prensa	*press*	Higher
la revista	*magazine*	la atención	*attention*	
popular	*popular*	reconocer	*to recognise, admit*	

Los famosos populares suelen participar en las series de telerrealidad.

Popular celebrities often participate in reality TV series.

exclusive interviews — entrevistas exclusivas

Muchas estrellas tienen una fuerte presencia en las redes sociales y ahora están compartiendo su vida allí.

Many stars have a strong presence on social media and they are now sharing their life there.

they get collaborations — consiguen colaboraciones

Para los famosos, puede ser difícil salir sin ser reconocidos. Muchos quieren evitar la prensa.

For celebrities, it can be difficult to go out without being recognised. Many want to avoid the press.

enjoy the attention — disfrutan la atención

Question

¿Te gustaría ser una persona famosa?

Would you like to be a famous person?

Simple Answer

Sí, porque mi sueño es ser un músico conocido.

Yes, because my dream is to be a well-known musician.

Extended Answer

No me interesa nada ser una estrella. No me gustaría ni la atención ni la presión.

I'm not interested at all in being a star. I would like neither the attention nor the pressure.

Lo bueno de ser famoso es... — The good thing about being famous is...

Vocabulary

lo bueno	*the good thing*	el dinero	*money*	influir	*to influence*	
positivo/a	*positive*	rico/a	*rich, wealthy*	fundar	*to set up, establish*	Higher
el éxito	*success*	el respeto	*respect, regard*	merecer	*to deserve, be worthy of*	
el premio	*prize, reward, award*	el apoyo	*support, backing*			

Lo bueno de ser famoso es que podría abrir las puertas a oportunidades emocionantes.

The good thing about being famous is that it could open doors to exciting opportunities.

Es increíble que un famoso tenga el poder de ser una influencia positiva para los jóvenes.

It's incredible that a celebrity has the power to be a positive influence for young people.

to change society for the better — cambiar la sociedad para mejor

Los famosos pueden ganar respeto y muchos premios por su trabajo.

Celebrities can gain respect and lots of awards for their work.

inspire others with — inspirar a otros con

earn a lot of money for — ganar mucho dinero por

Varios famosos quieren usar su fama para algo bueno y han apoyado causas importantes.

Various celebrities want to use their fame for something good and have supported important causes.

Los aspectos negativos — The negative aspects

Vocabulary

negativo/a	*negative*	molestarse	*to be offended*
la confianza	*confidence, trust*	la realidad	*reality*
mantener	*to keep, maintain*	la soledad	*loneliness, solitude*
la imagen	*image*	el comentario	*remark, comment*
la presión	*pressure*	la víctima	*victim*
criticar	*to criticise*	la vergüenza	*embarrassment, shame*

(Higher: la realidad, la soledad, el comentario, la víctima, la vergüenza)

Es posible que un famoso tenga una falta de confianza en otra gente. Por eso, podrían sufrir de soledad.

It is possible for a famous person to have a lack of trust in other people. Therefore, they may suffer from loneliness.

Existe presión por mantener siempre la imagen y parecer perfecto.

There is pressure to always maintain your image and to seem perfect.

La salud mental de una estrella podría ser afectada por un horario ocupadísimo.

A star's mental health could be affected by a really busy schedule.

Los famosos que consiguen atención en Internet pueden ser víctimas de un montón de comentarios intolerantes.

Celebrities who gain attention on the internet can be victims of a lot of intolerant comments.

Practice Questions

Q1 *A celebrity is discussing what they do and don't like about being famous.*

> Soy una estrella de la telerrealidad. Grabar mi vida es divertido porque hago muchas actividades diferentes. En cambio, puede ser duro mantener mi imagen todo el día.

SPEAKING

Top Tip For Higher Students
✓ Use 'lo mejor' and 'lo peor' to talk about the best and the worst things about being famous.

*Now it's your turn. Imagine you're a celebrity and talk about what you like and dislike about being famous. Aim to talk for **two** minutes.* [10 marks]

Q2 *You are reading a social media post from Tanvir, a famous influencer. Choose the correct option to complete the sentences below.*

READING

> Quiero promover mi nuevo libro sobre mi experiencia como influencer. Habla de todas las actividades locas que he grabado y explica cuánto me han ayudado mis aficionados. Además, describo cómo ser influencer ha cambiado mi vida. Aunque todavía me resulta difícil hablar con otra gente, ya tengo mucha más confianza.

(Higher)

a) Tanvir's book is...
- **A.** a novel.
- **B.** an autobiography.
- **C.** a guide book.

[1 mark]

b) He talks about...
- **A.** his fans.
- **B.** his promotion.
- **C.** his family.

[1 mark]

c) Being an influencer has...
- **A.** given him more confidence.
- **B.** made it difficult to talk to others.
- **C.** made him feel happier.

[1 mark]

Make sure you talk about the good and the bad...

In the exam, you could be asked to talk about the advantages and the disadvantages of fame. It'd be handy to have a few sentences in mind that cover both sides of celebrity life, so give these pages another read.

Listening Questions

Let's take a break from all the glitz and glamour and put what you've learned to the test. The questions on the next few pages will help you prepare for tackling questions on Celebrity Culture in your exams.

1   Four friends are chatting about celebrities. What are their opinions?

Write **P** for a **positive** opinion.

      N for a **negative** opinion.

      P + N for a **positive** and **negative** opinion.

Listening Track 27

1 a   Amira   ☐   *[1 mark]*

1 b   Cris   ☐   *[1 mark]*

1 c   Emilio   ☐   *[1 mark]*

1 d   Nadia   ☐   *[1 mark]*

2   You will hear 4 short sentences. Listen carefully and, using your knowledge of Spanish sounds, write down in **Spanish** exactly what you hear for each sentence.

You will hear each sentence **three** times: the first time as a full sentence, the second time in short sections and the third time again as a full sentence.

Use your knowledge of Spanish sounds and grammar to make sure that what you have written makes sense. Check carefully that your spelling is accurate.

Listening Track 28

Foundation

2 a **Sentence 1**

.... *[2 marks]*

2 b **Sentence 2**

.... *[2 marks]*

Higher

2 c **Sentence 3**

.... *[2 marks]*

2 d **Sentence 4**

.... *[2 marks]*

Speaking Questions

Candidate's Material

- You are talking to your Colombian friend.

- Your teacher will play the part of your friend and will speak first.

- You should address your friend as *tú*.

- When you see this – **?** – you will have to ask a question.

In order to score full marks, you must include a verb in your response to each task.

1. Say what your favourite celebrity does. (Give **one** detail.)

2. Say what your favourite celebrity looks like. (Give **one** detail.)

3. Describe your favourite celebrity's personality. (Give **one** detail.)

? **4.** Ask your friend a question about their favourite celebrity.

5. Describe an advantage of being famous. (Give **one** detail.)

6. Describe how you discovered your favourite celebrity. (Give **two** details.)

7. Say whether or not you would like to be famous and why.
(Give **one** detail and **one** reason.)

Higher

Teacher's Material

- You begin the role-play.

- You should address the candidate as *tú*.

- You must read out the teacher's role as shown below **without any changes**.

- You must begin the role-play by using the introductory text below.

Introductory text: *Estás hablando con tu amigo colombiano/tu amiga colombiana.
Yo soy tu amigo/tu amiga.*

1. ¿Qué hace tu famoso favorito?

2. ¿Cómo es tu famoso favorito físicamente?

3. Describe el carácter de tu famoso favorito.

? **4.** Allow the candidate to ask a question about your favourite celebrity.
Give an appropriate response.

5. ¿Cuál es una ventaja de ser famoso?

6. ¿Cómo descubriste a tu famoso favorito?

H

7. ¿Te gustaría ser famoso? ¿Por qué?

Reading Questions

1   You read these comments from some Spanish teenagers about celebrities.

> **[A] Álex**: El viernes pasado, conocí a una estrella de fútbol. Sin embargo, no me interesa seguir a los famosos. Prefiero las opiniones de mis amigos.
>
> **[D] David**: Sigo a muchos músicos famosos porque sus vidas me interesan, pero pienso que las canciones de los artistas actuales son aburridas.
>
> **[E] Elena**: Me encantaría conocer a mi artista favorita. La sigo en las redes sociales. La letra de sus canciones siempre me afecta.

Match the correct person with each of the following questions.
Write the correct letter in each box.

1 a   Who has met a famous person?

[1 mark]

1 b   Who is moved by an artist's songs?

[1 mark]

1 c   Who follows a lot of famous musicians?

[1 mark]

2   A Mexican musician has written about his life. When do the different events happen?

> *Actualmente hago actuaciones de mis canciones en vivo con una banda. Cuando era más joven, solía dar conciertos solo. Sin embargo, es bueno ahora tener a otros músicos conmigo. Llevo muchos meses escribiendo nuevas canciones, pero tengo la intención de dejar de la industria de la música. Pronto comenzaré a actuar para una serie de televisión. No he actuado nunca en mi carrera y estoy emocionado.*

Write **P** for something that happened in the **past**, **N** for something happening **now**, or **F** for something that is going to happen in the **future**. Write the correct letter in each box.

2 a   Working with a band

[1 mark]

2 b   Working alone

[1 mark]

2 c   Leaving the music industry

[1 mark]

2 d   Acting

[1 mark]

Writing Questions

1 Using your knowledge of grammar, complete the following sentences in **Spanish**. Choose the correct Spanish word from the three options in the grid. Write the correct **word** in the space.

1 a Yo .... a ese actor.

sigo	sigue	sigues

[1 mark]

1 b Ahora el grupo es muy ....

rico	rica	ricos

[1 mark]

1 c La directora .... recibido muchos premios.

han	ha	he

[1 mark]

2 You are writing an article about celebrity life. Write approximately **90** words in **Spanish**.

You must write something about each bullet point. Mention:

- what you think celebrity life is like
- a time when you or your friend have wanted to be like a celebrity
- what you would want to be famous for in the future. *[15 marks]*

3 Translate the following sentences into **Spanish**.

3 a I have been following my favourite author for two years.

.... *[2 marks]*

3 b When we were younger, we wanted to form a band.

.... *[2 marks]*

3 c The best thing about being a star is having lots of fans.

.... *[2 marks]*

3 d In my opinion, it's not worth being famous.

.... *[2 marks]*

Celebrity Culture — Vocabulary

Show the examiner you've got that star quality by using the celebrity-related vocab on this page.

Favourite Celebrities

el/la famoso/a	*celebrity, famous person*
la personalidad	*celebrity*
la actriz	*actor (f), actress*
el actor	*actor (m)*
el/la artista	*artist, performer*
el/la cantante	*singer*
el/la músico/a	*musician*
el/la director(a)	*director*
el/la modelo	*model*
el/la jugador(a)	*player*
el/la autor(a)	*writer, author*
el/la influencer	*influencer*
el grupo	*group*
la estrella	*star*
famoso/a	*famous, well-known*
conocido/a	*known, well-known*
importante	*important, influential*
seguir	*to follow*
el/la seguidor(a)	*follower, fan, supporter*
la voz	*voice*
de moda	*in fashion, fashionable*
el papel	*role, part*

la letra	*lyrics*
la novela	*novel*
el carácter	*personality, character*
listo/a	*clever, intelligent (after ser)*
hermoso/a	*handsome, beautiful*
artístico/a	*artistic*
gracioso/a	*funny*

Higher

el/la deportista	*sportsperson*
la banda	*(musical) band*
la actuación	*performance, acting*
actuar	*to act*
colgar	*to post (photo)*
el/la aficionado/a	*fan*
el/la representante	*representative (agent)*
la cara	*face, expression*
la belleza	*beauty*
el estilo	*style*
el talento	*talent*
el destino	*destiny*
el contenido	*content*
digital	*digital*

Celebrity Life

la telerrealidad	*reality TV*
la entrevista	*interview*
la revista	*magazine*
popular	*popular*
lo bueno	*the good thing*
positivo/a	*positive*
el éxito	*success*
el premio	*prize, reward, award*
el dinero	*money*
rico/a	*rich, wealthy*
el respeto	*respect, regard*
el apoyo	*support, backing*
compartir	*to share*
negativo/a	*negative*
la confianza	*confidence, trust*
mantener	*to keep, maintain*
la imagen	*image, picture*
la presión	*pressure*
criticar	*to criticise*
molestarse	*to be offended*
el comportamiento	*behaviour*
la juventud	*youth*

Higher

el público	*public*
la prensa	*press*
la tendencia	*tendency, trend*
la reacción	*reaction*
la atención	*attention*
conseguir	*to get, obtain*
reconocer	*to recognise, admit*
la influencia	*influence*
influir	*to influence*
la riqueza	*wealth, riches*
fundar	*to set up, establish*
merecer	*to deserve, be worthy of*
la realidad	*reality*
la soledad	*loneliness, solitude*
publicar	*to publish, post (online)*
el comentario	*remark, comment*
la víctima	*victim*
la vergüenza	*embarrassment, shame*

Revision Summary Test for Section Eight

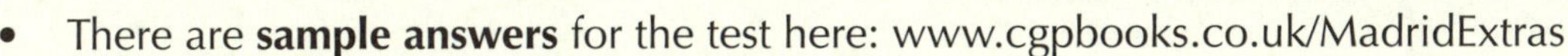

Work your way through this summary test to go over all the ups and downs of celebrity life.

- These questions are **hard**, but they'll really help you see **how well you know your stuff**.
- Tackle the **revision summary test** below, or scan the QR code to do it **online**. You can **track your progress** online and see **which areas need more work**.
- There are **sample answers** for the test here: www.cgpbooks.co.uk/MadridExtras

Favourite Celebrities ☑

1) Write the English for: a) el/la cantante   b) el/la director(a)   c) el/la jugador(a)   d) el/la autor(a) ☑

2) In Spanish, say what your favourite celebrity does. Give at least two details. ☑

3) There are 4 Spanish adjectives to describe a celebrity's personality in this section. How many can you remember? ☑

4) 'She is famous because she's a very important actress.' Say this in Spanish. ☑

5) In Spanish, describe what your favourite celebrity from your childhood looked like. Give one reason why you liked them. ☑

6) 'Me interesa seguir a los modelos porque puedo ver la ropa que está de moda.' Translate this sentence into English. ☑

7) What's the Spanish for: a) follower   b) voice   c) role, part   d) novel ☑

8) 'My favourite celebrity is really popular on the internet. He makes videos about computer games and he writes songs too.' How would you say this in Spanish? ☑

9) 'Después de tener una gran discusión con su representante, mi banda favorita ya no es un grupo.' Translate this sentence into English. ☑

10) Imagine you've just met your favourite celebrity. In Spanish, describe how you discovered them and why you like them. ☑

Higher (9–10)

Celebrity Life ☑

11) Write the English for: a) el éxito   b) el dinero   c) el respeto   d) la confianza   e) molestarse ☑

12) In Spanish, give one advantage and one disadvantage of being famous. ☑

13) 'La gente critica a los influencers por tener un efecto negativo en la sociedad.' Translate this sentence into English. ☑

14) ¿Qué piensas de las revistas que hablan de los famosos? ☑

15) Say these words in Spanish: a) interview   b) support   c) behaviour   d) youth ☑

16) 'Mis padres odian las series de telerrealidad.' Say this in English. ☑

17) In Spanish, say whether or not you would like to be famous and why. ☑

18) Sara says: 'The reality of being famous seems difficult to me. You can feel embarrassment due to the articles that journalists publish.' Translate what she says into Spanish. ☑

19) 'Ayer unos deportistas famosos anunciaron a la prensa que fundarán un nuevo estadio.' Say this sentence in English. ☑

20) ¿Crees que los famosos merecen la atención que reciben? ¿Por qué? ☑

Higher (18–20)

Where to Go

Grab some suncream and pack your suitcase — you're off on holiday.

Don't forget you can access your online content here: www.cgpbooks.co.uk/Madrid

Vamos de viaje — We're going on a trip

Vocabulary

las vacaciones	*holidays*	el extranjero	*abroad*	Sudamérica	*South America*
el viaje	*trip, journey*	el mundo	*world*	la nación	*nation*
el puente	*long weekend*	España	*Spain*	hispanohablante	*Spanish-speaking*

El próximo puente, quiero ir de vacaciones al extranjero.

The next long weekend, I want to go on holiday abroad.

→ *to another country* — a otro país

Todos querríamos ir de vacaciones juntos a Italia.

We would all like to go on holiday together to Italy.

→ *France* — Francia
Germany — Alemania
the USA — los Estados Unidos

Bashir va a Australia. Será un viaje largo al otro lado del mundo.

Bashir is going to Australia. It will be a long journey to the other side of the world.

¿Cómo es el paisaje? — What's the landscape like?

Vocabulary

el paisaje	*landscape, scenery*	el bosque	*forest, wood*	la costa	*coast*
hermoso/a	*beautiful*	la montaña	*mountain*	la playa	*beach*
tranquilo/a	*calm, tranquil*	el río	*river*	el monte	*hill, hills, countryside*
el campo	*countryside*	la isla	*island*	el lago	*lake*

Snowdonia es una región de Gales con muchas montañas.

Snowdonia is a region of Wales with lots of mountains.

Vamos a Menorca, una isla que tiene muchas playas de arena.

We go to Menorca, an island that has many sandy beaches.

→ *a lot of countryside* — mucho monte
beautiful views — vistas preciosas

Hay unos lagos hermosos en el norte de Inglaterra.

There are some beautiful lakes in the north of England.

→ *large areas of forest* — grandes zonas de bosque

Question

¿Adónde vas de vacaciones?

Where do you go on holiday?

Simple Answer

Voy de vacaciones a Irlanda del Norte.

I go on holiday to Northern Ireland.

Extended Answer

Voy de vacaciones a Irlanda del Norte para ver a mis abuelos. Solemos pasar unas semanas allí, en un pueblo cerca del mar.

I go on holiday to Northern Ireland to see my grandparents. We tend to spend a few weeks there, in a village near the sea.

¿Por qué quieres ir allí? — Why do you want to go there?

Vocabulary

al aire libre	*in the open air, outdoors*	el sitio	*place, site*
pasarlo bien/mal	*to have a good/bad time*	la arquitectura	*architecture*
disfrutar	*to enjoy*	conocido/a	*known, well-known*
visitar	*to visit*	histórico/a	*historic, historical*

Quiero ir a España porque tiene arquitectura hermosa.

I want to go to Spain because it has beautiful architecture.

Cada vez que he ido a Cádiz con mis amigos, lo hemos pasado muy bien.

Every time I've been to Cádiz with my friends, we have had a really good time.

Le gustaría ir a Sudamérica para ver una cultura diferente.

She would like to go to South America in order to see a different culture.

Espero ir a un sitio conocido como Machu Picchu algún día.

I hope to go to a well-known site like Machu Picchu one day.

on holiday to Iceland — de vacaciones a Islandia

Vamos a visitar Edimburgo porque es un sitio histórico.

We are going to visit Edinburgh because it is a historic place.

Rome — Roma
Berlin — Berlín
Athens — Atenas

Preferiría ir de vacaciones a un país donde se puede pasar mucho tiempo al aire libre.

I would prefer to go on holiday to a country where you can spend a lot of time outdoors.

enjoy the good weather — disfrutar del buen tiempo

Practice Questions

Q1 *Marina and Hugo are telling their Colombian friend about Barcelona. Choose the statement that is mentioned in each pair below.*

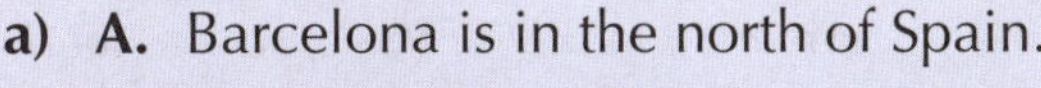

a) **A.** Barcelona is in the north of Spain.
   B. Barcelona has millions of tourists. *[1 mark]*

b) **A.** It's surrounded by the Mediterranean Sea.
   B. It's famous for its art and architecture. *[1 mark]*

c) **A.** Marina thinks that there is lots to do outdoors.
   B. In July and August, Marina loves spending all day on its beaches. *[1 mark]*

Q2 *You are writing an article about travel for a competition. You should write about 90 words in Spanish. Mention:*
   - *where you prefer to go on holiday*
   - *a recent holiday you went on*
   - *what holiday plans you have for this year.* *[15 marks]*

Top Tip for Higher Students
✓ Use the 'we' form of the conditional to talk about what you and your family would like to do.

Don't just name places — give opinions about them too...

There are plenty of Spanish words to help you describe different holiday destinations. Opinions are a great way to boost your marks in the exam, so try to mention what you like and dislike about a place.

Accommodation and Travel

Now you've chosen where you're going to visit, you need a place to stay and a way to get there...

Busco alojamiento... — I'm looking for accommodation...

Vocabulary

el alojamiento	*accommodation*	la tienda	*tent*
el hotel	*hotel*	quedar(se)	*to stay*
la habitación	*room*	reservar	*to book, reserve*
la recepción	*reception (hotel)*	el ascensor	*lift, elevator*
la instalación	*facility*	la calefacción	*heating*
el camping	*campsite, camping*	el lujo	*luxury*

[Higher] el ascensor / la calefacción / el lujo

Quisiera quedarme en un camping para cuatro noches.
I would like to stay on a campsite for four nights.

for a fortnight — para quince días

Siempre nos quedamos en un hotel de lujo.
We always stay in a luxury hotel.

Es esencial encontrar una habitación que tenga cuarto de baño y una cama cómoda.
It's essential to find a room that has a bathroom and a comfortable bed.

Me gustaría quedarme en un albergue juvenil para conocer a gente nueva.
I would like to stay in a youth hostel in order to meet new people.

to save money — ahorrar dinero

> **Grammar (Higher only)** — I need...
>
> When talking about the features of something you require, use the subjunctive (p.190).
>
> **Busco un hotel que tenga piscina.**
> ***I'm looking for a hotel that has a pool.***

Question
¿Qué tipo de habitación le gustaría a usted?
What type of room would you like?

Simple Answer
Me gustaría una habitación con vistas al mar.
I would like a room with sea views.

Extended Answer
Somos una familia de tres, así que necesitamos dos habitaciones — una individual y una doble.
We are a family of three, so we need two rooms — a single and a double.

¿Cuánto cuesta reservar...? — How much does it cost to book...?

Vocabulary

costar	*to cost*	el euro	*euro*	caro/a	*expensive*
pagar	*to pay (for)*	alto/a	*high*	barato/a	*cheap*
el precio	*price, cost*	bajo/a	*low*	[H] el costo	*price, cost*

Mi amigo y yo buscamos alojamiento barato.
My friend and I are looking for cheap accommodation.

have found a hotel with lower prices — hemos encontrado un hotel con precios más bajos

Una noche en este hotel cuesta ciento diez euros.
One night in this hotel costs one hundred and ten euros.

Preferiríamos pagar más para quedarnos en el centro de la ciudad.
We would prefer to pay more to stay in the city centre.

a room with modern facilities — una habitación con instalaciones modernas

Cómo llegar allí — How to get there

Vocabulary

llegar	*to arrive*	la estación	*station*
viajar	*to travel*	el tren	*train*
volver	*to go back, return*	el destino	*destination*
directo/a	*direct, straight*	la llegada	*arrival*
coger	*to take, catch*	el retraso	*delay*
el coche	*car*	la velocidad	*speed, velocity*
el puerto	*port, harbour*	la distancia	*distance*
el barco	*boat, ship*	la frontera	*border, frontier*
el aeropuerto	*airport*	internacional	*international*
el avión	*plane, aeroplane*	regresar	*to come back, go back, return*
el vuelo	*flight*		

(la estación to regresar marked **Higher**)

Viajar en avión me permite llegar a mi **destino** más pronto.
Travelling by plane allows me to arrive at my destination sooner.

Preferiría **coger un vuelo directo** desde el aeropuerto.
I would prefer to catch a direct flight from the airport.

Quieren **viajar en barco**, pero **prefiero ir en tren** porque es más rápido.
They want to travel by boat, but I prefer to go by train because it's faster.

Vamos a **viajar en coche** y esperamos **llegar a la frontera** a las once.
We are going to travel by car and we hope to arrive at the border at 11 o'clock.

Catching the high-speed train — Coger el tren de alta velocidad

They hate the delays at the station — Odian los retrasos en la estación

I get seasick — me mareo

Practice Questions

Q1 Read Lucía's diary entry about an upcoming trip and answer the questions below. **READING**

> En febrero voy de vacaciones a París. Ya he organizado el alojamiento y el transporte. Voy a viajar en tren porque es más barato que viajar en avión y más cómodo que viajar en autobús. Quedarme en un hotel costaría mucho, entonces he reservado un piso pequeño por un precio mejor. Tiene una cocina y un balcón* bonito. La estación está muy cerca también.

**balcón — balcony*

a) How will Lucía travel to Paris? *[1 mark]*

b) Give **one** reason why Lucía is going to use that type of transport. *[1 mark]*

c) What type of accommodation will she be staying in? *[1 mark]*

d) Give **two** details about the accommodation. *[2 marks]*

Q2 Listen carefully to 5 short sentences.
Use your knowledge of Spanish sounds and write down in Spanish exactly what you hear for each sentence. *[10 marks]*

(**Higher**)

 LISTENING

Listening Track 30

Use plenty of adjectives to describe your accommodation...

Get comfy with accommodation vocab because it'll be relevant to any holiday. Modes of transport will come up in different places too, so make sure you feel confident talking about how to get somewhere.

Find the CGP RevisionHub at cgpbooks.co.uk/Madrid

Getting Around and What to Do

There's no point planning a holiday if you're not going to enjoy yourself once you're there... Let's look at how you can get around, as well as what there is to see and do.

¿Coges el transporte público? — Do you take public transport?

Vocabulary

el transporte público	*public transport*	a pie	*on foot*
el billete	*ticket (for transport)*	conducir	*to drive*
la vuelta	*return, trip, ride*	el tráfico	*traffic*
el metro	*underground, tube, metro*	tardar	*to take (time)*
el autobús	*bus*	alquilar	*to hire, rent*
montar	*to ride*	caminar	*to walk*
la bicicleta, bici	*bicycle, bike*	el camino	*way, route, path*

(Higher: alquilar, caminar, el camino)

Cogeré el autobús porque será la opción más barata y tardará menos tiempo.

I will take the bus because it is the cheapest option and it will take less time.

Fuimos a la playa a pie ya que está cerca de nuestro hotel.

We went to the beach on foot since it's near our hotel.

by taxi because our feet were hurting — en taxi porque nos dolían los pies

Cogí el metro porque había mucho tráfico.

I took the underground because there was a lot of traffic.

the tram — el tranvía

I couldn't hire a car — no podía alquilar un coche

¿Cuál es la mejor manera de llegar al centro de la ciudad?

What is the best way to get to the city centre?

¿Qué te gustaría hacer? — What would you like to do?

Vocabulary

la excursión	*trip, excursion*	el puesto	*stall (market)*
el museo	*museum*	el turismo	*tourism*
el templo	*temple*	el/la guía	*guide (person)*
el castillo	*castle*	la guía	*guide book*
la plaza	*square*	la exposición	*exhibition, display*
el mercado	*market*	la torre	*tower*

(Higher: el turismo, el/la guía, la guía, la exposición, la torre)

No nos gusta nada más que dar un paseo por los puestos del mercado.

We like nothing more than to go for a stroll through the market stalls.

visit historic monuments — visitar monumentos históricos

Vamos a hacer una excursión a las ruinas antiguas de un templo.

We are going to go on an excursion to the ancient ruins of a temple.

El guía dice que hay que subir a la torre para ver la ciudad entera.

The guide says that you have to go up the tower to see the whole town.

explore the national park — explorar el parque nacional

Quiero ir a una exposición en la plaza mayor del pueblo.

I want to go to an exhibition in the town's main square.

Una actividad divertida es... — An enjoyable activity is...

Para mí, lo más importante es
buscar un parque temático.

*For me, the most important thing
is to look for a theme park.*

to buy a souvenir
— comprar un recuerdo
to do water sports
— hacer deportes acuáticos

Mañana iremos a un restaurante para
probar la comida típica de la región.

*Tomorrow we will go to a restaurant
to try the region's typical food.*

Quieren tomar el sol,
pero van a quemarse si no
se sientan a la sombra.

*They want to sunbathe,
but they're going to get sunburnt
if they don't sit in the shade.*

take my camera
— llevar mi cámara
buy some guide books
— comprar unas guías

Cuando estoy de vacaciones,
suelo tomar muchas fotos.

*When I'm on holiday, I usually
take lots of photos.*

Q&A Audio

Question

¿Qué hiciste durante
tus vacaciones?

*What did you do
during your holiday?*

Simple Answer

Fuimos a la playa y
fue muy relajante.

*We went to the beach
and it was very relaxing.*

Extended Answer

Pasamos mucho tiempo en la playa porque
hacía sol. Tomé el sol y jugué con mis primos.

*We spent a lot of time on the beach because it was
sunny. I sunbathed and played with my cousins.*

Grammar — la foto

<u>Watch out</u> for nouns that don't fit
the masculine / feminine rule of
ending with an '<u>-o</u>' or '<u>-a</u>' (p.151):

<u>la</u> fot<u>o</u>   *the photo*
<u>el</u> agu<u>a</u>   *the water*

('water' is actually a feminine noun,
but it takes '<u>el</u>' as its article because
'la agua' is too awkward to pronounce.)

Practice Questions

Q1 *Oleksii is discussing holiday activities with a friend.*

SPEAKING

*Cuando voy a un país extranjero, tengo ganas de hacer
actividades al aire libre. Iré a Portugal el próximo año.
Nadaré en el mar y participaré en clases de baile en la playa.*

Top Tip for Higher Students
✓ Use the subjunctive to
express something you want
to happen, e.g. 'Quiero
que haga buen tiempo.'

*Now it's your turn. Talk about what you like to do on holiday and what
you'd like to see and do on your next one. Aim to talk for about two minutes.*   **[10 marks]**

Q2 *You read this extract from a leaflet about Galicia, a
region of Spain. Answer the questions below in English.*

READING

*La región hermosa de Galicia está en el norte de España. Aquí se puede conocer ciudades como
Santiago de Compostela, la capital de la región. Si quieres explorar la ciudad, es posible coger
el autobús o montar en bici. Hay una catedral preciosa y varios museos que cuentan la historia
de la región. Para disfrutar de la belleza de los edificios, es mejor dar un paseo por las calles.*

a) Where is Galicia located?   *[1 mark]*

b) Write down two things you can
visit in Santiago de Compostela.   *[2 marks]*

c) What's the best way to
enjoy the architecture in
Santiago de Compostela?   *[1 mark]*

Higher

Think about the sorts of activities you might want to say...

I don't know about you, but this section has given me a few ideas for my next holiday... Before you check
out and head off for some exam-style practice, try jotting down as much vocab from this section as you can.

Listening Questions

Remember that these questions are a similar style to the ones that you'll see in the exam. They'll help you hone the skills you'll need and give you an idea of what areas you might need to work on.

1 Dolores is asking her friend for advice about a future holiday.
Answer the questions in **English**.

Listening Track 31

1 a When do Dolores and her husband want to go on holiday?

....   *[1 mark]*

1 b Why does Dolores's husband want to take a longer plane journey?

....   *[1 mark]*

1 c What does Dolores like to do on holiday?

....   *[1 mark]*

2 Nico is calling to make a reservation at Hotel Cristal.

Listening Track 32

Write **A** if only statement **A** is correct.
       B if only statement **B** is correct.
       A + B if both statements **A** and **B** are correct.

2 a Nico is trying to reserve a room for...

A	tonight.
B	tomorrow night.

[1 mark]

2 b He would like a...

A	view of the sea.
B	big bathroom.

[1 mark]

2 c The hotel is...

A	a twenty-minute walk from the station.
B	a fifteen-minute bus ride from the station.

[1 mark]

2 d The hotel restaurant...

A	is open until 9 pm.
B	closes at 11.30 pm.

[1 mark]

Speaking Questions

Candidate's Material

- Spend a few minutes looking at the two photos. Make notes on them to use during the test.

- Your teacher will ask you to talk about the content of the photos. You should talk for approximately **one minute** at Foundation tier and **one and a half minutes** at Higher tier. **You must say at least one thing about each photo**.

- After you have spoken about the content of the photos, your teacher will then ask you some questions related to **any** of the topics within the topic of **Travel and Tourism**.

Teacher's Material

- Candidates should talk about the photos above for approximately **one minute** at Foundation tier or **one and a half minutes** at Higher tier. They may use any notes they have made during the preparation time. Begin by asking the candidate to tell you about the photos:

  - Háblame de las fotos.

- When the candidate has finished talking about the photos, ask them the following unprepared conversation questions on the topic of **Travel and Tourism**:

  - ¿Qué tipo de transporte prefieres? ¿Por qué?

  - ¿Prefieres visitar sitios tranquilos o animados? ¿Por qué?

  - Describe la última vez que fuiste de vacaciones.

  - ¿Dónde te gusta quedarte cuando estás de vacaciones? ¿Por qué?

  - Háblame de las actividades que sueles hacer cuando estás de vacaciones.

  - En tu opinión, ¿cuál es el mejor destino para unas vacaciones? ¿Por qué?

Reading Questions

1   You read this email from your Spanish friend Mario.

> *El viaje más largo de mi vida fue el año pasado. Tuvimos que ir al aeropuerto en autobús, pero había mucho tráfico y el viaje duró dos horas en lugar de una. Luego, descubrimos que ningún vuelo podía salir del aeropuerto debido al mal tiempo. Tuvimos que esperar unas siete u ocho horas para coger el siguiente vuelo.*

Answer the following questions in **English**.

1 a   How did Mario get to the airport?

.... *[1 mark]*

1 b   Why did his journey to the airport take longer than expected?

.... *[1 mark]*

1 c   Why was Mario's flight cancelled?

.... *[1 mark]*

2   You read this article about Alba's recent holiday.

> *Acabo de volver de un viaje a las montañas con mis amigos. Hicimos muchas actividades que no se pueden hacer en la ciudad, como montar en bici por las montañas y nadar en los lagos naturales. Para mí, lo mejor de este tipo de vacaciones es el sentido de aventura que se siente al estar al aire libre todo el día. Esto no es posible cuando estás de vacaciones en una ciudad.*

Answer the following questions in **English**.

2 a   Where did Alba go on holiday?

.... *[1 mark]*

2 b   What two activities does Alba mention doing on the trip?

1. ....

2. .... *[2 marks]*

2 c   What does she say is the best thing about this type of holiday?

.... *[1 mark]*

Writing Questions

Foundation

1 You are writing a blog post about where you like to go on holiday.

Write approximately **50** words in **Spanish**.

You must write something about each bullet point.

Mention:

- the landscape
- accommodation
- transport
- things to do
- things to see.

[10 marks]

2 Translate the following sentences into **Spanish**.

2 a He organises a trip abroad.

.... *[2 marks]*

2 b The journey on the underground cost five euros.

.... *[2 marks]*

Higher

2 c My aunt hired a boat for the excursion.

.... *[2 marks]*

2 d If you come back by train, there will be a delay.

.... *[2 marks]*

2 e We would travel by car, but it would take a long time.

.... *[2 marks]*

3 You are writing an article about a recent holiday for a local magazine.

Write approximately **150** words in **Spanish**.

You must write something about both bullet points.

Mention:

- what you enjoyed about the place you visited
- what you would do differently on your next holiday. *[25 marks]*

Travel and Tourism — Vocabulary

Welcome to a world of vocab about travel and tourism. There's lots to explore and we hope that you enjoy your stay...

Where to Go

bienvenido/a	welcome
las vacaciones	holidays
de vacaciones	on holiday
el viaje	trip, journey
el puente	long weekend
el extranjero	abroad
el/la extranjero/a	foreigner
el/la turista	tourist
el mundo	world
España	Spain
Sudamérica	South America
el país	country
el paisaje	landscape, scenery
hermoso/a	beautiful
tranquilo/a	calm, tranquil
el campo	countryside
el bosque	forest, wood
la montaña	mountain
el río	river
la isla	island
la costa	coast
el mar	sea

la playa	beach
el calor	heat, hot
al aire libre	in the open air, outdoors
pasar	to pass, spend (time), happen
pasarlo bien/mal	to have a good/bad time
disfrutar	to enjoy
visitar	to visit
el sitio	place, site
la capital	capital (city)
la arquitectura	architecture
conocido/a	known, well-known
histórico/a	historic, historical
animado/a	lively

Higher

la nación	nation
hispanohablante	Spanish-speaking
precioso/a	beautiful, precious
el monte	hill, hills, countryside
el lago	lake
la arena	sand

Accommodation

el alojamiento	accommodation
el hotel	hotel
la habitación	room
cómodo/a	comfortable
moderno/a	modern
la recepción	reception (hotel)
la instalación	facility
el camping	campsite, camping
la tienda	tent
la vista	view
quedar(se)	to stay
reservar	to book, reserve
organizar	to organise
ahorrar	to save (time, money)

costar	to cost
pagar	to pay (for)
el precio	price, cost, value
el euro	euro
el peso	peso (currency)
alto/a	high
bajo/a	low
caro/a	expensive
barato/a	cheap

Higher

el costo	price, cost
la llave	key
el ascensor	lift, elevator
la calefacción	heating
el lujo	luxury

Travel

llegar	*to arrive*
viajar	*to travel*
volver	*to go back, return*
directo/a	*direct, straight*
coger	*to take, catch*
el transporte	*transport*
el coche	*car*
el puerto	*port, harbour*
el barco	*boat, ship*
el aeropuerto	*airport*
el avión	*plane, aeroplane*
el vuelo	*flight*
la estación	*station*
el tren	*train*

la mochila	*rucksack*
la maleta	*suitcase*
la entrada	*entrance*
la salida	*exit, departure*

Higher

el destino	*destination*
la visita	*visit, visitor*
la llegada	*arrival*
el retraso	*delay*
la velocidad	*speed, velocity*
la distancia	*distance*
la frontera	*border, frontier*
internacional	*international*
regresar	*to come back, go back, return*
acostumbrarse a	*to get accustomed, get used to*

Getting Around and What to Do

el transporte público	*public transport*
el billete	*ticket (for transport)*
la vuelta	*return, trip, ride*
perder	*to miss, lose*
el metro	*underground, tube, metro*
el autobús	*bus*
bajar	*to get off, lower*
montar	*to ride*
la bicicleta, bici	*bicycle, bike*
a pie	*on foot*
conducir	*to drive*
el tráfico	*traffic*
tardar	*to take (time)*
rápido/a	*quick, fast*
la excursión	*trip, excursion*
el parque temático	*theme park*
el edificio	*building*
el museo	*museum*
el templo	*temple*
el castillo	*castle*
la plaza	*square*
el mercado	*market*
el puesto	*stall (market)*
el recuerdo	*souvenir*
sacar	*to take out, get, obtain*
el plano	*map*
la cámara	*camera*
la foto	*photo, picture*

perdido/a	*lost*
perderse	*to get lost*
tomar el sol	*to sunbathe*

Higher

alquilar	*to hire, rent*
caminar	*to walk*
el camino	*way, route, path*
atraer	*to attract*
el turismo	*tourism*
el/la guía	*guide (person)*
la guía	*guide book*
la aventura	*adventure*
el deporte acuático	*water sport*
la exposición	*exhibition, display*
la torre	*tower*
la altura	*altitude*
la señal	*sign, signal*
la sombra	*shade, shadow*
quemarse	*to get sunburnt*
quejarse	*to complain*

Souvenirs are a great idea —
until you have to pack them…

Revision Summary Test for Section Nine

Get in the holiday mood with a revision summary to test all of the relevant words and phrases.

- These questions are **really tricky**, but they'll help you see **how well you know your stuff**.
- Tackle the **revision summary test** below, or scan the QR code to do it **online**.
  You can **keep track of your progress** online and see **which areas need more work**.
- There are **sample answers** here: www.cgpbooks.co.uk/MadridExtras

Where to Go ✓

1) Translate this into Spanish: 'I want to visit the capital of Spain in order to see its architecture.'

2) Daniela says: 'Muchos turistas viajan a Sudamérica para disfrutar de los sitios históricos conocidos.' How would you say this in English?

3) ¿Qué tipo de paisaje te gusta más? ¿Por qué?

4) 'El mar estaba tranquilo durante mi viaje a la costa de la isla.' Translate this sentence into English.

5) ¿Por qué te gusta ir de vacaciones?

6) In Spanish, how do you say: 'It is important to have a good time when you are on holiday.'

7) 'Pasaron el puente en una ciudad animada.' How would you say this in English?

Higher
8) A guidebook says: 'Esta nación hispanohablante tiene montañas altísimas. Además, uno de los ríos más largos del mundo corre por este país.' Translate this sentence into English.

9) ¿Prefieres las vacaciones en el extranjero o dentro de tu propio país? ¿Por qué?

Accommodation and Travel ✓

10) 'El hotel está cerca. Si sigues esta calle, verás la recepción.' What does this mean in English?

11) In Spanish, say you want to reserve a room for 4 nights. Say 2 features you want the room to have.

12) Julián says: 'En julio, me quedé en un camping en una tienda grande.' What is he saying?

13) List all the Spanish words in this section related to money and prices.
    There are 10 (plus 1 for Higher tier).

14) 'El tren es el tipo de transporte más directo al aeropuerto.' How would you say this in English?

15) How would you say that you need to take your suitcase and rucksack to the station in Spanish?

16) Imagine you're going on holiday to Cuba. Say how you'll travel there and describe where you'll stay.

Higher
17) 'I'll arrive at my destination late because we have returned to port.' Translate this into Spanish.

18) Belén says: 'Las fronteras internacionales están cerradas, entonces hay un retraso para las llegadas. Espero que el vuelo no tenga que regresar a Madrid.' Translate what she is saying into English.

Getting Around and What to Do ✓

19) In Spanish, how would you say: 'We are going to get off the bus in the main square.'

20) Pablo says: 'El viaje durará menos tiempo si monto en bici o voy a pie en lugar de conducir. El tráfico está muy lento hoy.' Translate what he is saying into English.

21) What do the following Spanish words mean in English?
    a) la entrada   b) el billete   c) la vuelta   d) perder   e) el metro   f) perderse

22) List all the places of interest from this section in Spanish. There are 7 (plus 1 for Higher tier).

23) 'There are lots of photos from the excursion on my camera.' Translate this sentence into Spanish.

24) Javi says: 'Pasé mucho tiempo en el puesto de recuerdos.' How would you say this in English?

25) Marta says: 'Voy a sacar un plano de la ciudad porque estoy perdida.' What is she saying?

H
26) Describe a problem that you had while you were on holiday.

27) ¿Cómo serían tus vacaciones ideales? ¿A qué destino irías y qué harías allí?

Technology

Mobile phones, computers, tablets... for your GCSE, you'll have to be able to talk about how you use technology, as well as giving some advantages and disadvantages to it.

Head to the CGP RevisionHub for all your online content: www.cgpbooks.co.uk/Madrid

La tecnología — Technology

Vocabulary

el ordenador	*computer*	el vídeo	*video*	la ventaja	*advantage*
el móvil	*mobile phone*	el juego	*game*	la desventaja	*disadvantage*
el teléfono	*phone, telephone*	la recepción	*reception*	el dispositivo	*device, gadget*
la tableta	*tablet (e.g. iPad)*	funcionar	*to function, work*	conectar	*to connect, plug in*

Question

¿Cómo usas tu móvil?

How do you use your mobile phone?

Simple Answer

Uso mi móvil para mandar mensajes.

I use my mobile phone to send messages.

Grammar — the conditional

To imagine what you 'could do' or 'couldn't do', use the conditional of 'poder' (see p.183) followed by the infinitive.

No podría hacer mis deberes sin un ordenador.

I couldn't do my homework without a computer.

Extended Answer

Tener un móvil es crucial para mí. Sin mi móvil, no podría ni mandar ni recibir mensajes.

Having a mobile phone is crucial to me. Without my mobile phone, I couldn't send or receive messages.

La tecnología es muy útil porque puedes encontrar información rápidamente.

Technology is really useful because you can find information quickly.

and it has improved our quality of life — y ha mejorado nuestra calidad de vida

Sin embargo, una desventaja es que siempre tienes que estar conectado.

However, one disadvantage is that you always have to be connected.

if you lose reception, your device won't work — si pierdes la recepción tu dispositivo no funcionará

Uso mucho la tecnología en mi tiempo libre. Me gusta jugar a juegos en mi portátil y uso mi tableta para ver vídeos.

I use technology a lot in my free time. I like playing games on my laptop and I use my tablet to watch videos.

Practice Question

Q1 Your friend Indra is talking to you about how her family uses technology.
What is her opinion on the following points?
*Write **P** for a **positive** opinion. Write **N** for a **negative** opinion.*
*Write **P + N** for a **positive** and **negative** opinion.*

a) Her cousins sending her messages   *[1 mark]*

b) Her sister playing computer games   *[1 mark]*

c) Her brother watching videos   *[1 mark]*

d) Watching movies on her tablet   *[1 mark]*

Use your own gadgets for vocabulary revision...

Practise your technology vocab by tracking how you use your devices over a fortnight. Write down the word for the device you used in Spanish, then add a short phrase or sentence to describe what you used it for.

Quick Quiz

The Internet

Ah, the internet — handy for so many things. It also has its downsides, though.
Have a read of these pages to learn how to talk about all of this in Spanish.

¿Qué haces en Internet? — What do you do on the internet?

Vocabulary

el Internet	*internet*	comunicar	*to communicate*
la Red	*internet*	descubrir	*to discover*
online	*online*	en línea	*online*
el sitio web	*website*	el usuario	*user*
la app	*app*	conectarse	*to connect*
la página	*page*	(a Internet)	*(to the internet)*
el correo electrónico	*email*	navegar	*to surf, browse*
bajar	*to download*	publicar	*to publish, post*

Higher: en línea, el usuario, conectarse (a Internet), navegar, publicar

No, Marcos... Not
that kind of surfing.

Me encanta usar Internet para
descubrir nuevas canciones y bajarlas.

*I love using the internet to discover
new songs and download them.*

share images
— compartir imágenes

Me gustan los sitios web que puedo
usar para comunicarme con otra gente.

*I like websites that I can use to
communicate with other people.*

Navego por diferentes páginas de
arte porque me encanta el dibujo.

*I browse different art pages
because I love drawing.*

I receive emails about art classes
— Recibo correos electrónicos
sobre clases de arte

Q&A Audio

Question

¿Por qué te gusta
tu app favorita?

*Why do you like
your favourite app?*

Simple Answer

Mi app favorita es un
juego de acción. Lo
encuentro divertido.

*My favourite app
is an action game.
I find it fun.*

Extended Answer

En mi app favorita hago compras online. Me gusta porque
me ha permitido encontrar mucha ropa de segunda
mano. Me divierto navegando por artículos diferentes.

*On my favourite app I do online shopping. I like
it because it has let me find a lot of second-hand
clothing. I entertain myself browsing different items.*

Las ventajas — Advantages

El uso de apps y sitios web nos
ayuda en nuestras vidas diarias.

*The use of apps and websites
helps us with our daily lives.*

Hay buenas opciones en
Internet para investigar un
tema que te interesa.

*There are good options on
the Internet for researching
a topic that interests you.*

Mis padres usan Internet para
sus cuentas bancarias porque
es más fácil que ir al banco.

*My parents use the internet for
their bank accounts because it's
easier than going to the bank.*

Gracias a la Red, es más
cómodo hacer las compras.
Ayer, compré unos regalos
en línea y ya están aquí.

*Thanks to the internet, it's more
comfortable to do your shopping.
Yesterday, I bought some presents
online and they're already here.*

Grammar — comparisons

In Spanish, you can compare one
thing to another using 'más ... que'
(more ... than) and 'menos ... que'
(less ... than) (see p.168).

**Hacer compras por Internet es
más rápido que ir a las tiendas.**

*Doing shopping on the internet
is faster than going to the shops.*

easier to find discounts for
— más fácil encontrar
descuentos para

Los peligros — Dangers

Vocabulary

la información	*information*
robar	*to rob, steal*
peligroso/a	*dangerous*
seguro/a	*safe, secure*
el dato	*data, information*
la contraseña	*password*
desconocido/a	*unknown*
la seguridad	*security, safety*
la protección	*protection*

(Higher) el dato, la contraseña, desconocido/a, la seguridad, la protección

Grammar (Higher only) — the ... thing is that...

In Spanish, you can say 'the good thing' or 'the bad thing' by using '<u>lo</u>' followed by '<u>bueno</u>' or '<u>malo</u>'.

<u>Lo bueno / malo</u> es que...   *<u>**The good / bad thing**</u> is that...*

You can do this with <u>any adjective</u>:

<u>Lo mejor / peor</u> es que...   *<u>**The best / worst thing**</u> is that...*

<u>Lo peligroso</u> es que...   *<u>**The dangerous thing**</u> is that...*

To say '<u>the most... thing</u>', just add '<u>más</u>' before the adjective:

<u>Lo más útil</u> es que...   *<u>**The most useful thing**</u> is that...*

Lo peor de Internet es que la gente puede usar tu contenido sin tu permiso.

The worst thing about the internet is that people can use your content without your permission.

share your photos with unknown people — compartir tus fotos con gente desconocida

Es fácil perder mucho tiempo en Internet y olvidarse de la vida real.

It's easy to waste a lot of time on the Internet and to forget about real life.

Es importante tener una contraseña segura para proteger tu identidad. Si alguien sabe tu contraseña, puede robar tu información.

It's important to have a secure password to protect your identity. If someone knows your password, they can steal your information.

use your account to post spam — usar tu cuenta para publicar basura

Hacer compras online me molesta porque es difícil saber si me gustará el producto sin verlo en realidad.

Shopping online annoys me because it's difficult to know if I will like the product without seeing it in reality.

the price of delivery is so expensive — el precio de entrega es muy caro

---

Practice Questions

Q1 *Write a description of ways you use the internet. You should write about 90 words in Spanish. Write about:*

- *how you use the internet*
- *what you used the internet for when you were younger*
- *something you will use the internet for in the future.*   [15 marks]

Top Tip for Higher Students
✓ Use adverbs, e.g. 'actualmente', 'normalmente', or 'pronto' to give more detail about the time periods that you mention.

Q2 *You are listening to Alba and Mario discuss internet usage. Answer the following questions in English.*

Listening Track 34

- **a)** What **two** activities does Mario prefer to going on the internet?   [2 marks]
- **b)** What does Alba say is the best thing about the internet?   [1 mark]
- **c)** What does Mario say is a great danger on the internet?   [1 mark]
- **d)** Why does Alba worry about junk email?   [1 mark]

Don't only use 'me gusta' — vary your language...

There are lots of phrases you can use to express your opinions, like 'me encanta' or 'me molesta' to say what you love or what annoys you. Make sure you use a variety in your answers — examiners will love them.

Find the CGP RevisionHub at cgpbooks.co.uk/Madrid   Section Ten — Media and Technology

Social Media

From posting content to using reactions, these pages dive into the different ways we use social media.

Las redes sociales — Social networks

Vocabulary

la red	*network*	mandar	*to send*
social	*social*	el contenido	*content*
la cuenta	*account*	el blog	*blog*
el/la seguidor(a)	*follower*	colgar	*to post (photo)*
compartir	*share*	comentar	*to comment*
subir	*to upload*	el comentario	*comment*
popular	*popular*	charlar	*to chat*
el mensaje	*message*	la reacción	*reaction*
enviar	*to send*	el emoticón	*emoji®*

(Higher: el contenido, el blog, colgar, comentar, el comentario, charlar, la reacción, el emoticón)

Grammar (Higher only)
— colgar (to post)

'Colgar' (to post) is a stem-changing verb (see p.176) that changes in the present tense:

Cuelgo las fotos que hago en mi blog.
I post the photos that I take on my blog.

Mis amigos **cuelgan** fotos en mi página.
My friends post photos on my page.

Hoy hay muchas apps de las redes sociales. Permiten al usuario hablar con otras personas y ver su contenido.

Nowadays there are many social networking apps. They allow the user to talk with others and to view their content.

to gain followers — ganar seguidores

Las redes sociales están cambiando la forma en la que nos comunicamos. Usamos reacciones e imágenes para expresarnos.

Social networks are changing the way in which we communicate. We use reactions and images to express ourselves.

Uso las redes sociales para... — I use social networks to...

Question

¿Usas las redes sociales?
Do you use social networks?

Simple Answer

Sí, comparto fotos con mis amigos en las redes sociales.
Yes, I share photos with my friends on social networks.

Extended Answer

Sí, las uso para encontrar nuevos cantantes porque muchos lanzan sus canciones en ellas. Sin embargo, intento poner un límite al tiempo que paso en las redes sociales.

Yes, I use them to find new singers because many release their songs on them. However, I try to put a limit on the time that I spend on social media.

Me encanta usar las redes sociales para hablar con mis amigos que viven lejos de mí.

I love using social networks to talk to my friends who live far away from me.

my cousins who live in Canada — mis primos que viven en Canadá

Uso mi cuenta para charlar con personas que comparten mis intereses. Además, cuelgo fotos de la comida que he preparado porque me gusta cocinar.

I use my account to chat with people who share my interests. Also, I post photos of food that I've prepared because I like cooking.

I've met in a game — he conocido en un juego

Paso demasiado tiempo en las redes sociales porque me pierdo leyendo comentarios.

I spend too much time on social media because I get lost reading comments.

when I could go out with my friends — cuando podría salir con mis amigos

Los problemas de las redes sociales — The problems of social media

Vocabulary

el contacto	*contact*		el ciberacoso	*cyberbullying*
contestar	*to answer, reply, respond*	**Higher**	la víctima	*victim*
guardar	*to keep, save*		la tendencia	*tendency, trend*

Gracias a las redes sociales, puedo seguir noticias mundiales y tendencias. Sin embargo, a veces es difícil apagar mi móvil.

Thanks to social networks, I can follow world news and trends. However, sometimes it's difficult to switch off my phone.

I always have someone I can chat to — siempre tengo alguien con quien puedo charlar

Por una parte, puedo ver una variedad de vídeos en las redes sociales. Por otra parte, la mayoría de los vídeos tienen muchos anuncios.

On the one hand, I can watch a variety of videos on social media. On the other hand, the majority of the videos have a lot of adverts.

I waste time looking at useless things — pierdo tiempo mirando cosas inútiles

'Pierdo' comes from 'perder', which is a stem-changing verb. See p.176.

Las redes sociales son útiles pero pueden ser preocupantes. Por ejemplo, el ciberacoso causa mucho daño a las víctimas.

Social networks are useful but they can be worrying. For example, cyberbullying causes a lot of hurt to victims.

Practice Questions

Q1 Your Spanish friend asks you the questions below about your thoughts on social media. Reply to the questions out loud in Spanish.

SPEAKING

a) ¿Cómo usas las redes sociales?

b) ¿Cuánto tiempo pasas en las redes sociales?

c) ¿Por qué te gusta tu red social favorita?

d) ¿Por qué es importante la tecnología?　　　*[8 marks]*

Top Tip for Higher Students
✓ Use 'lo más útil es que...' or 'lo más divertido es que...' to describe why you like social media in extra detail.

Q2 Toni has written a blog post about spending time on the internet and social networks. Read their comments and then answer the questions below in English.

READING

> *Mucha gente dice que los jóvenes pasan demasiado tiempo en Internet, pero yo no estoy de acuerdo. En mi familia mis padres pasan mucho más tiempo en Internet que mis hermanos. Uso las redes sociales bastante. Como vivo lejos de mis amigos del colegio y no puedo verlos por las tardes, hablamos por nuestros móviles. Sin embargo, me molesta cuando tengo que esperar mucho tiempo para recibir una respuesta a mis mensajes.*

a) In Toni's family, who spends the most time on the internet?　　*[1 mark]*

b) What does Toni use social media for?　　*[1 mark]*

c) What disadvantage of using social media does Toni give?　　*[1 mark]*

You can change the language of your social media to Spanish...

If you go into the settings of your social media apps, you should be able to change the language of them. Not only will it look really impressive, it will also show you the different terms from these pages in context.

Listening Questions

Doing loads of practice is a sure-fire way to improve. That's why we've come up with these questions for you to tackle — they'll have you feeling that you're on your way to GCSE glory.

1   You are listening to a Spanish podcast. Luisa and Javier are talking about how they use the internet. Answer the questions in **English**.

Listening Track 35

1 a   What does Javier use the internet for? Give **one** thing.

.... *[1 mark]*

1 b   For Luisa, what is a danger of the internet?

.... *[1 mark]*

1 c   What serious problem does Javier mention?

.... *[1 mark]*

1 d   What reason does he give for thinking it's a problem?

.... *[1 mark]*

2   A group of classmates are having a discussion about social media. Which use of social media and which problem does each person mention? Write the correct **letter** for the use. Write the correct **number** for the problem.

Listening Track 36

Use	
A	Learn about the news
B	Follow celebrities
C	Discover new places
D	Organise parties

Problem	
1	People don't talk in real life
2	Difficult to keep track of groups
3	Cyberbullying
4	Cause arguments with friends

		Use	Problem	
2 a	Elena	☐	☐	*[2 marks]*
2 b	Malek	☐	☐	*[2 marks]*
2 c	Gaby	☐	☐	*[2 marks]*

Speaking Questions

Candidate's Material

- When your teacher asks you, read aloud the following text **in Spanish**.

Foundation

- No puedo vivir sin tecnología.
- Uso las redes sociales para mandar mensajes.
- Podemos descubrir mucha información en Internet.
- Todas las noches juego a videojuegos en mi tableta.
- Intento apagar mi móvil cuando me voy a la cama.

Higher

- Ahora los dispositivos son muy caros.
- No puedo usar mi portátil porque acaba de romperse.
- El ordenador nuestro funciona muy despacio y hace mucho ruido.
- Paso muchísimo tiempo mirando una pantalla, lo cual no es saludable.
- Lo mejor de las redes sociales es que hacen la comunicación más fácil.
- Desafortunadamente, siento presión por seguir las tendencias online.

- You will then be asked four questions **in Spanish** that relate to the topic of **Media and Technology**.

- In order to score the highest marks, **answer all four questions as fully as you can**.

Teacher's Material

- Start by asking the candidate to read the text by saying *Lee el texto*.

- Allow the candidate to read the text aloud, then ask the following four questions for their tier.

- Allow the student to develop their answers as much as possible.

Foundation

- ¿Cómo usas la tecnología?
- ¿Cuánto tiempo pasas en tu móvil?
- ¿Qué piensas de las redes sociales?
- ¿Qué peligros tiene el Internet?

Higher

- Describe la app más útil que usas.
- ¿Por qué la gente pasa tanto tiempo online?
- ¿Cuáles son las desventajas de Internet?
- ¿Cuál es tu opinión sobre hacer las compras en Internet?

Reading Questions

1   You read this blog post from a student about technology at their school.
Answer the following questions in **English**.

> Me molestan los ordenadores del instituto porque son lentísimos. Sin embargo, hemos recibido nuevas tabletas para cada estudiante, y son mucho más modernas que los ordenadores. Otra cosa buena es que todos los alumnos tienen una cuenta de correo electrónico del instituto. La usamos para mandar los deberes a los profesores. El instituto tiene una página en las redes sociales y es muy útil. Sirve para compartir las noticias escolares* con los padres.

*escolares
— school

1 a   Why does the student dislike the school computers?

....   *[1 mark]*

1 b   What do the students use their school email account for?

....   *[1 mark]*

1 c   What does the school use social media for?

....   *[1 mark]*

2   Your friend messages you about a social media app they've tried.
What is their opinion about the following features of the app?
Write **P** for a **positive** opinion.
Write **N** for a **negative** opinion.
P + N for a **positive** and **negative** opinion.

> ¡Hola! Tengo que contarte algo sobre una nueva red social. Lo mejor de la app es que es muy fácil de navegar. Las opciones para enviar y contestar mensajes son efectivas. En cambio, diría que los emoticones que se pueden usar en la app son raros y un poco feos. No me gusta nada el diseño. Además, tengo que criticar el hecho de que no hay forma de controlar los comentarios en tus fotos. Debido a esto, ya he visto algunos casos del ciberacoso... Aunque tiene ventajas, no te recomendaría esta red social.

2 a   Navigation

[1 mark]

2 b   Emojis

[1 mark]

2 c   Commenting on photos

[1 mark]

Writing Questions

Foundation

1 You are writing an email to your Spanish friend about technology.
Write approximately **50** words in **Spanish**.
You must write something about each bullet point. Mention:

- phones
- computers
- tablets
- screens
- internet.

[10 marks]

2 Translate the following sentences into **Spanish**.

2 a I watch videos on social networks.

.... *[2 marks]*

2 b I like to download music on my mobile phone.

.... *[2 marks]*

Higher

2 c They should change their passwords if they are not secure.

....

.... *[2 marks]*

2 d I bought a device with better memory to save more photos.

....

.... *[2 marks]*

2 e My friend doesn't reply to messages until the next day, which annoys me.

....

.... *[2 marks]*

3 You are writing a blog post about what you think of social media.
Write approximately **150** words in **Spanish**.
You must write something about each bullet point. Mention:

- something you've used social media for recently
- the positive and negative aspects of social media.

[25 marks]

Media and Technology — Vocabulary

On this page you'll find all the handy words for talking about media, technology and their uses.

Technology

la tecnología	*technology*
moderno/a	*modern*
eléctrico/a	*electric*
el ordenador	*computer*
el móvil	*mobile phone*
el teléfono	*phone, telephone*
la tableta	*tablet (e.g. iPad)*
el teclado	*keyboard*
la pantalla	*screen, monitor*
el vídeo	*video*
el juego	*game*
el videojuego	*computer game*
la recepción	*reception (e.g. radio)*
funcionar	*to function, work*
apagar	*to turn off*
encender	*to turn on*

servir	*to serve*
la ventaja	*advantage, benefit*
la desventaja	*disadvantage*

Higher

el dispositivo	*device, gadget*
digital	*digital*
la radio	*radio*
el portátil	*laptop*
el diseño	*design*
el sistema	*system*
la memoria	*memory*
el volumen	*volume*
el sonido	*sound*
conectar	*to connect, plug in*
instalar	*to install*
cargar	*to charge (phone)*
la línea	*line (phone)*

The Internet

el Internet	*internet*
la Red	*internet*
los medios de comunicación	*media*
online	*online*
el sitio web	*website*
la app	*app*
la página	*page*
el correo electrónico	*email*
bajar	*to download*
comunicar	*to communicate*
descubrir	*to discover*
la información	*information*
robar	*to rob, steal*
el peligro	*danger*
peligroso/a	*dangerous*
seguro/a	*safe, secure*

Higher

en línea	*online*
el usuario	*user*
conectarse (a Internet)	*to connect (to the Internet)*
navegar	*to surf, browse*
publicar (en Internet)	*to publish, post (online)*
la investigación	*research*
investigar	*to research*
el dato	*data, information, fact*
la contraseña	*password*
desconocido/a	*unknown*
la seguridad	*security, safety*
la protección	*protection*
apropiado/a	*appropriate, suitable*

Social Media

la red	*network*
social	*social*
la cuenta	*account*
el seguidor	*follower*
el/la joven	*teenager, young person*
compartir	*to share*
subir	*to upload*
popular	*popular*
la conversación	*conversation*
el mensaje	*message*

enviar	*to send*
mandar	*to send*
el contacto	*contact*
contestar	*to answer, reply, respond*
guardar	*to keep, save*
grabar	*to record*

Higher

el contenido	*content*
el blog	*blog*
colgar	*to post (photo)*
comentar	*to comment*

Higher

el comentario	*remark, comment*
el diálogo	*conversation*
charlar	*to chat*
la reacción	*reaction*
el emoticón	*emoji*
el ciberacoso	*cyberbullying*
la víctima	*victim*
la tendencia	*tendency, trend*

Revision Summary Test for Section Ten

It's time for some summary questions to test just how well you've got on with this section.

- These questions are **hard**, but they'll really help you see **how well you know your stuff**.
- Tackle the **revision summary test** below, or scan the QR code to do it **online**.
  You can **track your progress** online and see **which areas need more work**.
- There are **sample answers** for the test here: www.cgpbooks.co.uk/MadridExtras

Technology ☑

1) How many words for technological devices and equipment can you remember from this section?
   There are 6 you need to know (plus 3 for Higher tier).

2) ¿Cómo y cuándo usas la tecnología?

3) Write the Spanish for:
   a) modern   b) electric   c) reception   d) to function   e) to turn on   f) to serve

4) What's the technology like at your school? Write about it in Spanish.

5) In Spanish, give at least one advantage and one disadvantage of technology.

6) Translate these sentences into Spanish: 'I bought a new laptop with more memory.
   I love the design and the sound quality. However, installing apps takes a long time.'

The Internet ☑

7) Translate this sentence into English: 'Uso mi correo electrónico y diferentes
   sitios web para comunicarme con otra gente y mirar páginas interesantes.'

8) In Spanish, give two ways that you use the internet. Include as much detail as you can.

9) a) List as many words as you can think of that are related to internet security.
      There are 5 you need to know (plus 5 for Higher tier).
   b) Use some of these words to write about potential dangers online.

10) 'There are lots of fun online games that you can play with friends.' Say this in Spanish.

11) Translate these sentences into English: 'Necesitaba hacer más investigación para un proyecto
    de geografía. Navegué por Internet para encontrar la información necesaria.'

Social Media ☑

12) Dolores says: 'There are too many young people that worry about being popular and having lots
    of followers.' Translate this sentence into Spanish. In Spanish, say whether you agree and why.

13) Which words can you think of from this section that would relate to sending messages and
    posting content online? There are 8 you need to know (plus 9 for Higher tier).

14) '¿Cómo usas las redes sociales? ¿Cuáles son las ventajas y desventajas?' Translate these
    questions into English, then answer them in Spanish, giving as much detail as you can.

15) Marcos says: 'Mis compañeros de clase piensan que las tendencias de las redes sociales son
    las más importantes del mundo. Para mí, es una idea tonta'. Translate this into English.

16) En español, escribe lo que piensas sobre la cuestión del ciberacoso.

Quick Quiz

At Home

This is your chance to describe your home, your daily routine and the various chores you do.

¿Cómo es tu casa? — What's your house like?

Don't forget you can access your online content here: www.cgpbooks.co.uk/Madrid

Vocabulary

vivir	*to live*	el salón	*living room*
la casa	*house*	el baño	*bathroom*
el piso	*flat, apartment*	la cocina	*kitchen*
la planta	*floor*	el jardín	*garden*
agradable	*pleasant, nice*	la escalera	*stairs, ladder*
cómodo/a	*comfortable*	la pared	*(interior) wall*
el cuarto	*room*	la puerta	*door*
el dormitorio	*bedroom*	la ventana	*window*
la habitación	*bedroom*	la cama	*bed*

Grammar — there is / are

To say what <u>there is</u> in your house, use '<u>hay</u>'. This word <u>stays the same</u> regardless of whether the thing you're talking about is <u>singular</u> or <u>plural</u>.

En mi casa, hay un salón.
*In my house, **there is** a lounge.*

Hay seis cuartos.
***There are** six rooms.*

Vivo en una casa muy agradable. Hay una cocina grande con muchas ventanas y tengo mi propio dormitorio también.

I live in a really nice house. There's a big kitchen with a lot of windows and I have my own bedroom too.

but I share my bedroom with my brother — pero comparto mi dormitorio con mi hermano

Vivimos en un piso pequeño con dos habitaciones. Está en la tercera planta y mi cuarto favorito es el salón.

We live in a small flat with two bedrooms. It's on the third floor and my favourite room is the living room.

I hate how many stairs there are — odio cuántas escaleras hay

Me gustaría vivir en una casa moderna.

I'd like to live in a modern house.

Q&A Audio

Question

¿Cómo sería tu casa ideal?
What would your ideal house be like?

Simple Answer

Mi casa ideal sería muy grande.
My ideal house would be really big.

Extended Answer

Mi casa ideal tendría una piscina de lujo y un jardín enorme. Quisiera tener espacio para invitar a todos mis amigos.

My ideal house would have a luxury swimming pool and a huge garden. I would like to have space to invite all of my friends over.

Un día típico — A typical day

Vocabulary

despertarse	*to wake (up)*
levantarse	*to get up*
lavarse	*to have a wash*
vestirse	*to get dressed*
cambiarse	*to get changed*
dormirse	*to fall asleep*

Grammar — reflexive verbs

These verbs are <u>reflexive</u> — they say what you do <u>to yourself</u>. To use them, <u>remove</u> the <u>reflexive pronoun</u> (se), <u>conjugate the verb</u> as normal and put the reflexive pronoun back <u>in front of the verb</u> in its <u>correct form</u> (see p.185).

<u>Me duermo</u> a las diez de la noche.   ***I fall asleep** at 10 pm.*

Some of these verbs are stem-changing. See p.176.

Cada mañana, me despierto a las siete y luego me lavo.

Every morning, I wake up at seven o'clock and then I have a wash.

I always get dressed quickly — siempre me visto rápidamente

Después de volver del colegio me cambio y hago mis deberes.

After returning from school, I get changed and I do my homework.

I shower — me ducho

Las tareas — Chores

Vocabulary

la tarea	*chore*	limpiar	*to clean*	sacar	*to take out*
hacer	*to do, make*	lavar	*to wash*	la basura	*rubbish, junk*
ayudar	*to help*	pasear	*to take for a walk*	cocinar	*to cook*
preparar	*to prepare*	el perro	*dog*	arreglar	*to tidy*

Cada mañana hago mi cama. También ayudo a preparar el desayuno.

Every morning, I make my bed. I also help to prepare breakfast.

— *I put the dishwasher on* — pongo el lavavajillas

Después de la cena, tengo que lavar los platos y quitar la mesa.

After dinner, I have to wash the dishes and clear the table.

— *tidy my bedroom* — arreglar mi dormitorio

Los fines de semana paseo al perro, pero durante la semana mis padres lo hacen.

On weekends I take the dog for a walk, but during the week my parents do it.

Una tarea que no me gusta hacer es sacar la basura.

One chore I don't like doing is taking out the rubbish.

— *organising my clothes* — ordenar mi ropa

Practice Questions

Q1 You are writing a blog about your house.
You should write about 90 words in Spanish. Mention:

- *what the house you live in is like*
- *what chores you did last week*
- *what your dream house would be like.*

(WRITING)

[15 marks]

Top Tip for Higher Students
✓ Use possessive adjectives to describe your house, e.g. 'el dormitorio grande es mío'.

Q2 Your pen-pal from Colombia sends you this email about their typical day at home.
Read the passage and then write the correct letter for each question.

(READING)

> Me encanta despertarme a las seis porque la casa está tranquila. Cuando me levanto, me visto y hago mi cama. Intento hacer mis deberes por la tarde, y a veces mis padres me ayudan. Cada noche, tengo que hacer una tarea. Anoche limpié el baño y ¡eso fue horrible!

a) They love...
  A. falling asleep late   **B.** waking up early   **C.** waking up late   *[1 mark]*

b) In the afternoon, they...
  A. do their homework   **B.** wash the dishes   **C.** get dressed   *[1 mark]*

c) Last night, they...
  A. made their bed   **B.** cleaned the bathroom   **C.** helped their parents   *[1 mark]*

Use your own home to practise your vocabulary...

To get to grips with this home vocab, you could try walking around your home and saying the room or part of the house in Spanish as you walk through it. You could even try doing this with your daily routine too.

The Local Area

For the exam, you'll need to know how to describe your local area and what's there.
You might also have to talk about shopping and clothing. So crack on with these pages...

Háblame de tu región — Talk to me about your region

Vocabulary

la región	*region*	el barrio	*neighbourhood, district*
el campo	*countryside*	la zona	*area, zone*
la ciudad	*city, town*	industrial	*industrial*
el pueblo	*village, small town*	principal	*main, principal*
el centro	*centre*	la comunidad	*community*

Simón lives in 'the zone'.

Vivo en la zona industrial de una ciudad.
No está en el centro, pero hay mucho ruido.

*I live in the industrial area of a city. It isn't
in the centre, but there is a lot of noise.*

Mi pueblo está en el campo. Es muy bonito
pero no hay muchos sitios para visitar.

*My village is in the countryside. It's very
pretty, but there aren't many places to visit.*

there are options for shopping —
hay opciones para hacer compras

Question

¿Dónde vives?
Where do you live?

Simple Answer

Vivo en un pueblo en Cumbria.
I live in a village in Cumbria.

Extended Answer

Vivo en un pueblito en el
campo. Preferiría vivir en una
ciudad porque hay más que
hacer. Aquí solo hay bosques.

*I live in a little town in the
countryside. I would prefer to live
in a city because there is more to
do. Here there are only forests.*

Grammar — adding 'ito'

In Spanish, you can add bits onto the ends of nouns and
adjectives to change their meanings. Adding 'ito/a/os/as'
makes the word smaller or cuter. Find out more on p.152.

En mi barrio hay... — In my neighbourhood, there is...

Vocabulary

se puede	*one can, you can*	el café	*café*	el estadio	*stadium*
el ayuntamiento	*town hall*	el gimnasio	*gym*	la iglesia	*church*
la biblioteca	*library*	la piscina	*swimming pool*	la mezquita	*mosque*
el parque	*park*	el banco	*bank, bench*	la sinagoga	*synagogue*

En mi barrio, hay un gran
parque, un gimnasio y dos cafés.

*In my neighbourhood, there's a
big park, a gym and two cafés.*

a famous restaurant
— un restaurante famoso

Mi ciudad tiene varios edificios
hermosos. Aquí se puede visitar
una biblioteca muy antigua.

*My city has various beautiful
buildings. Here one can
visit a really old library.*

a historic mosque
— una mezquita histórica

Me gustaría ver una nueva
piscina en mi pueblo.

*I'd like to see a new swimming
pool in my village.*

more green spaces
— más espacios verdes

¡Vamos de compras! — Let's go shopping!

Vocabulary

el centro comercial	*shopping centre*	la marca	*make, brand*	el zapato	*shoe*
la tienda	*shop*	la ropa	*clothes,*	el reloj	*clock, watch*
cerrar	*to close*		*clothing*	la venta	*sale*
comprar	*to buy*	la moda	*fashion*	la cola	*queue*
vender	*to sell*	la camiseta	*T-shirt*	cobrar	*to charge (money)*
el producto	*product*	el pantalón	*trousers*	devolver	*to return, give back*

(**Higher**: la venta, la cola, cobrar, devolver)

Los fines de semana me gusta ir de compras con mis amigos. Normalmente compramos caramelos y vemos una película en el cine.

On weekends, I like to go shopping with my friends. Normally we buy sweets and see a movie at the cinema.

Prefiero ver la ropa en una tienda. Cuando hago las compras online, los artículos nunca son mi talla exacta y tengo que devolverlos.

I prefer to see clothes in a shop. When I do online shopping, the items are never my exact size and I have to return them.

Las tiendas locales están cerrando porque mucha gente va a los centros comerciales más grandes. Creo que es triste para la comunidad.

The local shops are closing because many people are going to the bigger shopping centres. I think it's sad for the community.

Practice Questions

Q1 *Read aloud the following text.* [5 marks]

(SPEAKING)

> Mi región es bastante grande. Vivo en un pueblo industrial. Creo que mi pueblo necesita más parques. Me gusta ir al centro comercial. Mañana voy de compras con mi hermana.

Top Tip for Higher Students
✓ Use the subjunctive mood correctly, e.g. 'Es decepcionante que solo tenga un parque.'

Answer the questions below out loud in Spanish.

a) Describe tu pueblo.

b) ¿Qué no te gusta de tu pueblo?

c) ¿Qué se puede hacer en tu región?

d) ¿Qué piensas de los centros comerciales? [10 marks]

Q2 *Ridwan is writing to you about what his region is like.*
Read the passage and then answer the questions below in English.

(READING)

> La gente dice que no hay mucho que hacer en mi región. Es cierto que aquí no hay muchas tiendas y las que tenemos cobran mucho por sus productos. En cambio, hay que reconocer los edificios maravillosos que tenemos aquí. Por ejemplo, yo podría pasar un día entero en el museo de arte porque me parece muy interesante.

a) What is generally said about where Ridwan lives? [1 mark]

b) What does Ridwan say about existing shops in his local area? Give **one** detail. [1 mark]

c) What is **one** positive thing that Ridwan says about his local area? [1 mark]

(Higher — Q2)

'La ropa' is a noun that's always singular...

When you're talking about clothing in Spanish, remember that 'la ropa' will always be singular even when the English translation is plural. So 'I bought clothes' would be 'compré ropa' rather than 'compré ropas'.

Directions and Weather

These pages will prove very useful if you travel to Spain... and when you go into your exam.

¿Dónde está? — Where is it?

Vocabulary

aquí	*here*	detrás	*behind*		el metro	*metre*
allí	*there, over there*	entre	*between, among*		hacia	*towards*
cerca	*close, near, nearby*	la calle	*street*	Higher	fuera	*outside*
lejos	*far (away)*	la esquina	*corner (of a street)*		situado	*situated,*
delante	*in front, ahead*	el kilómetro	*kilometre*			*located*

El ayuntamiento está entre la biblioteca y el banco.

The town hall is between the library and the bank.

Mi casa no está lejos del centro del pueblo. Está en la esquina de la calle.

My house isn't far from the town centre. It's on the corner of the street.

Hay un café delante del parque. Está fuera de la ciudad.

There's a café in front of the park. It's outside of the city.

quite close to here — bastante cerca de aquí

Grammar — 'estar' for locations

In Spanish, there are two verbs for 'to be' — 'ser' and 'estar'. To describe where things are, you need to use 'estar' — see p.178. You can also use 'estar situado' to say where something is situated.

¿Cómo se llega a...? — How do you get to...?

Vocabulary

andar	*to walk*	el norte	*north*		encontrar	*to find*
tomar	*to take*	el sur	*south*		el lugar	*place, position*
la izquierda	*left*	el este	*east*	H	cruzar	*to cross*
la derecha	*right (direction)*	el oeste	*west*		el camino	*way, route, path*

Toma la salida de la derecha y el parque temático no está muy lejos.

Take the right exit and the theme park isn't too far.

Follow the road — Sigue la carretera

Si te pierdes, anda hacia el centro donde verás una iglesia alta.

If you get lost, walk towards the centre where you'll see a tall church.

El estadio está al oeste de la ciudad. Es muy fácil encontrarlo.

The stadium is to the west of the city. It's very easy to find it.

Ese camino te lleva en la dirección equivocada. Ve a la izquierda y el centro comercial está allí.

That path leads you in the wrong direction. Go left and the shopping centre is there.

Grammar — giving instructions

To give instructions, use the imperative. See how to form it on p.191.

Cruza la calle y luego **sigue** las señales.
Cross the street and then follow the signs.

Toma la segunda salida a la derecha.
Take the second exit on the right.

Ve en esta dirección — está cerca.
Go in this direction — it's nearby.

Hace buen / mal tiempo — The weather is good / bad

Vocabulary

el tiempo	*weather*	el calor	*heat, hot*	la temperatura	*temperature*
el clima	*climate*	el viento	*wind*	el grado	*degree*
hace (+ noun)	*it is (+ weather noun)*	la lluvia	*rain*	frío/a (adj.)	*cold*
el sol	*sun*	llover	*to rain*	fresco/a	*cool*

Question

¿Qué tiempo hace donde vives?

What's the weather like where you live?

Simple Answer

De momento hace mucho frío.

It's very cold at the moment.

'frío' can be used as an adjective (e.g. 'No me gusta el tiempo frío.') or as a noun with the verb 'hacer' (e.g. 'Hace frío hoy.')

Extended Answer

Hoy hace mucho sol en el sur, pero mañana habrá nubes. Eso me parece genial, porque prefiero el tiempo cuando no hace demasiado calor.

Today it's very sunny in the south, but tomorrow there will be clouds. This seems great to me, because I prefer the weather when it's not too hot.

Esta semana lloverá en el este del país, pero hará sol aquí.

This week it will rain in the east of the country, but it will be sunny here.

Ayer hizo mal tiempo en mi región. Había un viento fresco.

Yesterday the weather was bad in my region. There was a cool wind.

Espero que haga sol esta primavera. No me gusta la lluvia.

I hope that it's sunny this spring. I don't like the rain.

El verano pasado pasé mal las vacaciones debido a las temperaturas altas.

Last summer I didn't enjoy the holidays due to the high temperatures.

Grammar — hace + noun

To describe the weather in English, you often use '<u>to be</u>', e.g. '<u>it's sunny</u>'. In Spanish, you have to use the verb '<u>hacer</u>' instead:

<u>Hace</u> sol / viento / frío.
It's *sunny / windy / cold.*

Remember you can put the verbs into <u>different tenses</u> too.

Practice Questions

Q1 *A tour guide is giving you directions to different places in a city you're visiting. Listen to the description of where each place is and choose the correct letter from the box for each question.*

A. Behind   **B.** To the left of   **C.** To the right of   **D.** On the corner of

a) The town hall is ... the park.

b) The shopping centre is ... the cinema.

c) The clothes shop is ... this street.

d) The gym is ... the swimming pool.   *[4 marks]*

Q2 *Translate these sentences into Spanish.*

a) *My friend's house isn't far from mine.*

b) *We will ask for the right way.*

c) *Last autumn it barely rained.*

d) *Cold temperatures are the best.*

[8 marks]

Higher

Don't let revision rain on your parade...

You'll use 'estar' and 'hacer' a lot when talking about directions and weather, so it'd be useful exam prep to write out verb tables for them both. That way, you'll have a handy place to refer to when you're revising.

Listening Questions

These exam-style questions will test your knowledge so that you're prepared come rain or shine.

1 Nadia and Sebastian are telling you about where they live.

Choose the correct answer and write the correct letter in each box.

Listening Track 38

1 a Nadia's house is in...

A	the city centre.
B	the suburbs of the city.
C	the industrial area of the city.

[1 mark]

1 b At the house...

A	there is no garden.
B	they are going to build a garden.
C	they share a garden with the neighbours.

[1 mark]

1 c Sebastian wants his flat to...

A	be on a high floor.
B	have a lift.
C	have stairs.

[1 mark]

2 Your friends Amira and Jorge are talking about what they do around the house.

Answer the questions in **English**.

Listening Track 39

2 a Who does most of the chores in Amira's house?

.... *[1 mark]*

2 b What chore does Amira not want to do? Why not?

.... *[1 mark]*

2 c What is **one** chore that Jorge has to do during the week?

.... *[1 mark]*

2 d What is **one** advantage that Jorge gives for helping out at home?

.... *[1 mark]*

Speaking Questions

Candidate's Material

- You are talking to your Chilean friend.

- Your teacher will play the part of your friend and will speak first.

- You should address your friend as *tú*.

- When you see this — ? — you will have to ask a question.

> **In order to score full marks, you must include a verb in your response to each task.**
>
> **1.** Say what there is to do in your neighbourhood. (Give **one** detail.)
>
> **2.** Say one thing about the weather in your region last week. (Give **one** detail.)
>
> **?** **3**. Ask your friend a question about where they live.
>
> **4.** Describe what there is in your house. (Give **one** detail.)
>
> **5.** Say what chores you do at home. (Give **one** detail.)
>
> **Higher**
> **6.** Describe the last time you went shopping. (Give **two** details.)
>
> **7.** Say what your ideal house would be like and why.
> (Give **one** detail and **one** reason.)

Teacher's Material

- You begin the role-play.

- You should address the candidate as *tú*.

- You must read out the teacher's role as shown below **without any changes.**

- You must begin the role-play by using the introductory text below.

Introductory text: *Estás hablando con tu amigo chileno/tu amiga chilena.*
Yo soy tu amigo/tu amiga.

> **1.** ¿Qué se puede hacer en tu barrio?
>
> **2.** ¿Qué tiempo hizo en tu región la semana pasada?
>
> **?** **3.** Allow the candidate to ask a question about where you live.
> Give an appropriate response.
>
> **4.** ¿Qué hay en tu casa?
>
> **5.** ¿Qué tareas haces en casa?
>
> **H**
> **6.** Describe la última vez que fuiste de compras.
>
> **7.** ¿Cómo sería tu casa ideal? ¿Por qué?

Reading Questions

1 You see an online forum. Some young Spanish people are describing what they do in their local area. Write the correct letter in each box.

Write **E** for Emilio. **S** for Sofía. **H** for Hugo.

> **Emilio**: *Vivo en la capital y hay un montón de cosas que se puede hacer aquí. Por ejemplo, el sábado pasado fui al estadio para ver un concierto.*
>
> **Sofía**: *En mi pueblo pequeño no hay muchas opciones para ir de compras. En cambio, tenemos una variedad de espacios verdes para disfrutar.*
>
> **Hugo**: *Mi ciudad es muy moderna. Me gusta ir al centro comercial cada sábado porque hay un cine grande y algunos restaurantes geniales allí.*

1 a Who likes going to the shopping centre?

[1 mark]

1 b Who lives somewhere with lots of green spaces?

[1 mark]

1 c Who went to a stadium last Saturday?

[1 mark]

2 You see some headlines on a news website for your local area.

A	Los ciudadanos exigen mejores carreteras.
B	Una nueva biblioteca pública será fundada por el ayuntamiento.
C	Más bancos cierran por causa del Internet.
D	La nueva obra en el teatro local cierra después de su gran éxito.
E	El supermercado introduce descuentos enormes este puente.

Which headline matches each description? Write the correct letter in each box.

2 a Closed buildings

[1 mark]

2 b A new community building

[1 mark]

2 c Shopping sales

[1 mark]

Writing Questions

1 Using your knowledge of grammar, complete the following sentences in **Spanish**.
Choose the correct Spanish word from the three options in the grid.
Write the correct **word** in the space.

1 a Mi abuelo .... en un piso.

vive	vives	vivo

[1 mark]

1 b Es un salón ....

cómoda	cómodo	cómodos

[1 mark]

1 c La tienda .... aquí.

está	es	tiene

[1 mark]

2 You are writing an article about where you live.
Write approximately **90** words in **Spanish**.
You must write something about each bullet point.

Mention:

- what you think of your region

- what the weather was like last summer

- what your ideal area to live in would be like.

[15 marks]

3 Translate the following sentences into **Spanish**.

3 a I always get dressed quickly.

.... *[2 marks]*

3 b My ideal house would have art in each room.

.... *[2 marks]*

3 c Walk towards the bank and then cross the road.

.... *[2 marks]*

3 d The worst thing about my region is that the weather is always bad.

.... *[2 marks]*

Where People Live — Vocabulary

If you're looking for the vocabulary to describe where you live and what your region is like, look no further.

The Home

vivir	to live
la casa	house
el piso	flat, apartment, floor (of building)
la planta	floor
el/la vecino/a	neighbour
el/la dueño/a	owner, landlord
describir	to describe
agradable	pleasant, nice
cómodo/a	comfortable
el espacio	space, room
el cuarto	room
el dormitorio	bedroom
la habitación	bedroom
el salón	living room
el baño	bathroom
la cocina	kitchen
el jardín	garden
el estudio	study, studio
la escalera	stairs, ladder
bajar	to go down
subir	to go up
la pared	(interior) wall
la puerta	door
la ventana	window
la mesa	table
la cama	bed

despertar	to wake (someone) (up)
despertarse	to wake (up)
levantarse	to get up
lavarse	to have a wash
vestir	to dress
vestirse	to get dressed
cambiarse	to get changed
quitarse	to take off (clothes)
dormir	to sleep
dormirse	to fall asleep
la tarea	chore
hacer	to do, make
ayudar	to help
preparar	to prepare
limpiar	to clean
lavar	to wash
pasear	to take for a walk
el perro	dog
sacar	to take out
la basura	rubbish, junk

Higher

el hogar	home
el rincón	corner (inside shape, house)
acostar	to put to bed
acostarse	to go to bed
cocinar	to cook
arreglar	to tidy

The Local Area — Places

la región	region
el campo	countryside, pitch, field (sport)
la ciudad	city, town
el pueblo	village, small town
bonito/a	pretty, nice, beautiful
el centro	centre, middle
las afueras	outskirts, suburbs
el barrio	neighbourhood, district
la zona	area, zone
industrial	industrial
principal	main, principal
la comunidad	community
se puede	you can (general), one can
el edificio	building
el ayuntamiento	Spanish town council, city council, town hall
la plaza	square
el puente	bridge

la biblioteca	library
el parque	park
el café	café
el restaurante	restaurant
el cine	cinema
el teatro	theatre
el gimnasio	gym
la piscina	swimming pool
el hospital	hospital
el banco	(financial) bank, bench
la estación	station
el estadio	stadium
la iglesia	church
la mezquita	mosque
la sinagoga	synagogue

Higher

el/la ciudadano/a	citizen, member of the public
la construcción	building
la fuente	fountain

The Local Area — Shopping

el centro comercial	*shopping centre*
el supermercado	*supermarket*
la tienda	*shop*
abierto/a	*open, unlocked*
cerrado/a	*closed*
cerrar	*to close*
la(s) compra(s)	*shopping*
ir de compras	*to go shopping*
el cliente	*client, customer*
la caja	*till (in shop)*
la bolsa	*bag*
la tarjeta	*bank card*
comprar	*to buy, purchase*
gastar	*to spend (money)*
costar	*to cost*
vender	*to sell*
el producto	*product*
el artículo	*product, item*
la marca	*make, brand*

el tamaño	*size, dimension*
la ropa	*clothes, clothing*
la moda	*fashion*
de moda	*in fashion, fashionable*
la camisa	*shirt*
la camiseta	*T-shirt*
el pantalón	*trousers*
el vestido	*dress*
la falda	*skirt*
el zapato	*shoe*
el reloj	*clock, watch*

Higher

la sección	*department (in store)*
la cola	*queue*
la venta	*sale*
el descuento	*discount*
los gastos	*expenses, costs, spending*
cobrar	*to charge (money)*
devolver	*to return, give back*

Directions and Weather

la dirección	*address, direction*
aquí	*here*
allí	*there, over there*
cerca	*close, near, nearby*
lejos	*far (away)*
delante	*in front, ahead*
detrás	*behind*
entre	*between, among*
la calle	*street*
la esquina	*corner (of a street)*
la carretera	*road*
el kilómetro	*kilometre*
el metro	*metre*
perderse	*to get lost*
andar	*to walk*
tomar	*to take*
la izquierda	*left*
la derecha	*right (direction)*
el norte	*north*
el sur	*south*
el este	*east*
el oeste	*west*
encontrar	*to find*
el lugar	*place, position*
el tiempo	*weather*
el clima	*climate*
hace (+ noun)	*it is (+ weather noun or adjective)*

el sol	*sun*
el calor	*heat, hot*
el viento	*wind*
la lluvia	*rain*
llover	*to rain*
la temperatura	*temperature*
el grado	*degree (temperature)*
frío/a (adj.)	*cold*
fresco/a	*cool*
la estación	*season (of the year)*
la primavera	*spring*
el verano	*summer*
el otoño	*autumn*
el invierno	*winter*

Higher

hacia	*toward, towards*
fuera	*outside, out*
situado/a	*situated, located*
cruzar	*to cross*
el camino	*way, route, path*
la nube	*cloud*

Ah... The perfect weather for a walk.

Revision Summary Test for Section Eleven

Work through this summary test for a reminder of all you'll need to describe where you live.

- These questions are **really tricky**, but they'll help you see **how well you know your stuff**.
- Tackle the **revision summary test** below, or scan the QR code to do it **online**.
  You can **keep track of your progress** online and see **which areas need more work**.
- There are **sample answers** here: www.cgpbooks.co.uk/MadridExtras

At Home ☑

1) How many nouns can you remember that relate to rooms and parts of a house?
   There are 14 in this section (plus 1 for Higher tier).

2) In Spanish, write about what you like and dislike about your house.

3) Translate this sentence into Spanish: 'My bedroom has a comfortable bed and a small table.'

4) a) List the verbs from this section to do with a typical routine. There are 10 (plus 2 for Higher tier).
   b) Use some of these words to describe in Spanish what you typically do after school.

5) '¿Qué haces para ayudar en casa?' Translate this question into English, then answer it in Spanish.

6) Translate this sentence into English: 'Nuestros vecinos nos han dicho que querían
   alquilar una casa nueva, pero desafortunadamente el dueño de la casa los rechazó.'

7) In Spanish, describe two characteristics you would like your house to have.

The Local Area ☑

8) En español, y con frases completas, describe tu barrio. ¿Qué hay? ¿Qué te gusta?

9) 'Vivo en la zona principal de mi ciudad. Aquí se puede encontrar un estadio
   famoso y un parque grande.' Translate these sentences into English.

10) List the 3 religious buildings that appear in this section.

11) Write the Spanish for: a) pitch   b) industrial   c) town hall   d) café   e) bench

12) In Spanish, describe a time you went shopping, including as much relevant vocabulary as you can.

13) List the 9 nouns from this section to do with clothes.

14) Translate these words and give their opposites in Spanish: a) closed   b) to save (money)   c) to buy

15) '¿Cómo mejorarías tu región?' Translate this question into English and answer it in Spanish.

16) Translate these sentences into Spanish: 'To celebrate the building of a new section in the
    supermarket, there will be big discounts. However, the queues will be really long.'

Directions and Weather ☑

17) 'Para llegar al hospital, toma la carretera a la izquierda.' Translate this sentence into English.

18) a) In Spanish, give all the directions on a compass.
    b) List the words in this section that describe an object's position. There are 7 (plus 2 for Higher tier).

19) How would you say in Spanish that the gym is on the corner of the street, to the right of the theatre?

20) '¿Qué tiempo hace hoy?' Translate this question into English, then answer it in Spanish.

21) What's the English for...?
    a) la dirección   b) el kilómetro   c) el metro   d) andar   e) el clima

22) 'Mañana hará calor. Las temperaturas van a subir a los 32 grados.' What's tomorrow's forecast?

23) In Spanish, write about your favourite season of the year. Include as much detail as you can.

24) Translate this sentence into Spanish: 'My friend got lost on the route towards my house, which
    is situated outside the city. She waited in an obvious place to be able to find her easily.'

25) Pick two locations in your town, and in Spanish, say how to get from one to the other.

Environmental Problems

Time to think green and start talking about the issues that affect the environment.

Remember there's also lots of online content here: www.cgpbooks.co.uk/Madrid

El medioambiente — The environment

Vocabulary

el problema	*problem*	contaminar	*to pollute*	el aumento	*increase, rise*
destruir	*to destroy, ruin*	tirar	*to throw*	cortar	*to cut (up)*
el bosque	*forest, wood*	el plástico	*plastic*	emitir	*to emit, give off*
el daño	*harm, damage*	la basura	*rubbish, junk*	el humo	*smoke, fumes*
la contaminación	*pollution*	la energía	*energy, power*	el recurso	*resource*

(**Higher**: cortar, emitir, el humo, el recurso)

El mundo ha perdido muchos de sus bosques.
Se cortan árboles para producir más recursos.

The world has lost many of its forests. Trees are cut down to produce more resources.

El uso de ciertos combustibles contamina el aire.

The use of certain fuels pollutes the air.

En mi barrio... — In my neighbourhood...

Q&A Audio

Question

¿Qué problemas con el medioambiente hay en tu barrio?

What environmental problems are there in your neighbourhood?

Simple Answer

En mi barrio las calles están llenas de basura.

In my neighbourhood the streets are filled with rubbish.

Extended Answer

La contaminación acústica es un gran problema en el pueblo donde vivo. También hay muchas obras porque el pueblo está creciendo.

Noise pollution is a big problem in the town where I live. There are also lots of building works because the town is growing.

En mi región los ríos están sucios.
La gente tira plástico y basura a ellos.

In my region the rivers are dirty. People throw plastic and rubbish in them.

smell awful — huelen fatal

Vivo en una zona industrial. Las fábricas aquí usan mucha energía.

I live in an industrial area. The factories here use a lot of energy.

emit a lot of fumes — emiten muchos humos

Practice Question

Q1 *Look at the two photos below. Talk in Spanish about what is in the photos. You should talk for about a minute and say something about each photo.*

SPEAKING

Top Tip for Higher Students
✓ Start a relative clause by using relative pronouns, e.g. 'lo cual' or 'donde', to add more detail to your sentences.

[5 marks]

Make use of your preparation time in the speaking exam...

You'll get fifteen minutes of prep time before the speaking exam to read the questions and make notes. For the photo card question, you need to mention both photos — you'll lose marks if you only talk about one.

Environmental Impacts

Now you've seen some of the problems the environment faces, it's time to look at the impacts.

Los efectos — The effects

Vocabulary

la causa	*cause*	el río	*river*	el impacto	*impact*
la naturaleza	*nature*	el olor	*smell, odour*	desaparecer	*to disappear*
la especie	*species*	el cambio climático	*climate change*	contribuir	*to contribute*
la planta	*plant*	preocupar	*to worry*	el incendio	*fire*
el cielo	*sky*	debido (a)	*due (to)*	el desastre	*disaster*

Higher

El daño a la Tierra — The damage to Earth

Parece que no hay espacio suficiente para toda la basura que producimos. Sin embargo, si creamos más vertederos, podrían afectar a nuestros ríos.

It seems that there isn't enough space for all the rubbish that we produce. However, if we create more landfills, they could affect our rivers.

El uso excesivo de productos químicos puede matar muchos cultivos y plantas.

The excessive use of chemical products can kill many crops and plants.

Los científicos creen que la destrucción de los bosques contribuye al cambio climático. Si no actuamos, el nivel del mar va a aumentar aún más.

Scientists believe that the destruction of forests contributes to climate change. If we don't act, the sea level will rise even more.

Algunas personas dicen que no habrá recursos suficientes para las generaciones del futuro si seguimos usándolos al ritmo actual.

Some people say that there won't be enough resources for future generations if we keep using them at the current rate.

Me preocupo que más especies desaparecerán si no dejamos de destruir los hábitats.

I worry that more species will disappear if we don't stop destroying habitats.

Grammar — the inflectional/proper future

To talk about what things will be like in the <u>future</u>, you can use the <u>inflectional future</u> tense. See p.182.

Pienso que el cambio climático <u>afectará</u> a todos.   ***I think that climate change <u>will affect</u> everyone.***

Practice Question

Q1 Translate these sentences about environmental impacts into English.

a) *Construir más zonas industriales aumenta el uso de energía.*

b) *La contaminación del aire puede causar enfermedades graves.*

c) *Hemos perdido muchas especies debido al daño causado a los bosques.*

d) *Según varios estudios recientes, el clima está cambiando.*

[8 marks]

Don't let the inflectional future catch you out...

The inflectional future tense is really handy for talking about your predictions for the future. Make a verb table for revision with the inflectional future endings so that you've got them covered and ready to use.

Protecting the Environment

Time to round off these environment pages by looking at the ways we can protect it.

Proteger al medioambiente — Protecting the environment

Vocabulary

proteger	*to protect*	limpiar	*to clean*	conservar	*to conserve*
ayudar	*to help*	reducir	*to reduce*	fundar	*to set up*
resolver	*to solve, resolve*	apagar	*to turn off*	la campaña	*campaign*
salvar	*to save, rescue*	la organización	*organisation*	la manifestación	*protest*
reciclar	*to recycle*	en contra	*against*	efectivo/a	*effective*
recoger	*to pick up, tidy up*	a favor	*in favour*	el asunto	*matter, issue*

(*Higher*: conservar, fundar, la campaña, la manifestación, efectivo/a, el asunto)

¿Qué podemos hacer? — What can we do?

Question

¿Qué haces para proteger el medioambiente?
What do you do to protect the environment?

Simple Answer

Nunca compro bolsas nuevas y reciclo mi papel.
I never buy new bags and I recycle my paper.

Extended Answer

Intento no utilizar bolsas nuevas sino reciclar las viejas. Mi padre y yo vamos al centro de reciclaje para reciclar el vidrio. Además, camino al colegio para conservar la energía y reducir el uso de combustible.

I try not to use new bags but rather recycle old ones. My dad and I go to the recycling centre to recycle glass. Also, I walk to school to conserve energy and to reduce fuel use.

Apoyo a organizaciones que quieren salvar nuestros bosques y reducir la deforestación.

I support organisations that want to save our forests and reduce deforestation.

Estoy participando en una campaña de ahorro de energía. Apagaré las luces de casa para reducir la cantidad de energía que uso. Si todos hacen este cambio pequeño, podría tener un gran impacto.

I'm participating in an energy-saving campaign. I'll switch off the lights at home to reduce the amount of energy I use. If everyone makes this small change, it could have a big impact.

El mes pasado mi hermano mayor fue a una manifestación en contra de la moda rápida.

Last month my older brother went to a protest against fast fashion.

Practice Question

Q1 *Listen to Carmen talk about what her town is doing to protect the environment. Answer the following questions in English about what she says.*

    a) i) What are the people of her town going to do in March?   *[1 mark]*

        ii) Why is Carmen in favour of this idea?   *[1 mark]*

    b) i) What have the town council asked young people to do?   *[1 mark]*

        ii) What does Carmen suggest everyone does instead?   *[1 mark]*

Don't just say what you do — say why, too...

You'll get more marks in the exams if you give reasons for your answers. To practise this, try to add 'porque' to your sentences to add extra detail, e.g. 'Reciclo el plástico porque...', rather than just 'Reciclo el plástico.'

Social Issues

Time to move on to social problems. You'll have to be able to give opinions on them, so read on...

La falta de comida y el paro — Food shortages and unemployment

Vocabulary

la sociedad	*society*	el hambre	*hunger*	la economía	*economy*
la gente	*people*	la falta	*lack, shortage*	la preocupación	*worry, concern*
el tema	*issue, subject*	el paro	*unemployment*	la pobreza	*poverty*

Quiero que todo el mundo tenga acceso a la comida porque es un derecho básico. El hambre debería importarnos.

I want everyone to have access to food because it is a basic right. Hunger should matter to us.

we need it to survive — la necesitamos para sobrevivir

El paro es una preocupación muy grave porque sin empleo es difícil vivir bien.

Unemployment is a very serious concern because without a job it's difficult to live well.

it can affect people's mental health — puede afectar la salud mental de la gente

El delito — Crime

Vocabulary

la violencia	*violence*	el conflicto	*conflict*	cometer	*to commit (crime)*
el delito	*crime*	amenazar	*to threaten*	la culpa	*blame, fault*

El problema del delito es grave en mi barrio. Un grupo de ladrones robó a mi vecino el mes pasado pero por suerte la policía encontró a los culpables.

Crime is a serious problem in my neighbourhood. A group of thieves stole from my neighbour last month but luckily the police found the culprits.

Una manera en que podemos reducir la violencia es dar a la gente espacios seguros para expresar sus emociones y sentimientos.

One way that we can reduce violence is to give people safe spaces to express their emotions and feelings.

Las diferencias sociales — Social differences

Vocabulary

la diferencia	*difference*	la discriminación	*discrimination*	
justo/a	*fair, just*	la igualdad	*equality*	
comparar	*to compare*	la libertad	*freedom*	

> **Grammar** — the verb 'should'
>
> To say what someone should do, use '<u>deber</u>' in the conditional followed by the <u>infinitive</u>.
>
> **Deberías dar tu apoyo.**
> ***You should give your support.***

La discriminación es un problema grave. Muchas personas son juzgadas por el color de su piel, su sexualidad o su género. Deberíamos trabajar juntos para crear un mundo igual.

Discrimination is a serious problem. Many people are judged for the colour of their skin, their sexuality or their gender. We should work together to create an equal world.

Los muy ricos tienen vidas de lujo en comparación con la gente más pobre. No parece justo.

The very rich have lives of luxury compared to poorer people. It doesn't seem fair.

Ayudar a la sociedad — Helping society

Vocabulary

importar	*to matter, be important*	el apoyo	*support, backing*	elegir	*to choose, elect*
mejorar	*to improve, make better*	la actitud	*attitude*	la solución	*solution, answer*
dar	*to give*	la felicidad	*happiness*	el beneficio	*benefit*

(*Higher*: elegir, la solución, el beneficio)

Q&A Audio

Question

¿Qué haces para apoyar tu comunidad?
What do you do to support your community?

Simple Answer

Los lunes ayudo en un club deportivo del colegio.
On Mondays I help out in a sports club at school.

Extended Answer

Llevo un año ayudando en un banco de alimentos. Estoy agradecido de poder apoyar a la gente porque siento que estoy ayudando a mejorar la situación.
I've been helping out in a food bank for a year. I'm grateful to be able to support people because I feel like I'm helping to improve their situation.

Dar apoyo a las organizaciones benéficas es una solución para mejorar la sociedad.

Giving support to charitable organisations is one solution to improve society.

Participo en un club juvenil cerca de mí. Es una idea genial porque ofrece muchos beneficios a los jóvenes.

I'm participating in a youth club near me. It's a great idea because it offers a lot of benefits to young people.

Los fines de semana ayudo a los ancianos de mi comunidad. Para mí es importante traerles felicidad especialmente cuando tanta gente sufre de soledad.

At the weekend I help the elderly in my community. It's important to me to bring them happiness, especially when so many people suffer from loneliness.

Practice Questions

Q1 *Write a description of social problems relevant to you.*
You should write about 90 words in Spanish. Write about:

WRITING

* *a social problem that exists where you live*
* *something that you've done in the past to make a difference in your area*
* *something that people should do to improve a social problem in your area.*   *[15 marks]*

Top Tip for Higher Students
✔ Use the plural form of the conditional, e.g. 'deberíamos...' (we should...).

Q2 *In an interview, Juan is talking about social problems in his area.*
*Fill each gap in the sentences below with **one** word.*

LISTENING

Listening Track 41

a) Many people are affected by ______.
Others could help by supporting the appropriate ______.   *[2 marks]*

b) In schools, ______ is an issue.
It is important that each student has equal ______.   *[2 marks]*

(*Higher*)

Break down the vocabulary for these pages...

There's a lot of tricky vocab here, but don't panic — one way to make it easier is to sort the vocab into smaller topic groups (e.g. jobs, food, crime, equality and helping people), then learn the words one topic at a time.

Listening Questions

You know the drill now — four pages of exam-style questions are ready and waiting for you.
They say practice makes perfect and all that... So what are you waiting for?

1   Some young people are giving their views on environmental problems.
Complete the sentences in **English**.
Write **one** word in each space.

Listening Track 42

1 a   In the north of Spain, heavy rains have ☐ .

According to ☐ , climate change is the cause.   *[2 marks]*

1 b   Many people living in industrial areas are ☐

building more ☐ .   *[2 marks]*

Higher

1 c   The local people are worried about the damage to their ☐

as a result of ☐ .   *[2 marks]*

2   Andrea is in a radio interview discussing social problems.
Answer the questions in **English**.

Listening Track 43

2 a   Which social problem is Andrea talking about?

....   *[1 mark]*

2 b   Give **one** detail about **each** of the groups associated with this problem.

....

....   *[2 marks]*

2 c   What does Andrea think should be done to improve the situation?

....   *[1 mark]*

Higher

2 d   How does she suggest this solution is funded?

....   *[1 mark]*

Speaking Questions

Candidate's Material

- Spend a few minutes looking at the two photos. Make notes on them to use during the test.

- Your teacher will ask you to talk about the content of the photos. You should talk for approximately **one minute** at Foundation tier and **one and a half minutes** at Higher tier. **You must say at least one thing about each photo**.

- After you have spoken about the content of the photos, your teacher will then ask you some questions related to any of the topics within the topic of **The environment and social issues**.

Teacher's Material

- Candidates should talk about the photos above for approximately **one minute** at Foundation tier or **one and a half minutes** at Higher tier. They may use any notes they have made during the preparation time. Begin by asking the candidate to tell you about the photos:

  - Háblame de las fotos.

- When the candidate has finished talking about the photos, ask them the following unprepared conversation questions on the topic of **The environment and social issues**:

  - Describe un problema social que hay en tu barrio.

  - Háblame de la última vez que hiciste algo por tu comunidad.

  - ¿Cómo te afecta la contaminación?

  - ¿Cómo proteges el medioambiente?

  - ¿Qué podríamos hacer para conseguir una sociedad más igual?

  - ¿Qué pasará si no protegemos el medioambiente?

Reading Questions

1 Translate these sentences into **English**.

1 a La contaminación destruye la naturaleza.

.... *[2 marks]*

1 b Debes recoger y reciclar tu basura.

.... *[2 marks]*

1 c Me gustaría hacer algo para reducir el hambre en mi país.

.... *[2 marks]*

1 d Deberíamos actuar si queremos desarrollar una sociedad más justa.

.... *[2 marks]*

Foundation

2 You read this email from your friend Pilar about her new job at a charity.

> ¡Hola! Ahora trabajo para una organización que ayuda a gente que vive en la pobreza. Como consecuencia de las dificultades económicas, muchas personas están en paro y no tienen suficiente dinero para apoyar a sus familias. Les damos información sobre los trabajos que hay en la región y también les ayudamos a encontrar ropa y juguetes para sus niños. Después de haber empezado este empleo, comprendo de primera mano los beneficios de dar lo que puedes a los demás. Es la mejor parte del trabajo.

Complete these sentences. Write the letter for the correct option in each box.

2 a Due to economic difficulties, many people are...

A	struggling to afford clothing.
B	unemployed.
C	experiencing discrimination.

[1 mark]

2 b Her organisation gives people...

A	food and medicine.
B	free childcare.
C	information about jobs in the region.

[1 mark]

2 c After starting this job, she...

A	has been giving first-hand support to families.
B	sees the benefit of giving what you can to others.
C	better understands how to help others.

[1 mark]

Higher

Writing Questions

1 You are writing an article about problems in your area.
Write approximately **50** words in **Spanish**.
You must write something about each bullet point.

Mention:

- pollution
- energy use
- nature
- jobs
- an organisation that helps your community.

[10 marks]

2 Translate the following sentences into **Spanish**.

2 a We can make changes to improve society.

.... *[2 marks]*

2 b Each month I help to clean up the streets in my town.

.... *[2 marks]*

2 c Many species will not survive if pollution increases.

.... *[2 marks]*

2 d It's worth reducing the amount of plastic and glass you use.

.... *[2 marks]*

2 e For me, equality is the most important social concern.

.... *[2 marks]*

3 You are writing a post for a Spanish website about current social issues.
Write approximately **150** words in **Spanish**.
You must write something about both bullet points.

Mention:

- the social problem that worries you the most
- something that you think could be done to support other people.

[25 marks]

The Environment and Social Issues — Vocabulary

Have a read through these pages for the words you'll need to talk about environmental and social issues.

Environmental Problems

el medioambiente / el medio ambiente	*environment, natural world*
el problema	*problem*
grave	*serious, grave*
causar	*to cause*
producir	*to produce, cause*
aumentar	*to increase*
destruir	*to destroy, ruin*
gastar	*to use up*
el bosque	*forest, wood*
el árbol	*tree*
el daño	*harm, damage*
la contaminación	*pollution*
contaminar	*to pollute, contaminate*
tirar	*to throw*
el plástico	*plastic*
la basura	*rubbish, junk*
limpio/a	*clean*
sucio/a	*dirty*
la fábrica	*factory*
construir	*to build*
el ruido	*noise*
el aire	*air*
la luz	*light, electricity*

la energía	*energy, power*
usar	*to use*
el uso	*use*
el planeta	*planet*
el entorno	*environment, surroundings*
los alrededores	*surrounding area, vicinity*
el aumento	*increase, rise*
crecer	*to grow, increase*
existir	*to exist*
cortar	*to cut (up)*
el suelo	*ground, floor*
emitir	*to emit, give off*
el humo	*smoke, fumes*
químico/a (adj.)	*chemical*
fabricar	*to manufacture, produce*
las obras	*roadworks, building works*
utilizar	*to use*
el recurso	*resource*
el gas	*gas*
la piedra	*stone, rock*
la madera	*wood*
el oro	*gold*
el vidrio	*glass*

Higher applies from *el planeta* to *el vidrio*.

Environmental Impacts

la causa	*cause*
el efecto	*effect*
la naturaleza	*nature*
la especie	*species*
la planta	*plant*
la tierra	*earth, land, ground*
el cielo	*sky*
el río	*river*
el cambio climático	*climate change*
el fuego	*fire*
el olor	*smell, odour*
seco/a	*dry*
roto/a	*torn*
preocupar	*to worry, be a worry*
preocuparse por	*to worry about*
debido (a)	*owing (to), due (to)*
la prueba	*trial, proof*
la cifra	*figure, number, amount*
el/la científico/a	*scientist*
el impacto	*impact*
la consecuencia	*consequence*
como consecuencia	*in consequence, as a result*

acuático/a	*water, aquatic*
desaparecer	*to disappear*
matar	*to kill*
sufrir	*to suffer*
contribuir	*to contribute*
abandonar	*to abandon, leave (a place)*
el cultivo	*crop*
el incendio	*fire*
quemar	*to burn*
huele (a)	*it smells (of)*
el desastre	*disaster*
natural	*natural*
sobrevivir	*to survive*
advertir	*to warn*
negar	*to deny, refuse*
negarse a (+ infinitive)	*to refuse to*
la fuente	*source*
el factor	*factor*
el nivel	*level*

Protecting the Environment

proteger	*to protect*
ayudar	*to help*
la ayuda	*help*
resolver	*to solve, resolve*
el cambio	*change*
la acción	*action, act*
salvar	*to save, rescue*
reciclar	*to recycle*
recoger	*to pick up, collect, tidy up*
limpiar	*to clean*
reducir	*to reduce*
apagar	*to turn off, extinguish*
parar	*to stop (person, vehicle)*
responsable	*responsible*

práctico/a	*practical, useful*
la organización	*organisation*
público/a	*public*
en contra	*against*
a favor	*in favour*
en cambio	*on the other hand, whereas*

Higher

conservar	*to conserve, preserve*
puro/a	*pure, clean*
fundar	*to set up, establish*
la iniciativa	*initiative*
la campaña	*campaign*
la manifestación	*protest*
la responsabilidad	*responsibility*

el público	*public*
la esperanza	*hope*
profundo/a	*deep, profound*
mundial	*world(wide)*
consciente	*conscious, aware*

Higher

efectivo/a	*effective*
la cuestión	*issue, matter, question*
el asunto	*matter, issue, affair*
la clave	*key, crucial thing*
el motivo	*reason, motive*

Social Issues

la sociedad	*society*
el partido	*(political) party*
votar	*to vote*
la gente	*people*
el tema	*issue, subject, matter*
el aspecto	*aspect*
la ventaja	*advantage, benefit*
la desventaja	*disadvantage*
el hambre	*hunger*
la falta	*lack, shortage*
el paro	*unemployment, strike*
la economía	*economy*
la industria	*industry*
deber	*to have to, must*
la violencia	*violence*
el delito	*crime*
la diferencia	*difference*
justo/a	*fair, just*
pobre	*poor, unfortunate, without money*
rico/a	*rich, wealthy*
comparar	*to compare*
importar	*to matter, be important*
mejorar	*to improve, make better*
dar	*to give*
el apoyo	*support, backing*
la actitud	*attitude*
la felicidad	*happiness*

Higher

la población	*population*
el gobierno	*government*
la política	*politics, policy*
el documento	*document*
el informe	*report*
elegir	*to choose, elect*
el límite	*limit*

la dificultad	*difficulty, obstacle*
la preocupación	*worry, concern*
enorme	*enormous, vast*
temer	*to fear*
luchar	*to fight, struggle*
la soledad	*loneliness, solitude*
la pobreza	*poverty*
económico/a	*cheap, inexpensive, economic*
el comercio	*commerce, trade, business*
el impuesto	*tax*
la paz	*peace*
el conflicto	*conflict*
violento/a	*violent*
amenazar	*to threaten*
cometer	*to commit (crime)*

Higher

investigar	*to investigate*
la investigación	*investigation*
la culpa	*blame, fault*
entregarse	*to turn yourself in*
el derecho	*right (legal)*
la ley	*law, rule*
la autoridad	*authority*
el estado	*state, condition*
la discriminación	*discrimination*
igual	*equal, same, alike*
la igualdad	*equality*
la libertad	*freedom*
afortunado/a	*fortunate, lucky*
dirigir	*to direct, manage*
desarrollar	*to develop*
el desarrollo	*development*
la solución	*solution, answer*
el beneficio	*benefit*

Revision Summary Test for Section Twelve

This is a big section, but this page gives you summary questions to test what you need to know.

- Yep, these questions are **hard** — they'll really help you see **how well you know your stuff**.
- Tackle the **revision summary test** below, or scan the QR code to do it **online**.
  Use the CGP RevisionHub to **track your progress** and see **which areas need more work**.
- You can find **sample answers** here: www.cgpbooks.co.uk/MadridExtras

Environmental Problems ☑

1) 'In my city there are many factories. The air doesn't seem clean, the sky is never clear and there is always a lot of noise.' Translate this into Spanish.

2) Describe un problema con el medioambiente en tu región que te preocupa.

3) In Spanish, write about one thing that people do that harms the environment.

H 4) Translate these sentences into English: 'Las obras en los alrededores de mi barrio emiten muchos gases y mucho humo que contaminan el aire. También producen demasiado ruido.'

Environmental Impacts ☑

5) In Spanish, describe the impact of an environmental problem that concerns you.

6) Write down the Spanish for... :
   a) fire   b) smell   c) dry   d) torn   e) proof   f) figure   g) scientist

7) Translate this into Spanish: 'One of the main causes of climate change is that energy use is increasing.'

Higher 8) Lin says: 'Si negamos los efectos del cambio climático, tendrán un impacto aun más enorme. Habrá un aumento del nivel del mar y como consecuencia mucha tierra desaparecerá.' Translate what he says.

9) En tu opinión, ¿qué pasará con el medioambiente en el futuro?

Protecting the Environment ☑

10) List the 10 verbs (plus 2 for Higher tier) related to protecting the environment from this section.

11) What are two things you would like to do to help the environment? Write your answer in Spanish.

12) Translate this sentence into English: 'Apoyo a una organización pública que salva animales en peligro.'

13) Write about something you've done in the past to protect the environment.

H 14) Translate this into English: 'La esperanza es la clave de la iniciativa que dirijo. Quiero que la gente sea consciente de su responsabilidad por el planeta de una manera positiva porque es más efectivo.'

Social Issues ☑

15) List the 5 nouns (plus 4 for Higher tier) for the social issues covered in this section.

16) In Spanish, describe a social problem in your area and how you think it could be improved.

17) 'It's important to vote for parties that improve aspects of society that matter to you.' Translate this sentence into Spanish.

18) Write down the English for the following words:
    a) la ventaja   b) la desventaja   c) la economía   d) rico/a   e) la actitud   f) la felicidad

19) In Spanish, write about something you've done recently to help your community.

20) Raúl says: 'El paro y la falta de oportunidades laborales son temas graves. Tenemos que dar más dinero a varias industrias para crear más empleos.' Translate what he says into English.

Higher 21) ¿Cuál es el problema social del mundo que más te importa? ¿Por qué?

22) 'It isn't fair that so many people have to struggle to be equal to others. Equality and freedom of expression are rights that every person should have.' Translate this sentence into Spanish.

Nouns

Nouns are the words for people and objects — they're like the building blocks of a language.

Every Spanish noun is masculine or feminine...

1) Whether a word is <u>masculine</u>, <u>feminine</u> or <u>plural</u> affects lots of things.

When you learn a new noun, learn its gender too.

2) <u>Articles</u> (words for '<u>the</u>' and '<u>a</u>') change depending on the noun's gender, and so do any <u>adjectives</u> which describe it.

el árbol alto (m)   *the tall tree*
la casa alta (f)   *the tall house*

3) If you see a word with '<u>el</u>' or '<u>un</u>' before it, it's usually <u>masculine</u>. '<u>La</u>' or '<u>una</u>' in front of a word means it's <u>feminine</u>.

4) If you don't have these clues, you can look at a <u>word's ending</u> to help you guess.

Languages, days of the week, months, rivers, seas and mountains are also masculine in Spanish.

Most masculine nouns end in:
-o -l -n -r -s -ta -aje -ma -pa

Most feminine nouns end in:
-a -ción -sión -tad -tud -dad -umbre

5) You can't tell whether a noun ending in '<u>e</u>', '<u>ista</u>' or '<u>z</u>' is masculine or feminine — you just have to learn them.

el coche   *the car*   la gente   *the people*

...and some nouns can be both

1) Words for people often have a <u>masculine</u> and a <u>feminine</u> form. If the masculine noun ends in 'o', <u>drop the 'o'</u> and <u>add 'a'</u> to make it feminine.

Don't forget to change the article too.

el ingeniero → *la ingeniera (engineer)*

2) Nouns with other endings follow a different pattern. Here are a few examples:

Masc. ending	To make it feminine...	Example
-ante, -ente, -ista	no change	el turista *tourist (male)* → la turista *tourist (female)*
-or	add -a	el cuidador *carer (male)* → la cuidadora *carer (female)*

Making nouns plural

1) Some nouns in Spanish end in a <u>vowel</u>. To make them <u>plural</u>, just add '<u>s</u>' — 'una cam<u>a</u>' (*one bed*) becomes 'dos cam<u>as</u>' (*two beds*).

2) There are some <u>exceptions</u> to this rule though:

Noun ending	To make it plural...	Example
consonant except 'z'	add 'es'	una flor (*one flower*) → dos flores (*two flowers*)
'z'	drop the 'z' and add 'ces'	un disfraz (*one costume*) → dos disfraces (*two costumes*)
'(i)ón'	drop the accent and add 'es'	un avión (*one plane*) → dos aviones (*two planes*)

Grammar Questions

Write 'el' or 'la' for each of these words. Then write each one in the plural form with 'los' or 'las'.

1. zapato
2. camisa
3. tradición
4. color
5. vez
6. mitad
7. monte
8. dificultad
9. ciudadano
10. huelga
11. impresión
12. siglo

There are some exceptions to the gender rules...

Some nouns that end in 'a' are masculine, e.g. 'el día' (day), and some nouns that end in 'o' are feminine, e.g. 'la foto' (photo). You'll just have to learn these and all the other slippery exceptions off by heart.

Forming Nouns

This page is all about forming nouns from adjectives and using infinitive verbs as nouns.

You can turn some adjectives into nouns

See p.165 for more on adjectives and their uses.

1) In English, adding the suffix '-ity' to an adjective can turn it into a noun. For example, 'sec<u>u</u>re' becomes 'secu<u>rity</u>'.

2) You can form <u>nouns</u> from some <u>adjectives</u> in Spanish by adding the suffix '<u>-idad</u>'. For adjectives ending in a <u>vowel</u>, you often <u>remove the ending</u> and <u>add</u> '<u>-idad</u>'. If the adjective ends in a <u>consonant</u>, just add '<u>-idad</u>'.

| oportuno → oportun- → la oportun**idad** | | real → real- → la real**idad** |
| *opportune* | *opportunity* | real | *reality* |

3) You can also form the Spanish words for languages by <u>adding an article</u> to the <u>masculine form</u> of <u>nationality adjectives</u>.

español   *Spanish (person, object)*   **el** español   *Spanish (language)*

4) Adding an article also turns <u>nationality adjectives</u> into <u>nationality nouns</u>.

un inglés   *an English person*   **los** ingleses   *the English (people)*

When a masculine singular nationality has an accent on its final syllable, it loses the accent in the feminine or plural form. See p.165 for more.

Verbs can be used as nouns too

1) In Spanish, the <u>infinitive</u> form of a verb can be used as a <u>noun</u>. It's usually equivalent to the '<u>-ing</u>' form in English.

The infinitive is the form of the verb you'd find in a dictionary, e.g. 'hablar' (to speak, talk).

Andar es bueno para la salud.   *Walking is good for your health.*
Me encanta **bailar** por la tarde.   *I love dancing in the evening.*

2) When you use an <u>infinitive</u> as a noun, it's always <u>masculine</u> and usually <u>singular</u>. You'll need to make sure any <u>adjectives</u> you use <u>agree</u>.

Repasar es necesario para aprobar la prueba.   *Revising is necessary in order to pass the test.*

Add '-ito/a' to nouns to say 'little'

You can <u>take off</u> the final '<u>o</u>' or '<u>a</u>' from some nouns and <u>add</u> '<u>-ito/a</u>' instead to make something seem <u>smaller</u> or <u>show affection</u>.

Me encanta este **pueblito**.
I love this little town.

Grammar Questions

Translate the following sentences into **Spanish**.
1. I like eating Mexican food.
2. French is a fun language.
3. Smoking is prohibited.
4. The Spanish are friendly.
5. Being famous is complicated.
6. Renting a car is expensive.

Remember — nouns can be formed in several different ways...

Nouns crop up all over the place, so make sure you can recognise all the different ways they are formed. Plus, don't forget that you can make some nouns seem smaller by replacing the final 'o' or 'a' with '-ito/a'.

Articles

Articles are words like 'a' and 'the'. Where there's a Spanish noun, there's usually an article introducing it, so it's important you know how and when to use them correctly.

El, la, los, las — the

1) 'El', 'la', 'los' and 'las' are definite articles. They all mean 'the'.

2) The definite article changes depending on the gender of the noun, and whether it's singular or plural.

	Masculine	Feminine
Singular	el	la
Plural	los	las

3) Use 'el' before feminine nouns that start with a stressed 'a'.

> El agua está fría.   *The water is cold.*

4) When the masculine definite article 'el' is placed after the prepositions 'a' and 'de', it becomes 'al' and 'del'.

> Al final del día...   *At the end of the day...*

For more on prepositions, see p.158.

5) Sometimes you need a definite article in Spanish where you wouldn't use one in English:

a) With nouns used in a general sense: No me gusta el café.   *I don't like coffee.*
b) In front of the days of the week and times: los lunes a las seis   *Mondays at six o'clock*
c) In front of weights and measurements: dos euros el kilo   *two euros a kilo*
d) When you use a person's title: ¿Cómo está el señor Gómez?   *How is Mr Gómez?*

6) There's a neuter article 'lo' for things that aren't masculine or feminine.

> lo mejor / peor es que...   *the best / worst thing is that...*

When you use 'lo' in front of an adjective, the adjective has to be in the masculine form — see p.165.

Un, una, unos, unas — 'a' and 'some'

1) 'Un' and 'una' are indefinite articles. They both mean 'a'.

2) 'Un' is used for masculine words and 'una' is used for feminine words.

> un gato   *a cat*
> una casa   *a house*

3) When you make 'un' or 'una' plural, they become 'unos' and 'unas' — they mean 'some' or 'a few'.

> unos gatos   *some cats*
> unas casas   *some houses*

4) Watch out, though — 'a' is left out...

a) ...after the verb 'ser' when talking about someone's occupation or nationality: Soy estudiante.   *I'm a student.*

b) ...after a negative verb: No tengo perro.   *I haven't got a dog.*

Grammar Questions

Translate these sentences into **Spanish**.

1. I ate a chicken sandwich.
2. The water runs fast.
3. She is an English teacher.
4. He wants some chips.
5. I play basketball on Thursdays.
6. It took a few hours.

Check you know when to use each of the articles on this page...

You'll need to use an article to introduce most nouns in Spanish. Just remember to check the noun's gender and whether it's singular or plural — this will help you decide which form of the article you need to use.

Subject Pronouns

Subject pronouns are handy little words that save you from needing to repeat nouns all the time.

Yo, tú, él, ella — I, you, he, she

1) <u>Pronouns</u> are words that <u>replace nouns</u> — like '<u>you</u>' or '<u>them</u>'. You use them to <u>avoid repeating nouns</u>.

2) <u>Subject pronouns</u> replace the subject of a sentence. The <u>subject</u> is the noun <u>doing the action</u>.

> Khadija went to the beach and she sat on the sand. ← In English, the pronoun 'she' replaces Khadija's name. 'She' is a subject pronoun because it replaces the subject of the sentence — Khadija.

3) You <u>don't normally</u> include <u>subject pronouns</u> in Spanish sentences — but you <u>still</u> need to know them.

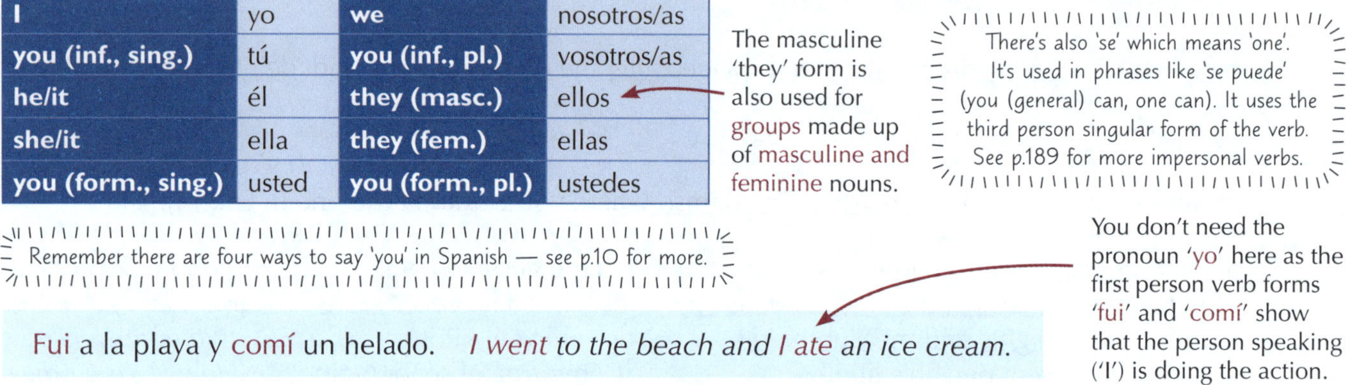

I	yo	we	nosotros/as
you (inf., sing.)	tú	**you (inf., pl.)**	vosotros/as
he/it	él	**they (masc.)**	ellos
she/it	ella	**they (fem.)**	ellas
you (form., sing.)	usted	**you (form., pl.)**	ustedes

The masculine 'they' form is also used for groups made up of masculine and feminine nouns.

There's also 'se' which means 'one'. It's used in phrases like 'se puede' (you (general) can, one can). It uses the third person singular form of the verb. See p.189 for more impersonal verbs.

Remember there are four ways to say 'you' in Spanish — see p.10 for more.

You don't need the pronoun 'yo' here as the first person verb forms 'fui' and 'comí' show that the person speaking ('I') is doing the action.

> Fui a la playa y comí un helado. *I went to the beach and I ate an ice cream.*

4) You can use the indefinite pronoun '<u>alguien</u>' (*someone*) to talk about an <u>unidentified person</u>.

> Alguien cerró la puerta.
> *Someone closed the door.*

> ¿Alguien dijo algo?
> *Did someone say something?*

You can use subject pronouns for emphasis

Although you <u>don't usually</u> need <u>subject pronouns</u> in Spanish, they help <u>emphasise</u> exactly <u>who</u> does what:

> ¿Qué queréis hacer el fin de semana que viene?   *What would you (inf., pl.) like to do next weekend?*

> Yo quiero ir de compras, pero él quiere ir al cine.
> *I want to go shopping, but **he** wants to go to the cinema.*

You include the pronouns here to emphasise who wants what. They're used in Spanish in cases when extra stress is put on pronouns in English.

> ¿Quieren visitar el museo?   *Do they / you (form., pl.) want to visit the museum?*
> Yo sí, pero ella no.   *I do, but **she** doesn't.*

Remember that if you're using 'ustedes', you need the 'they' form of the verb.

Grammar Questions

Write down the Spanish subject pronoun you'd use to replace each of these subjects.

1. Mosi (m) y Jorge (m)
2. el señor Pérez y usted
3. Alberto (m) y Tania (f)
4. Tidam (m) y tú (m)
5. tu tío (m)
6. Biyu (f) y yo (f)
7. Miranda (f)
8. Nico (m)

You don't usually need subject pronouns in Spanish...

If you want to know the subject of a sentence in Spanish, take a look at the verb — it'll look different depending on who it's talking about. Make sure you only use subject pronouns for clarity or emphasis.

Object Pronouns

Now you've got to grips with subject pronouns, it's time to learn about object pronouns...

Me, te, los, las — me, you, them

1) <u>Object pronouns</u> replace the <u>object</u> of a sentence. This is the thing <u>having the action done to it</u>.
2) Use <u>direct object pronouns</u> when you're talking about <u>who</u> or <u>what</u> an action is <u>done to</u>.

me	me
you (inf., sing.)	te
him/it/you (form., sing)	lo
her/it/you (form., sing)	la
them (m/f)/you (form., pl.)	los/las

us	nos
you (inf., pl.)	os

The pronoun usually goes before the verb and it needs to agree with the noun it replaces.

Cruz lava el coche. Cruz lo lava.
Cruz washes the car. Cruz washes it.

Me, te, les — to me, to you, to them

1) If you want to talk about doing something '<u>to</u>' or '<u>for</u>' <u>someone</u>, you need an <u>indirect object pronoun</u>.

El niño da la flor a su abuela. → El niño le da la flor.
The boy gives the flower to his grandmother. → *The boy gives the flower to her.*

2) These pronouns are the same ones you use with the verb '<u>gustar</u>' when you say you <u>like something</u>. This is because 'me gusta el chocolate' literally means 'chocolate is pleasing <u>to me</u>'.

me	me
you (inf., sing.)	te
him/her/it/you (form., sing.)	le
them/you (form., pl.)	les

us	nos
you (inf., pl.)	os

Getting the order right

1) Object pronouns <u>normally</u> come <u>before the verb</u>, but they can go <u>before</u> or <u>after</u> the verb if it's an <u>infinitive</u> (p.175) or a <u>present participle</u> (p.186).

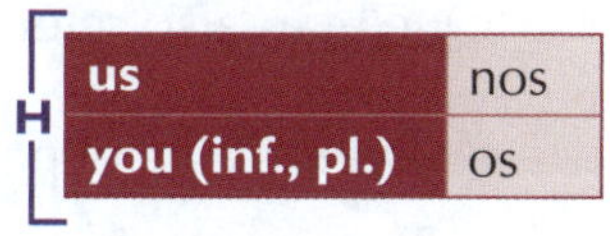

Often you need to add an accent to keep the right pronunciation.

Lo quiero ver. **OR** Quiero verlo.
I want to see it.

Le estamos hablando. **OR** Estamos hablándole.
We're talking to him.

2) With <u>commands</u>, the pronoun is <u>tacked on to the end</u>.

Escríbeme, por favor. *Write to me, please.*

Grammar Questions

Translate these sentences into **Spanish**, replacing the words in bold with the correct pronouns.

1. She breaks **the window**.
2. I drink **the water**.
3. He bought **her** a skirt.
4. I will send **them** an email.
5. I gave **you (inf., pl.)** the cat.
6. He told **us** the secret.

Pronouns are tricky — but if you can use them, you'll be flying...

Make sure you know the difference between direct and indirect object pronouns — use object pronouns for the thing having the action done to it, and use indirect object pronouns to say 'to' or 'for' someone.

More Pronouns

Pronouns can be a bit confusing, but they're useful for adding extra detail and asking questions.

Algo, alguno, ninguno — something, one, none

> 'Algo', 'alguno' and 'ninguno' are indefinite pronouns.

1) You can use the pronoun 'algo' to talk about an unidentified object.

> ¿Dijiste algo a alguien?   *Did you (inf., sing.) say something to someone?*

'Alguien' ('someone') is another indefinite pronoun. See p.154 for more.

2) When you use 'alguno' to replace a singular noun, it can mean 'one' or 'any'. For plural nouns, it means 'some (of them)'. 'Ninguno' can mean 'none' or 'no one'.

> Vi a algunos.   *I saw some (of them).*
>
> Ninguno de ellos lo tiene.   *None of them has it.*

3) For feminine nouns, you need 'alguna(s)' or 'ninguna(s)'.

Que — that, who

1) 'Que' can mean 'that' or 'who' — it's a relative pronoun. You can use it to start a relative clause, which is a way of adding detail to a sentence.

2) 'Que' can be used to refer to the subject of a clause — the person or thing doing the action:

> Allí está el hombre que vive en nuestra calle.   *There's the man who lives on our street.*

Higher

3) 'Que' can also refer to the object of a clause — the person or thing something is done to:

> ¿Dónde está el pan que compré ayer?   *Where's the bread that I bought yesterday?*

4) After prepositions, like 'con', 'a' and 'de', use 'el / la que' or 'el / la cual' for 'that / which'. When talking about plural nouns, you need to use 'los / las que' or 'los / las cuales' instead.

> el mercado del cual compro flores
> *the market from which I buy flowers*
>
> los cafés a los que fui ayer
> *the cafés that I went to yesterday*

5) If you're talking about a general idea instead of a specific subject, you need 'lo que'.

> Van a venir, lo que es maravilloso.   *They're going to come, which is wonderful.*

6) You can also use 'cuando' (*when*) and 'donde' (*where*) as relative pronouns.

> Suelo ir a la playa cuando hace calor.
> *I usually go to the beach when it's hot.*
>
> la tienda donde compré las uvas
> *the shop where I bought the grapes*

Some pronouns change after certain prepositions

> Watch out — 'mí' needs an accent, but 'ti' doesn't.

Higher

1) The words for 'me' and 'you' (inf., sing.) become 'mí' and 'ti' after prepositions like 'a' (to), 'para' (for), and 'sobre' / 'de' (about).

me	mí	us	nosotros/as
you (inf., sing.)	ti	you (inf., pl.)	vosotros/as
him/her	él/ella	them (m/f)	ellos/as
you (form., sing.)	usted	you (form., pl.)	ustedes

> Lo hice para ti.   *I made it for you (inf., sing.).*

2) You can use these pronouns after the preposition 'a' to put extra emphasis on who you're talking about.

> Me dio la pizza a mí.   *He gave the pizza **to me**.*

3) You can't say 'con mí' or 'con ti' in Spanish — you need 'conmigo' and 'contigo' instead.

> Está conmigo.   *He's with me.*

Section Thirteen — Nouns, Articles and Linking Words

Using pronouns to ask questions

Pronouns for asking questions are called 'interrogative pronouns'.

1) Normally, you can use '¿Qué...' to ask a question that starts with 'What...' in English.

> ¿Qué te gustaría hacer?   *What would you (inf., sing.) like to do?*

2) Use '¿Cuál(es)...' when you'd use 'Which...' or 'Which one(s)...' in English. But remember — sometimes you need '¿Cuál...' when you'd actually use 'What...' in English — see p.8.

> ¿Cuál es mejor?   *Which (one) is better?*
>
> ¿Cuál es su apellido?   *What is his surname?*

3) '¿Cuánto(s)/a(s)...' means 'How much...' or 'How many...'.

> ¿Cuánto cuesta la paella?   *How much does the paella cost?*

4) '¿Quién...' means 'Who...'. It changes to '¿Quiénes...' when you're referring to more than one person.

> ¿Quién es?   *Who is it?*

Higher: You often use '¿Quién(es)...' with prepositions.

> ¿Con quién?   *With whom?*

Esto, eso — this, that

If you don't know the gender of the noun you're replacing, or you want to talk about something more generally, you can use demonstrative pronouns like 'esto' and 'eso'.

'Esto' and 'eso' are invariable, which means they don't change to agree with a noun's gender.

> No me gusta esto.   *I don't like this.*
>
> ¿Qué es eso?   *What's that?*

H Use 'aquello' instead of 'eso' when the object is farther away.

> ¿Qué es aquello?   *What's that (thing)?*

El mío, el tuyo — mine, yours

1) 'El mío', 'el tuyo', etc. are possessive pronouns. You use them to say 'mine' or 'yours'.

2) Possessive pronouns agree in gender and number with the noun they're replacing.

Higher:

Possessive pronoun	Masc. sing.	Fem. sing.	Masc. pl.	Fem. pl.
mine	el mío	la mía	los míos	las mías
yours (inf., sing.)	el tuyo	la tuya	los tuyos	las tuyas
his/hers/its/yours (form., sing.)	el suyo	la suya	los suyos	las suyas
ours	el nuestro	la nuestra	los nuestros	las nuestras
yours (inf., pl.)	el vuestro	la vuestra	los vuestros	las vuestras
theirs/yours (form., pl.)	el suyo	la suya	los suyos	las suyas

Kwesi really didn't want to admit that the bread was his...

> ¿Es su casa?   *Is it their house?*
> No, la suya es más alta.   *No, theirs is taller.*
>
> ¿Es tu pan?   *Is it your (inf., sing.) bread?*
> No, el mío está allí.   *No, mine is there.*

Grammar Questions

Translate these sentences into **English**.

1. ¿Cuál es tu color favorito?
2. Leeré el libro que me dio.
3. ¿Has comido algo?
4. Eso no es verdad.
5. La tuya está aquí. **H**
6. Cociné para ti.
7. Irían contigo.
8. Querré aquello. **H**

These pages, which are very useful, will help you greatly...

It's well worth being able to use these pronouns. Getting to grips with them all can be tricky, but don't panic — just keep going over these pages until you feel confident about how and when to use them.

Prepositions

Prepositions are very useful words that you can use to talk about direction, time or location.

Use these words to say where something is

Don't forget to use 'estar' (see p.178) to say where something is.

al lado de	*to the side of*	contra	*against, opposite*	dentro de	*inside of*
delante de	*in front of*	encima de	*on top of*	fuera de	*outside of*
entre	*between, among*	desde	*from, since*	hacia	*toward(s)*

Higher — dentro de, fuera de, hacia

A — to, at

To say '<u>to</u>' in Spanish, you <u>normally</u> say '<u>a</u>'. But you can sometimes also use '<u>a</u>' to mean '<u>at</u>'.

Va **a** Hull.   *She's going to Hull.*

Vine **a** la fiesta.   *I came to the party.*

a las seis   *at six o'clock*

En — in, on

You can <u>normally</u> use '<u>en</u>' when you want to say '<u>in</u>'. You can also use '<u>en</u>' to say '<u>on</u>'.

En Leeds...   *In Leeds...*

Lo vi **en** la tele.   *I saw it on TV.*

El lunes...   *On Monday...*

You don't need 'on' for days of the week.

De — of, from

'<u>De</u>' usually means '<u>of</u>' or '<u>from</u>'. You can also use '<u>de</u>' to say what something's <u>made of</u> or <u>who</u> something <u>belongs to</u>.

un vaso **de** agua *a glass of water*

Es **de** oro. *It's made of gold.*

la casa **de** Xavi *Xavi's house*

Hasta — up to, as far as, until

You can use '<u>hasta</u>' to say '<u>up to</u>' or '<u>as far as</u>'. It can also mean '<u>until</u>'.

Solo va **hasta** Kent. *It only goes as far as Kent.*

Está abierto **hasta** las dos. *It's open until two o'clock.*

Sobre — on top of, over, about

For '<u>on top of</u>', use '<u>sobre</u>'. You can also use '<u>sobre</u>' when you want to say '<u>over</u>' or '<u>about</u>'.

Está **sobre** el armario. *It's on top of the wardrobe.*

Vuela **sobre** el mar. *It flies over the sea.*

Discuten **sobre** sus planes. *They argue about their plans.*

Grammar Questions

Use what you know about prepositions to translate these sentences into **Spanish**.

1. We talked about the weather.
2. The train goes as far as Spain.
3. I saw it on the wall.
4. They're from Valencia.
5. The dog ran towards me. (H)
6. I live outside of the city. (H)

Location prepositions — you can often make them from adverbs...

Adding 'de' to certain adverbs helps you make useful location prepositions. For example, you can take 'cerca' (*close, near, nearby*) and make it 'cerca de' (*close to, near to*). There's also 'detrás de' (*behind*).

Prepositions with Verbs and Nouns

Prepositions aren't just for describing where something is — you'll often see them before an infinitive or noun and after certain verbs. When they follow a verb, they can change its meaning.

Some prepositions are followed by an infinitive...

1) 'Para' followed by an infinitive means 'to' or 'in order to'.

> Veo la tele para descansar.   *I watch TV to relax.*

2) The preposition 'sin' means 'without'. Use it with an infinitive when you want to say 'without -ing'.

> Salió sin decir una palabra más.   *He left without saying another word.*

3) You can use 'antes de' + infinitive to say 'before -ing'.

> Compré la entrada antes de llegar al cine.   *I bought the ticket before arriving at the cinema.*

4) If you want to say 'after -ing', use 'después de' + infinitive.

> Después de terminar el examen, iré a una fiesta.   *After finishing the exam, I will go to a party.*

...and some are followed by a noun

In some verb phrases, the preposition is followed by a noun.

> Voy de vacaciones en julio.   *I'm going on holiday in July.*

> Los trabajadores están en huelga.   *The workers are on strike.*

Verb phrase	Meaning
ir de vacaciones	to go on holiday
estar de acuerdo	to be in agreement
preocuparse por (+ noun)	to worry about
estar en huelga	to be on strike
huele a (+ noun)	it smells of...

Some verbs are followed by a preposition

1) Sometimes you need to use a preposition after the verb. The preposition can change the verb's meaning:

Verb	Verb + preposition	Example sentence
llegar (*to arrive*)	llegar a (*to manage to, succeed in*)	Llegué a encontrarlo. (*I managed to find it.*)
dejar (*to let, leave*)	dejar de (*to stop -ing*)	He dejado de leerlos. (*I've stopped reading them.*)
volver (*to go back, return*)	volver a (*to do again*)	Volví a mirarlo. (*I looked at it again.*)
tratar (*to treat, deal with*)	tratar de (*to try to*)	Trataré de hacerlo rápido. (*I'll try to do it quickly.*)

2) The verb that comes after the preposition is always an infinitive.

Grammar Questions

Translate these sentences into **English**.

1. Hablé sin pensar.
2. Vuelven a hacer la tarea.
3. Ha dejado de fumar.
4. Juego para ganar.
5. Cerraré la puerta antes de salir.
6. Trato de beber más agua.

You'll just have to learn which verbs are followed by a preposition...

You might find it helpful to learn these verb phrases with some specific examples — they'll be easier to remember if you've got a sentence or two in mind. Now, get ready for some more prepositions...

'Por', 'Para' and the Personal 'a'

The prepositions 'por' and 'para' both mean 'for', but you use them in different situations.

Use 'por' to...

1) ...say 'around'.   El museo está **por** aquí.   *The museum is around here.*

2) ...say 'because of'.   No salí **por** el mal tiempo.   *I didn't go out because of the bad weather.*

3) ...say 'by'.   Fue pintada **por** un artista famoso.   *It was painted by a famous artist.*

4) ...say 'for' or 'on behalf of'.   Vivió allí **por** un año.   *He lived there for a year.*

5) ...say 'through'.   Entré **por** la puerta.   *I came through the door.*

You usually use 'por' to talk about the past, but sometimes you need it for the future, e.g. 'Estaré en Galicia por dos años'.

Use 'para' instead...

Using 'para' with an infinitive helps you say 'in order to' (see p.159).

1) ...in future time phrases like 'for X number of days' or 'for / by X time'.   Quiero el coche **para** un día.   *I want the car for one day.*

2) ...when you're talking about destinations.   el tren **para** Bilbao   *the train for Bilbao*

3) ...to say who something is for.   El artista la pintó **para** su cliente.   *The artist painted it for his client.*

H 4) ...to give your opinion.   **Para** mí, es importante.   *For me, it's important.*

The personal 'a'

You need an extra 'a' before the word for any human being or pet after every single verb.

Estoy buscando **a** Ozan.
I'm looking for Ozan.

BUT

Estoy buscando un libro.
I'm looking for a book.

You don't usually use the personal 'a' after 'tener' or 'ser'.

Grammar Questions

Translate these sentences into **English**.

1. Ahora llega el tren para París.
2. Lo haré para mañana.
3. La salida está por aquí.
4. Yo andaba por el campo.
H 5. Lo guardaban para sus hijos.
H 6. Salían raramente por el calor.

Decide whether you need a personal 'a' in each of these sentences.

7. Vieron ___ la película ayer.
8. Conocía ___ mucha gente.
9. Sacará ___ la basura.
10. Visito ___ mi abuelo.
H 11. Iban a ver ___ las mascotas.
H 12. Eso mata ___ las plantas.

Don't confuse the personal 'a' with the preposition 'a'...

You use the preposition 'a' in sentences with an indirect object, e.g. 'Doy la comida al perro' (I give the food to the dog). When you use the personal 'a', the human being or pet you're talking about is a direct object.

Conjunctions

Conjunctions help you link your ideas together to make longer, more complex sentences.

Y — and

1) '<u>Y</u>' means '<u>and</u>' — you use it just like you would in English.

> Me gusta jugar al fútbol. **AND** Me gusta jugar al rugby. **=** Me gusta jugar al fútbol y al rugby.
> *I like playing football.* *I like playing rugby.* *I like playing football and rugby.*

2) '<u>Y</u>' changes to '<u>e</u>' <u>before</u> a word starting with '<u>i</u>' or '<u>hi</u>'.

> Hablo español e inglés. *I speak Spanish and English.*

O — or

1) '<u>O</u>' means '<u>or</u>'.

> Juego al fútbol los sábados. **OR** Juego al rugby los sábados. **=** Juego al fútbol o al rugby los sábados.
> *I play football on Saturdays.* *I play rugby on Saturdays.* *I play football or rugby on Saturdays.*

2) When '<u>o</u>' comes just <u>before</u> a word starting with '<u>o</u>' or '<u>ho</u>', it changes to '<u>u</u>'.

> Cuesta siete u ocho euros. *It costs seven or eight euros.*

Pero — but

1) '<u>Pero</u>' means '<u>but</u>'.

> Me gusta el fútbol. **BUT** No me gusta el rugby. **=** Me gusta el fútbol, pero no me gusta el rugby.
> *I like football.* *I don't like rugby.* *I like football, but I don't like rugby.*

2) When '<u>but</u>' means '<u>but rather</u>', it becomes '<u>sino</u>'.

> No es español, sino francés. *He isn't Spanish, but (rather) French.*

Porque — because

> There's more about 'porque' and opinions on p.12.

'<u>Porque</u>' means '<u>because</u>'. It helps you <u>give opinions</u>:

> Me gusta esta comida porque está rica. *I like this food because it's tasty.*

Other conjunctions you need to know

> You usually use 'ni' with a negative verb to say 'neither...nor...'. See p.188 for more on negatives.

que	*that*	en cambio	*on the other hand, whereas*	como	*as*
si	*if*	aunque	*although, even though*	(no) ni... ni...	*nor, neither ... nor*
sin embargo	*however*	mientras	*while, whilst*	para que	*so that, in order that*

Grammar Questions

Translate these sentences into **Spanish**, deciding which conjunctions you need to use.

1. Geography is fun, but it's hard.
2. I like history because it's easy.
3. As I'm ill, I'll stay at home.
4. If it's hot, I go to the beach.
5. I speak French and Italian.
6. Do you prefer blue or green?

You don't want to sound like a robot, so start using conjunctions...

Conjunctions are really handy for giving opinions and reasons, which will help you impress the examiner.

Nouns, Articles & Linking Words — Grammar List

There's a lot to take in from this grammar section — check out these handy pages for some of the essentials.

Nouns

Common endings for masculine nouns are:
-o, -l, -n, -r, -s, -ta, -aje

Common endings for feminine nouns are:
-a, -ción, -sión, -tad, -tud, -dad, -umbre

For nouns ending in 'e' or 'ista', see p.151.

Some masculine nouns can be made feminine:

el médic**o** → **la** médic**a**	*doctor (m/f)*
el escrit**or** → la escrit**ora**	*writer (m/f)*
un ingl**és** → una ingl**esa**	*English person (m/f)*
el periodista → **la** periodista	*journalist (m/f)*
el cantante → **la** cantante	*singer (m/f)*
el cliente → **la** cliente	*client, customer (m/f)*

There are different ways to make singular nouns plural:

el gato → **los** gatos	*cat(s)*
la amistad → **las** amistad**es**	*friendship(s)*
la actri**z** → **las** actri**ces**	*actor(s) (f)*
la estac**ión** → **las** estac**iones**	*station(s)*
el coraz**ón** → **los** coraz**ones**	*heart(s)*

Some nouns can be formed from adjectives:

activo → la activ**idad**	*activity*
español → **el** español	*Spanish (language)*

You can also use the infinitive of a verb as a noun:
Reciclar es importante. — *Recycling is important.*

Add -ito/a to make a noun seem smaller:
la cosa → la cos**ita** — *thing → little thing*

Articles

Articles (words like 'the' and 'a') introduce nouns. They change depending on the noun's gender and whether it's singular or plural.

Definite articles:

el	*the (m, sing.)*
la	*the (f, sing.)*
los	*the (m, pl.)*
las	*the (f, pl.)*

Indefinite articles:

un	*a, an (m, sing.)*
una	*a, an (f, sing.)*
unos	*some (m, pl.)*
unas	*some (f, pl.)*

The masculine singular article 'el' changes when combined with the prepositions 'a' or 'de':
a + el → al
de + el → del

The article 'lo' can be used to talk about general things, e.g. 'lo bueno' (*the good thing*).

Subject Pronouns

Subject pronouns replace the subject of the sentence.

yo	*I*
tú	*you (inf., sing.)*
él	*he, it (m)*
ella	*she, it (f)*
usted	*you (form., sing.)*
nosotros/as	*we*
vosotros/as	*you (inf., pl.)*
ellos	*they (m)*
ellas	*they (f)*
ustedes	*you (form., pl.)*

Some subject pronouns change after certain prepositions.
con + mí → conmigo — *with me*
con + ti → contigo — *with you (inf., sing.)*

Emphatic Pronouns

Use subject pronouns after the preposition 'a' for emphasis.

(a) mí	*(to) me*
(a) ti	*(to) you (inf., sing.)*
(a) él / ella	*(to) him / her*
(a) usted / ustedes	*(to) you (form., sing./pl.)*
(a) nosotros/as	*(to) us*
(a) vosotros/as	*(to) you (inf., pl.)*
(a) ellos / ellas	*(to) them (m/f)*

Higher

Direct Object Pronouns

Direct object pronouns replace the person or thing the action is being done to.

me	*me*
te	*you (inf., sing.)*
lo	*him, it (m), you (form., sing.)*
la	*her, it (f), you (form., sing.)*
los	*them, you (form., pl.) (m)*
las	*them, you (form., pl.) (f)*
nos	*us*
os	*you (inf., pl.)*

Indirect Object Pronouns

Indirect object pronouns replace the person or thing being indirectly affected by the action.

me	*(to) me*
te	*(to) you (inf., sing.)*
le	*(to) him, her, it, you (form., sing.)*
les	*(to) them, you (form., pl.)*
nos	*(to) us*
os	*(to) you (inf., pl.)*

Indefinite Pronouns

Indefinite pronouns refer to nouns that are general and unspecific.

alguien	*someone*
algo	*something*
alguno	*one*
algunos	*some (of them)*
ninguno	*no one, none*
todo	*everything, all of it*
los/las demás	*the others (m/f)*

Demonstrative Pronouns

These demonstrative pronouns replace things in a sentence that are unspecific. They don't have to agree in gender or number.

esto	*this*
eso	*that*
aquello	*that (thing)*

Prepositions with Verbs and Nouns

Some prepositions are followed by an infinitive:

para (+ infinitive)	*in order to (+ verb)*
sin (+ infinitive)	*without (+ -ing)*
antes de (+ infinitive)	*before (+ -ing)*
después de (+ infinitive)	*after (+ -ing)*

Some verb phrases use a preposition + noun:

ir de vacaciones	*to go on holiday*
estar de acuerdo	*to be in agreement*
preocuparse por	*to worry about*
estar en huelga	*to be on strike*
huele a (+ noun)	*it smells of...*

The meaning of some verbs changes when they're followed by a preposition:

E.g. llegar → llegar a
to arrive → *to manage to, succeed in*

Prepositions

a	*to, at*	al lado de	*to the side of*
al	*to the (m, sing.)*	delante de	*in front of*
en	*in, on*	entre	*between, among*
de	*of, from*	contra	*against, opposite*
del	*of the (m, sing.)*	debajo de	*underneath, below*
hasta	*up to, as far as, until*	encima de	*on top of*
sobre	*on top of, over, about*	desde	*from, since*
		durante	*during*
		según	*according to*
con	*with*	sin	*without*
por	*around, because of, by, for, through*	dentro de	*inside of*
		fuera de	*outside of*
para	*for*	hacia	*toward(s)*

Relative Pronouns

Relative pronouns introduce extra information to a sentence. 'Que' can mean 'who' (if you're referring to someone) or 'that' (if you're referring to something).

que — *who, that*

E.g. Es el vecino que cuidó a mi gato.
He's the neighbour who took care of my cat.

Higher

After prepositions, you use 'el/la que', 'los/las que', 'el/la cual' or 'los/las cuales' to say 'that / which'.

el/la que	los/las que	*that / which*
el/la cual	los/las cuales	

E.g Lo vi durante el evento al que asistí.
I saw it during the event that I attended.

If you're talking about a general idea, you need 'lo que'.

lo que — *what, that which*

E.g. La carta nunca llegó, lo que era una sorpresa.
The letter never arrived, which was a surprise.

You can use 'cuando' and 'donde' as relative pronouns.

cuando	*when*	donde	*where*

Possessive Pronouns

Possessive pronouns show what belongs to who.

Higher

el/la mío/a los/las míos/as	*mine*
el/la tuyo/a los/las tuyos/as	*yours (inf., sing.)*
el/la suyo/a los/las suyos/as	*his, hers, its,* *yours (form., sing./pl.), theirs*
el/la nuestro/a los/las nuestros/as	*ours*
el/la vuestro/a los/las vuestros/as	*yours (inf., pl.)*

Remember — the personal 'a' is different to the preposition 'a'. See p.160 for more.

Conjunctions

y	*and*
o	*or*
pero	*but*
porque	*because*
que	*that*
si	*if*
por eso	*so, therefore*
sin embargo	*however*
en cambio	*on the other hand*
aunque	*although, even though*
mientras	*while, whilst*
como	*as*
para que	*so that, in order that*
sino	*but (rather), except*
(no) ni...(ni)...	*nor, neither...nor*

(Higher: para que, sino, (no) ni...(ni)...)

Section Thirteen — Nouns, Articles and Linking Words

Revision Summary Test for Section Thirteen

Nice job getting through this chunky grammar section. Now have a go at some questions.

- These questions are **hard**, but they'll really help you see **how well you know your stuff**.
- Tackle the **revision summary test** below, or scan the QR code to do it **online**.
  You can **track your progress** online and see **which areas need more work**.
- There are **sample answers** for the test here: www.cgpbooks.co.uk/MadridExtras

Nouns and Articles ☑

1) Write either 'm' or 'f' to show whether each noun is masculine or feminine.
   a) azúcar   b) canción   c) pájaro   d) papel   e) playa   f) árbol   g) falda   h) clase ☐

2) Make these nouns feminine: a) el periodista   b) el médico   c) un alemán   d) el pintor ☐

3) Make each of these nouns plural — don't forget to include 'los' or 'las':
   a) examen   b) mes   c) sábado   d) enfermedad   e) estación   f) actriz   g) camisa ☐

4) Translate these sentences into Spanish: a) Reading is interesting.   b) Singing is really boring. ☐

5) Choose the correct article in bold to complete each of these sentences: a) **El** / **La** agua está limpia.
   b) **Los** / **Las** chicas juegan al fútbol.   c) Dame **un** / **una** bolígrafo, por favor. ☐

6) Fill in the gaps with 'a' or 'de' combined with the correct definite article ('el' or 'la'):
   a) Voy ...... restaurante.   b) Salió ...... biblioteca.   c) Le gustaría ir ...... fiesta.   d) al lado ...... río ☐

7) Translate the following into Spanish: a) I'm a teacher.   b) I don't have a cat.   c) Are you Spanish? ☐

Pronouns ☑

8) List all the Spanish subject pronouns in this section. There are 12 you need to know. ☐

9) Rewrite these sentences, replacing the words in bold with the correct direct object pronoun.
   a) Buscaba **la caja**.   b) Estudio **las ciencias**.   c) Vi **al músico**.   d) He encontrado **mis zapatos**. ☐

10) Now rewrite these sentences, replacing the words in bold with the correct indirect object pronoun.
    a) Di los libros **a los alumnos**.   b) Envié la carta **a mi tía**.   c) Hablará **a sus amigos** mañana. ☐

11) Translate these sentences into Spanish using the correct indefinite pronouns.
    a) I have something in my eye.   b) Did they buy some (of them)?   c) None of them made dinner. ☐

12) What type of pronoun is the word 'que'? How would you say 'que' in English? ☐

13) Translate these sentences into Spanish using the correct interrogative pronouns.
    a) Who called you (inf., sing.)?   b) What did they do yesterday?   c) Which one is worse? ☐

14) Translate these sentences into Spanish using the correct demonstrative pronouns.
    a) I never wanted this.   b) I'd like to do that.   c) Have you read this?   d) That doesn't seem fair. ☐

15) Complete each sentence by circling the correct option:
    a) Ese pan es para **tú** / **ti**.   c) Pensaba en **ella** / **suya**.   e) ¿Las uvas son para **me** / **mí**?
    b) A **ellos** / **él** le gustan mucho.   d) ¿Vamos **contigo** / **con tú**?   f) Hablábamos de **ti** / **tú**. ☐

16) Translate these sentences into English: a) ¿Es la tuya o la mía?   b) Puse el vuestro en la cocina. ☐

(Higher)

Prepositions and Conjunctions ☑

17) Fill in the gaps with the correct preposition in Spanish: a) Queremos las bicis ...... una semana.
    b) Pagué treinta euros ...... el vestido.   c) La vi ...... la tele.   d) Me preguntaron ...... este tema. ☐

18) Translate these sentences into English: a) Entré en la casa por la ventana.   b) Fui al café de Diego.
    c) Destruí la carta sin leerla.   d) Van a quedarse hasta noviembre.   e) Bailé mucho durante la fiesta. ☐

19) What do these verbs mean in English? a) dejar de   b) llegar a   c) volver a   d) preocuparse por ☐

20) Choose the correct conjunction in bold, then translate these sentences into English:
    a) Es una fiesta tradicional **y** / **e** importante.   b) Comí esas naranjas **porque** / **pero** me encantan. ☐

21) Translate these sentences into English: a) Leo antes de acostarme.   b) Lo haré después de cenar. ☐

22) Say what the conjunction 'sino' means in English, then give a sentence in Spanish that uses it. ☐

(H)

Adjectives

Jazz up your work with some flashy describing words — and collect more marks while you're at it.

Adjectives describe things

1) In Spanish, adjectives have to <u>agree</u> with the <u>noun</u> they refer to, <u>even if they aren't right next to it</u>.

2) This means the <u>adjective changes</u> depending on the <u>gender</u> of the <u>noun</u> and whether it's <u>singular</u> or <u>plural</u>.

3) Adjectives that end in '<u>o</u>' in the <u>masculine singular</u> form change the '<u>o</u>' to '<u>a</u>' in the <u>feminine</u> form. When <u>plural</u>, the adjective ends in '<u>os</u>' (masculine) or '<u>as</u>' (feminine).

el chico alto *the tall boy*

la chica alta *the tall girl*   los chicos altos *the tall boys*   las chicas altas *the tall girls*

4) Adjectives with <u>certain endings</u> follow <u>different</u> rules:

Ending	Example	Masc. sing.	Fem. sing.	Masc. pl.	Fem. pl.
-e	triste (*sad*)	triste	triste	tristes	tristes
-ista	optimista (*optimistic*)	optimista	optimista	optimistas	optimistas
-z	feliz (*happy*)	feliz	feliz	felices	felices
-és	francés (*French*)	francés	francesa	franceses	francesas
-ol	español (*Spanish*)	español	española	españoles	españolas

When you look up a Spanish adjective in the dictionary, it will be in the masculine singular form.

Nationality adjectives that end in <u>consonants</u> add an ending in the <u>feminine</u> and <u>plural forms</u>. If they have an <u>accent</u> in the masculine singular, they <u>drop it</u> in the <u>feminine</u> and <u>plural</u>.

You can add -able to some verb stems to make adjectives

For some verbs that end in '<u>-ar</u>', you can add the suffix '<u>-able</u>' to the <u>verb stem</u> to form an adjective.

acept<u>ar</u> (*to accept*) ⟶ acept<u>able</u> (*acceptable*)

Spanish adjectives with this ending often end in '-able' in English too.

'ser' and 'estar' can change an adjective's meaning

1) Adjectives that <u>follow</u> 'ser' describe a <u>permanent</u> trait.

2) Adjectives that <u>follow</u> 'estar' describe someone <u>at a given moment</u>.

For more on using 'ser' and 'estar' with adjectives, see p.178.

3) Some adjectives <u>change their meaning completely</u> depending on whether they follow 'ser' or 'estar':

Dilip es listo.   *Dilip is clever.*   Mis primos son aburridos.   *My cousins are (always) boring.*
Dilip está listo.   *Dilip is ready.*   Mis primos están aburridos.   *My cousins are (feeling) bored.*

Grammar Questions

Translate these phrases into **Spanish**, making sure the adjectives agree.

1. the happy dog   **3.** the blue car   **5.** the German sister   **7.** The group is tired.

2. a vegan salad   **4.** a recyclable bottle   **6.** an avoidable problem   **8.** Is she ready?

Learn how different adjective endings change to agree...

That way, you'll know exactly how to make an unfamiliar adjective agree with whatever noun it's describing.

More Adjectives

Adjectives are really useful for saying what's yours and for pointing things out. Once you know loads of adjectives, you'll also need to know where to place them in a sentence.

Most adjectives go after the word they describe

1) In Spanish, most adjectives go <u>after the noun</u> (the word they describe).

2) But that's not always the case — some adjectives always go <u>in front of the noun</u> they're describing, like these ones:

> Es un vestido bonito.
> *It's a nice dress.*

mucho/a	*much, a lot*	alguno/a	*a/an, some*	pocos/as	*few,*	próximo/a	*next*
muchos/as	*many, lots of*	ninguno/a	*no, not...any*		*not many*	último/a	*last, final*
otro/a	*other,*	tanto/a	*so much + noun*	primero/a	*first*	cada	*each,*
	another	tantos/as	*so many + noun*	segundo/a	*second*		*every*
otros/as	*other*	poco/a	*little, not much*	tercero/a	*third*		

algunos parques	*some parks*	tanta gente	*so many people*
pocas casas	*few houses*		

Some adjectives change before masculine nouns...

primer	*first (m) (pre-noun)*	mal	*bad (m) (pre-noun)*	gran	*big, great (pre-noun)*
tercer	*third (m) (pre-noun)*	algún	*a/an, any (m) (pre-noun)*		
buen	*good (m) (pre-noun)*	ningún	*no, not...any (m) (pre-noun)*		

1) Some adjectives <u>lose</u> the final '<u>o</u>' when they go in front of a <u>masculine noun</u>.

> el tercer libro   *the third book*   un buen día   *a good day*

2) '<u>Alguno</u>' and '<u>ninguno</u>' <u>drop</u> the final '<u>o</u>' and <u>add an accent</u>.

> No hay ningún taxi libre.   *There's no taxi free.*

3) '<u>Grande</u>' is the only adjective that <u>drops</u> '<u>de</u>' in front of both <u>masculine and feminine</u> words.

> un gran paso   *a great step*   una gran señora   *a great lady*

...and some change their meaning depending on their position

Adjective	Before the noun...	After the noun...
grande	un gran hombre *a great man*	un hombre grande *a big man*
único	el único edificio *the only building*	el edificio único *the unique building*
nuevo	un nuevo coche *a new (to owner) car*	un coche nuevo *a newly-made car*
viejo	un viejo amigo *an old (long-standing) friend*	un amigo viejo *an old (elderly) friend*
antiguo	un antiguo templo *a former temple*	un templo antiguo *an ancient temple*

"I should've checked that advert more carefully..."

Mi, tu, nuestro — my, your, our

'Mi', 'tu', 'nuestro' etc. are possessive adjectives.

1) Words like '<u>my</u>' and '<u>your</u>' show <u>possession</u>. In Spanish they go <u>before</u> the noun and have to <u>agree</u> with the <u>noun</u> they're describing — <u>not the owner</u>. You only need to learn the forms in brackets if you're doing Higher tier (see below).

Possessive	Masc. sing.	Fem. sing.	Masc. pl.	Fem. pl.
my (mine)	mi (mío)	mi (mía)	mis (míos)	mis (mías)
your(s) (inf., sing.)	tu (tuyo)	tu (tuya)	tus (tuyos)	tus (tuyas)
his/her(s)/its/your(s) (form., sing.)	su (suyo)	su (suya)	sus (suyos)	sus (suyas)
our(s)	nuestro	nuestra	nuestros	nuestras
your(s) (inf., pl.)	vuestro	vuestra	vuestros	vuestras
their(s)/your(s) (form., pl.)	su (suyo)	su (suya)	sus (suyos)	sus (suyas)

'Su(s)' can mean 'his', 'her', 'its', 'their' and 'your' (formal). Use the rest of the sentence to work out which of these it is.

mi libro — *my book*
su perro — *his dog*

H 2) The forms in brackets are <u>long-form</u> adjectives. You use them for emphasis and put them <u>after the verb</u>:

el gato es nuestro — *the cat is ours*

The 'our(s)' and 'your(s) (inf., pl.)' forms are the same in the short and long forms.

Este, ese — this, that

'Este', 'ese' and 'aquel' are demonstrative adjectives.

1) Use '<u>este</u>' to say '<u>this</u>'. It's an adjective, so it changes to agree with the noun. When the noun is <u>feminine</u>, use '<u>esta</u>', and when it's <u>plural</u>, use '<u>estos</u>' (masculine) or '<u>estas</u>' (feminine).

este tigre *this tiger*   esta leche *this milk*   estos huevos *these eggs*   estas mesas *these tables*

2) Use '<u>ese</u>' to say '<u>that</u>' in English. Use '<u>esa</u>' for feminine nouns, and '<u>esos</u>' or '<u>esas</u>' for plural nouns.

ese tigre *that tiger*   esa leche *that milk*   esos huevos *those eggs*   esas mesas *those tables*

Higher

3) '<u>Aquel</u>' also means <u>that</u>. It's used for things that are <u>further away</u> — in English, you might say '<u>that over there</u>'.

4) 'Aquel' changes to '<u>aquella</u>' in the <u>feminine</u> form and '<u>aquellos</u>' and '<u>aquellas</u>' for the <u>plural</u> forms.

aquel tigre — *that tiger (over there)*
aquella leche — *that milk (over there)*
aquellos huevos — *those eggs (over there)*
aquellas mesas — *those tables (over there)*

Indefinite adjectives describe words in a more general way

1) '<u>Otro</u>' (*other, another*), '<u>todo</u>' (*all, the whole*), '<u>alguno</u>' (*some*), '<u>ninguno</u>' (*no, not any*) and '<u>mismo</u>' (*same*) are all examples of indefinite adjectives. They <u>change</u> to agree with the <u>noun</u>.

otro tigre — *another tiger*
algunos tigres — *some tigers*
cada tigre — *each tiger*

2) '<u>cada</u>' (*each, every*), is also an indefinite adjective, but it <u>never</u> changes to agree with what it's describing.

Grammar Questions

Translate these phrases into **Spanish**, making sure the adjectives go in the right place.

1. the first day
2. few products
3. each family
4. no plate
5. their books
6. those films

H 7. The pen is mine.
H 8. that apple over there

Don't let those fancy adjective names trip you up...

Possessive adjectives show who something belongs to, and demonstrative adjectives show where something is compared to where you are. Indefinite adjectives generally describe how much of something there is.

Comparative and Superlative Adjectives

To make your Spanish even more brilliant, learn how to compare things.

Más, menos — more, less

'More' is a comparative. 'The most' (Higher only) is a superlative.

1) In Spanish you can't say 'cheaper' or 'cheapest' — you have to say '<u>more cheap</u>' or '<u>the most cheap</u>'.

Este piso es barato.	Este piso es **más** barato.	Este piso es **el más** barato.
This flat is cheap.	*This flat is cheaper.*	*This flat is the cheapest.*

2) To say '<u>less cheap</u>' or '<u>the least cheap</u>', use '<u>menos</u>'.

Este piso es barato.	Este piso es **menos** barato.	Este piso es **el menos** barato.
This flat is cheap.	*This flat is less cheap.*	*This flat is the least cheap.*

3) To say 'the most / least' if the word you're describing is <u>feminine</u>, use 'la más / menos'. For <u>plural</u> words, use 'los/las más / menos'.

Zeynab es **la más** baja.   *Zeynab is the shortest.*

Más / menos ... que — more / less ... than

1) Use '<u>más</u> ... <u>que</u>' (more ... than) and '<u>menos</u> ... <u>que</u>' (less ... than) to <u>compare</u> two things <u>directly</u>.

2) If you want to say something is '<u>more than...</u>' followed by a <u>number</u>, use '<u>más de</u>'.

3) To say two things are <u>as</u> young or old or brilliant <u>as</u> each other, use '<u>tan</u> ... <u>como</u>' (as ... as).

Catalina es **más** tranquila **que** Minho, pero ella es **tan** tranquila **como** Daniel.

Catalina is more calm than Minho, but she is as calm as Daniel.

There are some exceptions...

All these comparatives and superlatives add 'es' for the plural forms.

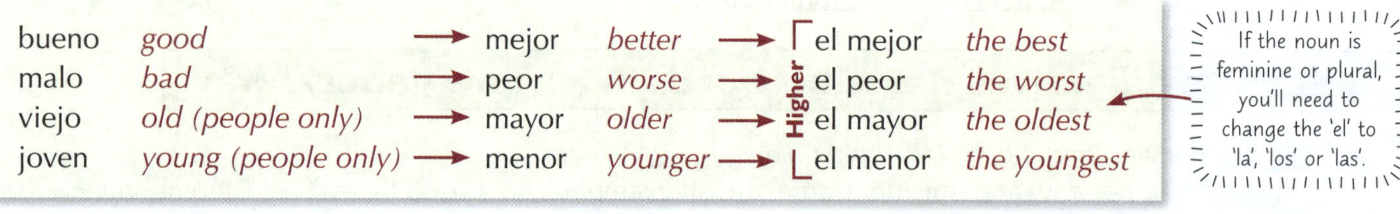

bueno	*good*	→	mejor	*better*	→	el mejor	*the best*
malo	*bad*	→	peor	*worse*	→	el peor	*the worst*
viejo	*old (people only)*	→	mayor	*older*	→	el mayor	*the oldest*
joven	*young (people only)*	→	menor	*younger*	→	el menor	*the youngest*

If the noun is feminine or plural, you'll need to change the 'el' to 'la', 'los' or 'las'.

Sara es **mayor que** Javier.   *Sara is older than Javier.*

Aya es **la mayor**.   *Aya is the oldest.*

Grammar Questions

Translate these sentences into **Spanish** — watch out for the irregular adjectives though.

1. This page is easier.
2. I am as tall as my father.
3. Faiza is older than Emilio.
4. Books are better than films.
5. Today is the worst day.
6. She is the youngest.

Using comparisons makes your writing better...

Just remember that comparatives have to agree with what they're describing. So to say 'Sara and Javier are more serious' in Spanish, you must say 'Sara y Javier son más seri<u>os</u>' because 'Sara y Javier' is a plural.

Adverbs

Adverbs describe verbs — use them to make your Spanish more interesting and complex.

Adverbs describe how actions are done

1) If you wanted to <u>describe how you run</u>, you could say 'I run <u>slowly</u>' — '<u>slowly</u>' is an <u>adverb of manner</u>.

2) In English, you add '-<u>ly</u>' to the adjective '<u>slow</u>' to make '<u>slowly</u>'.

3) It's similar in Spanish — to form an adverb of manner, you add '-<u>mente</u>' to the end of the <u>adjective</u>. <u>However</u>, you need to make sure the adjective is in the <u>feminine form</u> first.

lento (*slow*) ⟶ lenta (*feminine form of 'slow'*) **+** -mente ⟶ lentamente (*slowly*)

4) With adjectives that <u>don't end</u> in '<u>o</u>', you can just add '-<u>mente</u>'.

fácil (*easy*) **+** -mente ⟶ fácilmente (*easily*)

You can also use the Higher tier word 'despacio' to say slowly, e.g. 'Escribes despacio'. It's irregular and doesn't add -mente or change its ending.

5) Unlike with adjectives (see p.165), adverbs don't need to <u>agree</u>. This is because they're <u>describing</u> an <u>action</u>, not the <u>person</u> doing the action.

6) Adverbs of manner come <u>after</u> the <u>verb</u>.

Comemos rápidamente.	*We eat quickly.*
Habla alegremente.	*She speaks happily.*
Estudio tranquilamente.	*I study calmly.*
Contestan correctamente.	*They answer correctly.*

Some adverbs are formed differently

You don't say 'I sing <u>goodly</u>' in English, and you can't say '<u>buenamente</u>' in Spanish either.

bueno/a	*good*	⟶	bien	*well*
malo/a	*bad*	⟶	mal	*badly*

Canto bien.	*I sing well.*
Canto mal.	*I sing badly.*

Some adverbs describe possibility

<u>Adverbs of certainty</u> describe how <u>possible</u> something is. They normally come <u>before</u> the <u>verb</u>.

probablemente	*probably*
completamente	*completely*
quizás	*perhaps, maybe*
claro	*of course, clearly*

Probablemente seré profesor.	Quizás visitaré.
I will probably be a teacher.	*I'll maybe visit.*

Grammar Questions

Turn these adjectives into adverbs, then translate the **adverb** into **English**.

1. positivo	3. social	5. exacto	7. posible	9. evidente	11. nacional
2. directo	4. diferente	6. perfecto	8. tradicional	10. estricto	12. efectivo

(9–12 are Higher tier questions.)

Adjectives change to agree — adverbs don't...

Unlike adjectives, your adverbs don't need to agree with what they're describing. However, if you're forming an adverb with an adjective and '-mente', you need to make sure that you use the adjective's feminine form.

Adverbs and Adverbial Phrases

And here's another page on adverbs — these ones say where or when something is happening.

Adverbs can tell you where something is done...

Adverbs of place say <u>where</u> things happen. They come <u>after</u> the <u>verb</u> in a phrase or sentence.

aquí	*here*	lejos	*far (away)*	dentro	*inside, within*
allí	*there, over there*	detrás	*behind*	abajo	*down, below, downstairs*
cerca	*close, near, nearby*	delante	*in front, ahead*	arriba	*above, upstairs*

Higher (dentro / abajo / arriba)

Mi tía trabaja **aquí**.   *My aunt works here.*   —there — allí

Está muy **cerca**.   *It's very near.*   —far away — lejos

...or when it's happening

Adverbs of time say <u>when</u> or <u>how often</u> something is done. They can come at the <u>beginning</u> or <u>end</u> of a sentence, or <u>after</u> the verb they describe.

ya	*already*	después	*after, afterwards*	a veces	*sometimes*
ahora	*now, these days*	luego	*then, later*	pronto	*soon, early*
de momento	*at the moment*	siempre	*always, forever*	todavía	*still, yet*
antes	*before, beforehand*	nunca	*never*	jamás	*never*

Higher (pronto / todavía / jamás)

Ya tengo un reloj.   *I already have a watch.*

Siempre veo la tele.   *I always watch TV.*

Adverbial phrases work like adverbs

Adverbial phrases can often be used like adverbs and describe <u>how, when or where</u> something is happening. They are placed at the <u>beginning</u> or <u>end</u> of a sentence, or <u>after</u> the verb they describe.

aparte de	*besides, apart (from)*	
por fin	*finally, at last*	
por la noche	*at night*	

Aparte de leer me gusta jugar a los videojuegos.   *Apart from reading, I like to play videogames.*

Por fin gané una carrera.   *I finally won a race.*

Me lavo **por la noche**.   *I have a wash at night.*

Grammar Questions

Translate these phrases into **Spanish**.
1. My shoes are here.
2. I want to leave now.
3. Sometimes I travel.
4. We live far away.
5. I can finally sleep.
6. The shop is over there.

Por fin — it's time for a tip about adverb placement...

Adverbs of manner and adverbs of place come after the verb they describe, while adverbs of certainty usually come before the verb. Adverbs of time can go at the beginning or end of a sentence, or come after the verb.

Comparative and Superlative Adverbs

You can use similar techniques to those you learned on p.168 to compare how people do things.

Comparative adverbs compare how people do actions

1) To say that something is done 'more ...ly', use 'más ... que'.

>   Pilar trabaja **más** alegremente **que** Hani. *Pilar works more happily than Hani.*

2) If you want to say that something is done 'less ...ly', use 'menos ... que'.

>   Hani trabaja **menos** alegremente **que** Pilar. *Hani works less happily than Pilar.*

3) To say that someone does something 'as ... as' someone else, use 'tan ... como'.

>   Pilar trabaja **tan** alegremente **como** Hani. *Pilar works as happily as Hani.*

Paula and Alazne found that pizza always helped them work more happily.

Superlative adverbs say who does something the 'most ...ly'

Higher

To say someone does something 'the most ...ly', follow this pattern. Remember to change 'el' to 'la' if the subject is feminine, 'los' if it's a masculine plural subject, and 'las' for a feminine plural subject.

>   Ligaya es **la que** trabaja **más** alegremente. *Ligaya is the one who works the most happily.*
>   Juan es **el que** baila **menos** rápidamente. *Juan is the one who dances the least quickly.*

Watch out for irregulars...

| bien | *well* | → | mejor | *better* | → | el que mejor... | *the one who ... the best* |
| mal | *badly* | → | peor | *worse* | → | el que peor... | *the one who ... the worst* |

>   Juego **mejor** que él. *I play better than him.*   Nado **peor** que Lin. *I swim worse than Lin.*

Higher

>   Él es **el que peor** cocina. *He's the one who cooks the worst.*
>   Ellas son **las que mejor** actúan. *They are the ones who act the best.*

In Spanish, irregular superlative adverbs come straight after the 'que' and before the verb.

Grammar Questions

Complete the sentences in **Spanish** so that they match the words in the brackets.

1. Wafa come .... yo. (more quickly than)
2. Yo pinto .... ella. (better than)
3. Luis baila .... tú. (as well as)

Higher

4. Alba (f) es .... habla .... (the most calmly)
5. Ellos son .... conducen. (the best)
6. Inoke (m) es .... corre. (the worst)

Higher

Most comparative adverbs follow the same structure...

For regular comparative adverb structures, remember to sandwich the adverb in between 'más / menos / tan' and 'como / que'. For irregular comparative adverb structures, just stick the adverb straight before the 'que'.

Quantifiers and Intensifiers

You can use quantifiers and intensifiers with other words to give more detailed descriptions.

Quantifiers say how many or how much

1) Just saying 'I have apples' is boring. Use <u>quantifiers</u> to say you have <u>lots of</u> apples — or <u>too many</u>.

2) Quantifiers go <u>before the noun</u>, and most <u>change their endings</u> to agree with it, just like adjectives do.

mucho(s)	*much, a lot (many)*	tanto(s)	*so much (so many) + noun*
poco(s)	*little, not much (few, not many)*	bastante(s)	*quite a lot, enough*
demasiado(s)	*too much/many + noun*		

Tengo muchos deberes.	Escribes pocas cartas.	Tienen bastantes zapatos.
I have a lot of homework.	*You (inf., sing.) write few letters.*	*They have enough shoes.*

3) You don't just have to use these quantifiers with nouns — you can also use them with <u>verbs</u>. When you use them with verbs, they work like <u>adverbs</u>, so they go <u>after the verb</u> and <u>don't change their endings</u>.

Hablas demasiado.	*You (inf., sing.) talk too much.*	Comen mucho. *They eat a lot.*

Intensifiers strengthen what you're saying

1) You can use <u>intensifiers</u> like '<u>very</u>' and '<u>quite</u>' to <u>add detail</u> to what you're saying.

2) Intensifiers go <u>before the word they're modifying</u>, but their <u>endings don't change</u> at all.

muy	*very, really*	tan	*so*	bastante	*quite*	demasiado	*too*

Simón está muy feliz. *Simón is very happy.*	Comemos bastante bien. *We eat quite well.*

Adding 'ísimo' makes adjectives stronger

1) If you add 'ísimo/a/os/as' to an adjective, it's like adding '<u>really</u>' — it makes the meaning <u>stronger</u>.

2) The <u>ending</u> of 'ísimo' <u>changes</u> like other regular adjectives to <u>agree</u> with the <u>noun</u> it describes.

Su voz es hermosísima. *Her voice is really beautiful.*	Él es divertidísimo. *He is really funny.*

Grammar Questions

Rewrite each sentence, changing the quantifier or intensifier so it's used correctly.

1. Hay demasiado gatos aquí.
2. Es interesante bastante.
3. Tengo muchas amigos.
4. Tan hablan rápidamente.
5. Es un libro mucho bueno.
6. Hay una playa buenísimo.

I can't get enough of quantifiers and intensifiers...

Remember — you only need to change a quantifier to agree if it's used with a noun. Quantifiers that are used with verbs don't need to agree, so they just stay the same. Intensifiers don't need to change to agree either.

Adjectives and Adverbs — Grammar List

On this page you'll find all the words and phrases you need to add extra details to your nouns and verbs.

Adjectives

Adjectives often change to match the gender and number of what they're describing. Many feminine adjectives change an '-o' ending to '-a'.

bueno/a — *good*
malo/a — *bad*
ambos/as — *both*
propio/a — *own (pre-noun)*

For more on adjective agreement, see p.165.

Other adjectives only change to become plural.

grande — *big, large*   alegre — *cheerful*

Some adjectives change when they go in front of a masculine singular noun.

buen — *good (pre-noun)*   gran — *big, great (pre-noun)*
mal — *bad (pre-noun)*

An adjective's position can change its meaning.

único/a — *only (pre-noun), unique (post-noun)*
nuevo/a — *new, another (pre-noun), new, newly-made (post-noun)*
viejo/a — *old, long-standing (pre-noun), old, elderly (post-noun)*
antiguo/a — *former (pre-noun), old, ancient (pre- and post-noun)*

Possessive Adjectives

mi — *my*
tu — *your (inf., sing.)*
su — *his, her, its, your (form.), their*

nuestro/a/os/as — *our*
vuestro/a/os/as — *your (inf., pl.)*
mío/a/os/as — *mine*
tuyo/a/os/as — *yours (inf., sing.)*
suyo/a/os/as — *his, hers, its, yours (form.), theirs*
nuestro/a/os/as — *ours*
vuestro/a/os/as — *yours (inf., pl.)*

These Higher words are long-form possessive adjectives.

Higher

Demonstrative Adjectives

este/a — *this*   ese/a — *that*   aquel/la — *that*
estos/as — *these*   esos/as — *those*   aquellos/as — *those*

Indefinite Adjectives

cada — *each, every*   alguno/a — *a/an, any*
otro/a — *other, another*   ningún — *no, not...any (pre-noun)*
todo/a — *all, the whole*
mismo/a — *same*   ninguno/a — *no, not...any*
algún — *a/an, any (pre-noun)*

Only use 'algún' and 'ningún' with singular masculine nouns.

Adverbs

Most adverbs are formed by adding '-mente' to the feminine form of an adjective.

rápidamente — *quickly*
normalmente — *normally*
probablemente — *probably*
actualmente — *now, at present*
desafortunadamente — *unfortunately*
afortunadamente — *fortunately*

Adverbs don't need to change to agree — they stay the same.

Others don't follow this pattern.

también — *also, too, as well*   aun — *even*
además — *also, as well, besides*   incluso — *even, including*

Adverbs of manner describe how something is done.

bien — *well*   mal — *badly*   así — *like this/that*

Adverbs of certainty describe how likely something is.

quizás — *perhaps, maybe*

Adverbs of place describe where something happens.

aquí — *here*   abajo — *down, below, downstairs*
detrás — *behind*
dentro — *inside, within*   arriba — *upstairs, above*

Adverbs of time show when or how often something occurs.

ya — *already*   casi — *almost, nearly*
siempre — *always, forever*   pronto — *soon, early, quick*
por fin — *finally, at last*   todavía — *still, yet*
entonces — *then, so*   jamás — *never*
aún — *still*   enseguida — *straight away*
solo — *only, just*   apenas — *hardly, barely*

Higher

Comparative & Superlative Adjectives and Adverbs

más (...que) — *more (...than), adj. / adv. + er (...than)*
más de (+ number) — *more than (+ num)*
menos (...que) — *less (...than), fewer (...than)*
menos de (+ number) — *less than (+ num)*
tan...como — *as...as*
mejor — *better, best*
peor — *worse, worst*
el/la/los/las mejor(es) — *the best*
el/la/los/las peor(es) — *the worst*

Quantifiers & Intensifiers

Quantifiers say how much of something there is.

mucho(s) — *much, a lot (many)*
poco(s) — *little, not much (few, not many)*
demasiado(s) — *too much (many)*
tanto(s) — *so much (many)*
bastante(s) — *quite a lot, enough*

Intensifiers add detail to adjectives.

muy — *very, really*   bastante — *quite*
tan — *so*   demasiado — *too*

Revision Summary Test for Section Fourteen

Have a go at these questions to test yourself on what you've learnt about adjectives and adverbs.

- These questions are **really tricky**, but they'll help you see **how well you know your stuff**.
- Tackle the **revision summary test** below, or scan the QR code to do it **online**.
  You can **keep track of your progress** online and see **which areas need more work**.
- There are **sample answers** here: www.cgpbooks.co.uk/MadridExtras

Adjectives ☑

1) Add the adjective in brackets to each phrase so that it agrees with the noun.
   a) las chicas (feliz)   b) el hombre (optimista)   c) los exámenes (difícil)   d) una bebida (fresco)

2) Turn these verbs into adjectives using '-able': a) emplear   b) aceptar   c) separar

3) Translate each sentence into Spanish. Decide whether each sentence needs 'ser' or 'estar'.
   a) She is feeling sick.   b) His parents are uptight.   c) I think that football is boring.

4) Rewrite each sentence, putting the adjective in brackets into the right position.
   a) Quiero pantalones. (esos)   c) Es una casa. (gran)   e) Es mi móvil. (primer)
   b) Es la película. (tercera)   d) Es una casa. (grande)   f) Hay tiendas. (muchas)

5) Translate these sentences into Spanish using long-form possessive adjectives.
   a) The black dress is yours *(inf., sing.)*.   b) Those shirts over there are hers.

Adverbs ☑

6) Turn these adjectives into adverbs: a) sencillo   b) estupendo   c) malo   d) fácil   e) bueno

7) Choose the adverb or adverbial phrase in these sentences, then translate each sentence into English.
   a) Casi he terminado el libro.   c) A veces voy al teatro.   e) Quizás beberé café.
   b) Me encantaría estudiar allí.   d) El coche llegó por fin.   f) Hago mi cama por la mañana.

8) Rewrite each sentence so that the adverbs are in the correct position.
   a) Es divertido independientemente viajar.   b) Lejos vivo de mi colegio.   c) Está ahora trabajando.

9) Fill in the gaps by choosing the most appropriate adverb from each list.
   a) Vamos a hacer las compras .... (apenas / enseguida / jamás)
   b) Han limpiado todos los cuartos, ... el baño. (incluso / ya / solo)

Comparatives and Superlatives ☑

10) Correct the mistakes in these sentences.
    a) Carmen habla más rápidamente como Dani.   c) Odio estudiar. Estudio más mal que tú.
    b) Mi prima es tan directa que mi tía.   d) Monika puede cantar mayor que yo.

11) Translate each sentence into Spanish: a) Raúl is older than his sister.   b) We write better than them.

12) Translate these sentences into Spanish:
    a) Jorge (m) is the most ambitious.   c) Those girls are the youngest of the class.
    b) Paula (f) is the one who paints the worst.   d) They are the ones who run the slowest.

Quantifiers and Intensifiers ☑

13) Complete each sentence by adding the quantifier or intensifier in brackets.
    a) Es una asignatura .... divertida. (quite)   c) Mi amigo estudia .... (too much)
    b) Tengo .... videojuegos. (so many)   d) .... gente vive en este pueblo. (few)

14) For each sentence, say if the bold word is a quantifier (Q) or intensifier (I), then translate the sentence.
    a) La fiesta fue **muy** emocionante.   c) El café está **demasiado** caliente.
    b) Tenemos **tanta** comida.   d) Has puesto **bastante** leche en el vaso.

15) Translate these sentences into Spanish, adding the ending in brackets to form the adjective.
    a) Paella is really good. (-ísima)   b) The castle is really big. (-ísimo)

Verbs in the Present Tense

You can't do a lot without verbs — your Spanish won't make very much sense without them.

Verbs are actions

1) A <u>verb</u> is an <u>action word</u> like 'speak', 'eat' and 'live'.

2) Verbs can be put into <u>different tenses</u>, such as the <u>future</u> or <u>past</u>. For example, 'Yesterday, I <u>ate</u> a pie'.

3) To use a verb, you need to know its <u>infinitive</u> — the form you find in a <u>dictionary</u>, e.g. 'hablar' (*to speak*).

Forming the present tense

1) <u>Regular</u> verbs in Spanish end in '-<u>ar</u>', '-<u>er</u>' or '-<u>ir</u>'. To form the <u>present tense</u> of these regular verbs, you need to find the <u>stem</u>. To do this, <u>remove</u> the <u>last two letters</u> from the <u>infinitive</u>.

Infinitive	Remove last two letters	Stem
hablar	-ar	habl-

2) Then <u>add</u> the <u>endings</u> below to the <u>stem</u>.

-ar verbs

I speak	hablo	hablamos	we speak
you (inf., sing.) speak	hablas	habláis	you (inf., pl.) speak
he/she/it/you (form., sing.) speak(s)	habla	hablan	they/you (form., pl.) speak

Cantan. *They sing.*

Grita. *He shouts.*

Some verb forms change the spelling in their stem to avoid changing the pronunciation.

-er verbs

I eat	como	comemos	we eat
you (inf., sing.) eat	comes	coméis	you (inf., pl.) eat
he/she/it/you (form., sing.) eat(s)	come	comen	they/you (form., pl.) eat

Cojo. *I catch.*

Depende. *It depends.*

-ir verbs

I live	vivo	vivimos	we live
you (inf., sing.) live	vives	vivís	you (inf., pl.) live
he/she/it/you (form., sing.) live(s)	vive	viven	they/you (form., pl.) live

Abren. *They open.*

Escribe. *She writes.*

When to use the present tense

For another way to say what you're doing now, see p.186-187.

1) Use the <u>present tense</u> for actions taking place <u>now</u>...   Hablo español.   *I speak / I'm speaking Spanish.*

2) ...or for things that take place <u>regularly</u>.   Canto todos los días.   *I sing every day.*

3) You can also use it for things that are <u>about to happen</u>.   Mañana voy al cine.   *Tomorrow I'm going to the cinema.*

Grammar Questions

Put each of these infinitives into the present tense. The form of the verb is given in brackets.

1. bailar (yo)	**3.** discutir (ustedes)	**5.** aprender (él)	**7.** escribir (tú)
2. beber (nosotros)	**4.** romper (ellas)	**6.** nadar (vosotros)	**8.** visitar (ellos)

Get to grips with the present before you revise the other tenses...

Make sure you know how to conjugate regular verbs in the present tense — you'll be using them a lot.

Irregular Verbs in the Present Tense

Sadly, not all Spanish verbs are regular — some of the worst offenders are really common verbs...

Some verbs are stem-changing

These are also called 'radical-changing verbs'.

Adva was excited about all types of stem changes.

1) A stem-changing verb is a verb that changes its spelling in the present tense.

2) Usually, the 'e' in the stem changes to 'ie', or the 'o' or 'u' changes to 'ue'. Some verbs change the 'e' in their stem to 'i'.

3) The stem changes in every form apart from the 'we' and 'you (inf., pl.)' forms.

pensar — to think (e to ie)	
I think	pienso
you (inf., sing.) think	piensas
he/she/it/you (form., sing.) think(s)	piensa
we think	pensamos
you (inf., pl.) think	pensáis
they/you (form., pl.) think	piensan

Even though their stems change, their endings are regular.

These verbs also change their 'e' to 'ie'...

cerrar	*to close*	despertarse	*to wake up*
comenzar	*to begin*	querer	*to want, love*
empezar	*to begin*	preferir	*to prefer*

encontrar — to find (o to ue)	
I find	encuentro
you (inf., sing.) find	encuentras
he/she/it/you (form., sing.) find(s)	encuentra
we find	encontramos
you (inf., pl.) find	encontráis
they/you (form., pl.) find	encuentran

These verbs also change their 'o' or 'u' to 'ue'...

doler	*to hurt*	jugar	*to play*
dormir	*to sleep*	llover	*to rain*
poder	*to be able to*	volver	*to return*

pedir — to ask for (e to i)	
I ask for	pido
you (inf., sing.) ask for	pides
he/she/it/you (form., sing.) ask(s) for	pide
we ask for	pedimos
you (inf., pl.) ask for	pedís
they/you (form., pl.) ask for	piden

You also drop the 'u' in the present tense 'I' form of seguir — 'sigo'.

These verbs also change their 'e' to 'i'...

decir	*to say, tell*	servir	*to serve*
repetir	*to repeat*	seguir	*to follow*
vestirse	*to get dressed*	H elegir	*to choose, elect*

Some stem-changing verbs follow a different pattern

1) In some stem-changing verbs, the stem only changes its spelling in the 'I' form. All the other forms of the verb follow the same pattern as regular verbs in the present tense.

poner — to put (add g)	
I put	pongo

Pongo mis dibujos sobre la mesa. *I put my drawings on the table.*

conocer — to know (c to zc)	
I know	conozco

Conozco a unas personas aquí. *I know a few people here.*

2) Here are a couple of examples of verbs that follow a similar pattern to 'poner'...

salir — to go out, leave	salgo	I go out, I leave
traer — to bring	traigo	I bring

'Traer' is a little different — the 'e' changes to 'i' as well.

3) ...and here are some that follow a similar pattern to 'conocer':

conducir — to drive	conduzco	I drive
H ofrecer — to offer	ofrezco	I offer

'Hacer', 'ir' and 'tener'

In Spanish, the verbs 'to do / make', 'to go' and 'to have' are irregular.

hacer — to do, make

I do, make	hago
you (inf., sing.) do, make	haces
he/she/it/you (form., sing.) do(es), make(s)	hace
we do, make	hacemos
you (inf., pl.) do, make	hacéis
they/you (form., pl.) do, make	hacen

Only the 'I' form is irregular in the present tense.

Hago mis deberes. *I do my homework.*

Lo hago sonreír. *I make him smile.*

ir — to go

All of the present tense forms of 'ir' are irregular.

I go	voy
you (inf., sing.) go	vas
he/she/it/you (form., sing.) go(es)	va
we go	vamos
you (inf., pl.) go	vais
they/you (form., pl.) go	van

The verb 'dar' (to give) follows the same pattern as 'ir' in the present tense — 'I give' is 'doy', 'you give' is 'das', etc.

Va al concierto. *He's going to the concert.*

Siempre van allí. *They always go there.*

tener — to have

I have	tengo
you (inf., sing.) have	tienes
he/she/it/you (form., sing.) has/have	tiene
we have	tenemos
you (inf., pl.) have	tenéis
they/you (form., pl.) have	tienen

'Venir' (to come) follows a similar pattern to 'tener'. It also has an irregular 'I' form — 'vengo'.

Tengo cinco primos. *I have five cousins.*

Tiene mucho papel. *She has a lot of paper.*

'Tener' can also sometimes mean 'to be'

You can sometimes use 'tener' + noun to mean 'to be' + adjective.

You don't need an article for the nouns when you use them in this way with 'tener'.

Tienen hambre. *They are hungry.*

¿Tiene sed? *Is she thirsty?*

Tengo miedo. *I'm afraid.*

Tiene quince años. *He is fifteen.*

Tenemos calor. *We are hot.*

¿Tienen frío? *Are they cold?*

Grammar Questions

Correct the spelling mistake in each of these sentences.

1. Comenza a las tres.
2. Quieremos leche.
3. Yo do el libro a Lola.
4. Podes conducir.
5. Repeten las direcciones.
6. Penso que es importante.

Translate these sentences into **Spanish**, making sure the stem of each verb is spelt correctly.

7. I'm also coming to the party.
8. We're going there tomorrow.
9. I get dressed quickly.
10. I don't have a pen.
11. The students are hungry.
12. I recognise her from the film.

Practise using these irregular verbs over and over again...

Stem-changing verbs crop up all the time in Spanish. They can be tricky to remember, so take all the time you need to practise spelling them in all their forms. Look over these pages again if you're feeling stuck.

Quick Quiz

'Ser' and 'Estar' in the Present Tense

The verbs 'ser' and 'estar' both mean 'to be'. They're used differently, so it's really important to know which you need in each situation. Oh, and one more thing — they're irregular too...

Use 'ser' for permanent things

The verb 'ser' means 'to be'. It's used for permanent things. You need it to...

ser — to be	
I am	soy
you are (inf., sing.)	eres
he/she/it/you (form., sing.) is/are	es
we are	somos
you are (inf., pl.)	sois
they/you (form., pl.) are	son

1) ...talk about nationalities.

Somos ingleses.   *We are English.*

2) ...talk about someone's job.

Mi tío es profesor.   *My uncle is a teacher.*

3) ...say someone's name or say who someone is in relation to you.

Nerea y Sabina son mis primas.   *Nerea and Sabina are my cousins.*

4) ...describe the physical characteristics of a person or thing.

Es largo.   *It is long.*   Eres muy alto.   *You (inf., sing.) are very tall.*

5) ...describe someone's personality.

Sois amables.   *You (inf., pl.) are kind.*   Son listos.   *They are clever.*

Juma was ser-tain he wasn't that tall...

Use 'estar' for temporary things and locations

'Estar' also means 'to be'. You use it to...

1) ...talk about things that might change in the future.

Estoy bastante enfermo.   *I'm quite ill.*
(But you might not be ill next week.)

Estás muy triste hoy.   *You (inf., sing.) are very sad today.*
(But you might not be sad tomorrow.)

estar — to be	
I am	estoy
you are (inf., sing.)	estás
he/she/it/you (form., sing.) is/are	está
we are	estamos
you are (inf., pl.)	estáis
they/you (form., pl.) are	están

2) ...talk about where someone or something is.

Madrid está en España.   *Madrid is in Spain.*   Estamos en casa.   *We are at home.*

Grammar Questions

Decide whether you need 'ser' or 'estar' in each of these sentences.
1. Es / Está muy enojado hoy.
2. Siempre es / está trabajador.
3. Somos / Estamos de Hull.
4. Soy / Estoy en Bradford.
5. Es / Está mi hermano.
6. Mi padre es / está médico.

Always ask yourself whether you need 'ser' or 'estar'...

'Ser' and 'estar' are two of the most important verbs in Spanish — you'll need them all the time. Make sure you learn all their present tense forms so you can use them confidently and correctly in your exams.

The Preterite Tense

Use the preterite tense to describe actions that were completed at a specific point in the past.

I went — The preterite tense

To form the <u>preterite tense of regular verbs</u>, find the <u>stem</u> (see p.175) and then <u>add these endings</u>...

-ar verb endings

I	-é	-amos	we
you (inf., sing.)	-aste	-asteis	you (inf., pl.)
he/she/it/ you (form., sing.)	-ó	-aron	they/ you (form., pl.)

-er and -ir verb endings

I	-í	-imos	we
you (inf., sing.)	-iste	-isteis	you (inf., pl.)
he/she/it/ you (form., sing.)	-ió	-ieron	they/ you (form., pl.)

Don't forget the accent — without it, you'd be saying 'I speak to Sonal'.

Habló con Sonal. *He spoke to Sonal.*

Some verbs are irregular in the preterite tense

1) Here are three important <u>irregular verbs</u> in the <u>preterite tense</u>. Watch out — '<u>ser</u>' and '<u>ir</u>' are the <u>same</u>.

ser — to be; ir — to go

I was / went	fui
you (inf., sing.) were / went	fuiste
he/she/it/you (form., sing.) was (were) / went	fue
we were / went	fuimos
you (inf., pl.) were / went	fuisteis
they/you (form., pl.) were / went	fueron

dar — to give

I gave	di
you (inf., sing.) gave	diste
he/she/it/you (form., sing.) gave	dio
we gave	dimos
you (inf., pl.) gave	disteis
they/you (form., pl.) gave	dieron

2) Some verbs <u>change their stem</u> in the <u>preterite tense</u>. If you know what the stem change is, you can predict what the verb is going to be in its other forms.

Infinitive	I	he/she/it/you (form., sing.)	Infinitive	I	he/she/it/you (form., sing.)
decir (*to say*)	dije	dijo	tener (*to have*)	tuve	tuvo
poder (*to be able to*)	pude	pudo	estar (*to be*)	estuve	estuvo
poner (*to put*)	puse	puso	hacer (*to do, make*)	hice	hizo
querer (*to want*)	quise	quiso	venir (*to come*)	vine	vino
traer (*to bring*)	traje	trajo			

The 'he/she/it/ you (form., sing.)' form is sometimes different to what you might expect.

3) Verbs ending in '<u>-aer</u>' and '<u>-eer</u>' add '<u>y</u>' in the <u>third person</u> forms, e.g. '<u>cayó</u>' (*she fell*), '<u>leyeron</u>' (*they read*).

4) Other verbs only have stem changes in the '<u>he/she/it</u>' and '<u>they</u>' forms. Some change their 'e' to 'i' ('pedir' becomes '<u>pidió</u>' / '<u>pidieron</u>'). Some change their 'o' to 'u' ('<u>dormir</u>' becomes '<u>durmió</u>' / '<u>durmieron</u>').

5) Some verbs have <u>spelling changes</u> in the '<u>I</u>' form of the preterite tense. Verbs ending in '<u>-car</u>' change from '<u>c</u>' to '<u>qu</u>' ('<u>tocar</u>' becomes '<u>toqué</u>'). Verbs ending in '<u>-zar</u>' change from '<u>z</u>' to '<u>c</u>' ('<u>cruzar</u>' becomes '<u>crucé</u>'). Verbs ending in '<u>-gar</u>' change from '<u>g</u>' to '<u>gu</u>' ('<u>llegar</u>' becomes '<u>llegué</u>').

Higher

Grammar Questions

Put these verbs into the preterite tense. The subject is given in brackets.

1. venir (tú)   **2.** cenar (ellos)   **3.** dar (yo)   **4.** ir (él)   **H 5.** pedir (usted)   **6.** jugar (yo) **H**

Remember — 'ser' and 'ir' are the same in the preterite tense...

... but you should be able to work out which verb is being used by looking at the context of the sentence.

The Imperfect Tense

The imperfect helps you say what you 'were doing', what 'was happening' or what you 'used to do'.

I was going / I used to go — The imperfect tense

1) To form the <u>imperfect tense</u>, find the <u>stem</u> (see p.175) and then <u>add these endings</u>. The '<u>I</u>' form and the '<u>he/she/it/you (form., sing.)</u>' form look the <u>same</u>, so you'll have to use the <u>context</u> to tell which is which.

-ar verb endings

I	-aba	*Higher* → we	-ábamos	
you (inf., sing.)	-abas	you (inf., pl.)	-abais	
he/she/it/you (form., sing.)	-aba	they/you (form., pl.)	-aban	

Compraba manzanas.
I was buying / used to buy apples.

-er and -ir verb endings

I	-ía	*Higher* → we	-íamos	
you (inf., sing.)	-ías	you (inf., pl.)	-íais	
he/she/it/you (form., sing.)	-ía	they/you (form., pl.)	-ían	

Comía carne.
I was eating / used to eat meat.

2) Some verbs have slightly different translations too — '<u>estar</u>' can mean '<u>was/were</u>' and '<u>tener</u>' can mean '<u>had</u>'.

There are three irregular verbs in the imperfect tense

1) '<u>Ser</u>', '<u>ir</u>' and '<u>ver</u>' are the only three verbs which <u>don't</u> follow the pattern. '<u>Ser</u>' and '<u>ir</u>' are <u>irregular</u>...

ser — to be

I	era	*Higher* → we	éramos	
you (inf., sing.)	eras	you (inf., pl.)	erais	
he/she/it/you (form., sing.)	era	they/you (form., pl.)	eran	

Era rubio.
He was / used to be blond.

ir — to go

I	iba	*Higher* → we	íbamos	
you (inf., sing.)	ibas	you (inf., pl.)	ibais	
he/she/it/you (form., sing.)	iba	they/you (form., pl.)	iban	

Iba de compras.
I was going / used to go shopping.

2) ...but '<u>ver</u>' is <u>almost regular</u> — just add the '<u>-er</u>' endings onto '<u>ve-</u>', e.g. '<u>veía</u>'.

Veía la tele. *I was watching / used to watch TV.*

Había — There was / There were

'Hay' and 'había' come from the verb 'haber'.

In the <u>present tense</u>, '<u>hay</u>' means '<u>there is</u>' or '<u>there are</u>'. The <u>imperfect</u> form of '<u>hay</u>' is '<u>había</u>', which means '<u>there was</u>' or '<u>there were</u>' — it <u>stays the same</u>, regardless of whether the noun is <u>singular</u> or <u>plural</u>.

Había tráfico. *There was traffic.*　　　Había pájaros en el árbol. *There were birds in the tree.*

Grammar Questions

Put these verbs into the imperfect tense. The subject is given in brackets.

1. cantar (tú)　　3. aprender (usted)　　5. estar (yo)　　**H** 7. volver (ustedes)　　9. ser (nosotros) **H**
2. decir (él)　　4. nadar (ella)　　6. tener (tú)　　8. seguir (vosotros)　　10. ir (ellos)

Learning the imperfect — a perfect way to spend your time...

Everyone has to learn the singular imperfect forms, but only Higher tier students need to learn the plural forms.

Using the Past Tenses

Choosing which past tense to use can be a tricky business — here are some handy tips...

Learn when to use the preterite tense vs. the imperfect tense

1) Use the <u>preterite tense</u> to talk about a <u>single completed action</u> in the past or an event that happened during a <u>set period of time</u>.

> Fui al cine el jueves.   *I went to the cinema on Thursday.*   Ayer hizo calor.   *Yesterday it was hot.*

2) Use the <u>imperfect tense</u> to talk about what you <u>used to do repeatedly</u> or to <u>describe something</u> in the past.

> Hacía calor.   *It was hot.*   Iba al cine cada jueves.   *I used to go to the cinema every Thursday.*

3) You can also use the imperfect tense to talk about <u>something that was happening</u> when <u>something else happened</u>. You need to use the <u>preterite tense</u> for the action that <u>interrupts</u> the imperfect.

> Cuando paseaba al perro, vi a mi amigo.   *When I was walking the dog, I saw my friend.*

I have done — The present perfect tense

1) You use the <u>present perfect tense</u> to say '<u>have done</u>' or to talk about something that happened <u>recently</u>. To form it, you need the <u>present tense</u> of the verb '<u>haber</u>' and the <u>past participle</u>.

haber — to have...			
I	he	hemos	we
you (inf., sing.)	has	habéis	you (inf., pl.)
he/she/it/you (form., sing.)	ha	han	they/you (form., pl.)

> Han jugado al tenis.
> *They have played tennis.*

'Jugado' is a past participle.

2) To <u>form a past participle</u>, you <u>remove</u> the '<u>ar</u>' from '-ar' verbs and <u>add</u> '-ado'.

> ayudar *(to help)* ⟶ ayudado *(helped)*

3) For '-er' and '-ir' verbs, you <u>remove</u> the '<u>er</u>' or '<u>ir</u>' and <u>add</u> '-ido'.

> comer *(to eat)* ⟶ comido *(eaten)*

The past participle always stays the same — you don't need to make it feminine or plural.

4) There are some <u>irregular participles</u> that don't follow these rules. You'll just have to learn them.

Infinitive	Past participle
abrir	abierto *(opened, unlocked)*

Higher

Infinitive	Past participle	Infinitive	Past participle
cubrir	cubierto *(covered)*	ver	visto *(seen)*
decir	dicho *(said, told)*	hacer	hecho *(done, made)*
escribir	escrito *(written)*	volver	vuelto *(returned)*
poner	puesto *(put)*		

Grammar Questions

Translate these sentences into **Spanish**.

1. He has travelled to Spain.
2. She has run 500 metres.
3. They have finished the test.
4. Have you (tú) eaten already?
5. We have written a letter. **[H]**
6. They have returned home. **[H]**

Present perfect, preterite or imperfect — it's all in the timing...

To say what 'has happened' very recently, use the present perfect tense. To say what 'happened' once or over a set time period, use the preterite. For repeated actions in the past or descriptions, use the imperfect tense.

The Future Tenses

You'll need to talk about things that are going to happen at some point in the future.
There are two ways you can do it — and the first one's a piece of cake...

I'm going to... — The immediate future tense

This tense is also known as the 'periphrastic future'.

1) The immediate future tense can be used to talk about something that's about to happen, as well as something further on in the future.

2) To form the immediate future, take the present tense of 'ir' (to go) that goes with the person you're talking about.

3) Then, add 'a' and a verb in the infinitive.

ir — to go	
I am going	voy
you (inf., sing.) are going	vas
he/she/it/you (form., sing.) is/are going	va
we are going	vamos
you (inf., pl.) are going	vais
they/you (form., pl.) are going	van

voy
I am going
This is the present tense of 'ir'.

+ a **+**

comer
to eat
This is another verb in the infinitive.

=

Voy a comer.
I am going to / will eat.
This is a sentence about the future.

I will... — The proper future tense

This tense is also known as the 'inflectional future'.

1) Use the proper future tense to say what will happen.

2) To form it, take the 'future stem' of the verb — for most verbs, this is the infinitive.

3) Add the ending that matches the person you're talking about (the endings are the same for all verbs).

hablar
infinitive

+

é
future ending

=

hablaré
I will talk.

Future endings	
I	-é
you (inf., sing.)	-ás
he/she/it/you (form., sing.)	-á

Higher

we	-emos
you (inf., pl.)	-éis
they/you (form., pl.)	-án

4) There are a few verbs that have a special future stem, so you just have to learn them off by heart. These are the most important ones.

Infinitive	'I' form
tener (to have)	tendré
hacer (to do, make)	haré
poder (to be able to)	podré
poner (to put)	pondré

Infinitive	'he/she/it' form
haber (to have...)	habrá

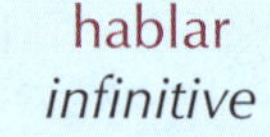

'Haber' is a bit different to other verbs — you only really need to use it in the 'he/she/it' form.

Higher

Infinitive	'I' form
saber (to know)	sabré
querer (to want)	querré
venir (to come)	vendré
decir (to say)	diré
salir (to go out)	saldré

Grammar Questions

Put these present tense verbs into the immediate and proper future tenses, keeping the subject the same.

1. haces	3. baila	5. puedes	7. ponen	9. queremos	11. dice
2. tiene	4. doy	6. juego	8. venimos	10. vivís	12. sabéis

(7, 8 and 11, 12 are marked **H**.)

Show off your skills by using both types of future tense...

Remember — the immediate future tense is useful for talking about something that's going to happen soon, but you'll need to use the proper future tense to talk about things that 'will happen' further ahead in the future.

The Conditional

Now it's time to talk about what 'could' or 'would' happen in the future...

Future stem + imperfect -er / -ir endings — The conditional

1) The <u>conditional</u> can be used for saying '<u>would</u>'. It uses the <u>same stems</u> as the <u>proper future tense</u> (see p.182) and adds these endings:

Conditional endings

I	-ía		we	-íamos
you (inf., sing.)	-ías	**Higher**	you (inf., pl.)	-íais
he/she/it/you (form., sing.)	-ía		they/you (form., pl.)	-ían

Pepe would eat the whole bowlful — if only Isuri would put it down...

comer
to eat
This is the <u>infinitive</u>. <u>Not</u> all verbs use the same future stem though (see p.182).

+

comía
I was eating.
This is the -er / -ir ending of the imperfect tense.

=

comería
I would eat.
This is a sentence in the <u>conditional</u>.

2) You can <u>combine</u> the conditional with other tenses to make more <u>complicated</u> sentences:

Bailaría, pero me duelen los pies.   *I would dance, but my feet hurt.*

Le gustaría ir a la playa, pero no puede ir porque está lloviendo.
She would like to go to the beach, but she can't go because it's raining.

For more on conjunctions, check out p.161.

Irregular verbs in the conditional

The <u>stems</u> for <u>irregular verbs</u> are the <u>same</u> ones you use for the <u>proper future tense</u> (see p.182). You just add the <u>conditional endings</u> instead:

Infinitive	'I' form
tener *(to have)*	tendría
hacer *(to do, make)*	haría
poder *(to be able to)*	podría
poner *(to put)*	pondría

Infinitive	'I' form
saber *(to know)*	sabría
querer *(to want)*	querría
venir *(to come)*	vendría
decir *(to say)*	diría
salir *(to go out)*	saldría

(Higher)

Infinitive	'he/she/it' form
haber *(to have...)*	habría

Saldría de la casa, pero estoy cansado.
I would leave the house, but I'm tired.

¿Podría ayudarme?   *Could you (form., sing.) help me?*

Using 'poder' (to be able to) in the conditional lets you say 'could'.

Grammar Questions

Write these verbs in the conditional. The subject has been given to you in brackets.

1. ir (yo)
2. cantar (él)
3. poner (tú)
4. hablar (usted)
5. hacer (ella)
6. pedir (yo)
7. decir (vosotros)
8. venir (nosotros)
9. querer (ustedes)
10. saber (ellos)

It's your lucky day — the conditional only has one set of endings...

It doesn't matter whether a verb ends in 'ar', 'er' or 'ir' (or whether it's regular or irregular) — you add the same conditional endings. Take some time to master the irregular stems before you turn to the next page.

Modal Verbs

Modal verbs help you express desire, ability or obligation, so you might find this page rather useful...

Deber, poder, querer, tener que, saber

1) <u>Modal verbs</u> are usually <u>followed by an infinitive</u>.

> **Debo terminar** la tarea ahora.
> *I must finish the task now.*

> **Deben llevar** un disfraz para la fiesta.
> *They have to wear a costume for the party.*

Using 'deber' in the conditional helps you say 'should'.

2) As well as '<u>deber</u>' (*to have to, must*), there are <u>four other</u> modal verbs you <u>need to know</u>:

a) Use '<u>poder</u>' to say '<u>can</u>' or '<u>could</u>'.

> No **puedo ir** al cine.   *I can't go to the cinema.*

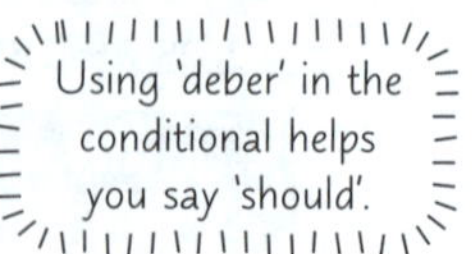

b) Use '<u>querer</u>' to say '<u>want to</u>'.

> **Quiero viajar** a más países.   *I want to travel to more countries.*

c) You can also use '<u>tener que</u>' when you want to say '<u>have to</u>' or '<u>must</u>'.

> **Tengo que volver** a casa a las seis.   *I have to go back home at six o'clock.*

'Tener' by itself isn't a modal verb. You need to add the 'que' to show the action that you have to do.

d) You can use '<u>saber</u>' to say '<u>know how to</u>'.

> **Sabe montar** en bici.   *She knows how to ride a bike.*

You could also translate this sentence as 'She can ride a bike.'

Quisiera, me gustaría — I would like

1) '<u>Quisiera</u>' and '<u>me gustaría</u>' are two common ways of saying '<u>I would like</u>'.
Just like other modal verbs, they are <u>followed by an infinitive</u>.

> **Quisiera / Me gustaría visitar** el museo.   *I would like to visit the museum.*

See p.12 for more on how to use verbs like 'gustar'.

2) You can use 'quisiera' and 'me gustaría' in <u>polite requests</u>.

> **Quisiera / Me gustaría reservar** una mesa para tres personas.   *I would like to reserve a table for three.*

3) Using other pronouns with '<u>gustar</u>' in the <u>conditional</u> helps you say what other people '<u>would like</u>'.

> ¿**Te gustaría leer**?   *Would you (inf., sing.) like to read?*

> **Le gustaría comer**.   *She would like to eat.*

Grammar Questions

Translate these sentences into **English**.

1. Debes repasar para la prueba.
2. Juanjo no sabe hablar español.
3. ¿Pueden venir a la boda?
4. Tenemos que escuchar bien.
5. No quiero volver a casa.
6. Quisiera pagar la cuenta.

Be careful when you change the tense of modal verbs...

Using modal verbs in different tenses can change their meaning slightly. For example, using 'poder' in the present tense helps you say 'can', but it becomes 'could' in the conditional. Now, I could use a snack break...

Reflexive Verbs and Pronouns

Quick Quiz

Sometimes you'll have to talk about things you do to yourself — like 'washing yourself' or 'getting yourself up' in the morning. It sounds weird in English, but in Spanish they do it all the time.

Me, te, se... — Reflexive pronouns

1) <u>Reflexive pronouns</u> usually mean '<u>self</u>'. They <u>change form</u> depending on <u>who's doing</u> the action:

myself	me	nos	ourselves
yourself (inf., sing.)	te	os	yourselves (inf., pl.)
himself/herself/oneself/ yourself (form., sing.)	se	se	themselves/ yourselves (form., pl.)

You can tell which verbs need 'self' by checking in the dictionary. 'To have a wash' is 'lavarse'.

2) When you use a reflexive verb on its own, the pronoun goes <u>before</u> it. **Me** lavo.   *I have a wash.*

3) If you have a verb followed by a <u>reflexive infinitive</u>, the reflexive pronoun goes <u>before</u> the <u>first verb</u> or at the <u>end</u> of the <u>infinitive</u>.

   Me debo levantar.   *I have to get up.*   Debes levantar**te**.   *You (inf., sing.) have to get up.*

4) You can also use <u>reflexive pronouns</u> for reciprocal actions where two people do something to <u>each other</u>.

   Nos hablamos.   *We talk to each other.*   ¿**Os** visteis?   *Did you (inf., pl.) see each other?*

Lavarse, despertarse, levantarse... — Reflexive verbs

1) Reflexive verbs follow a straightforward pattern, e.g. '<u>lavarse</u>' = to have a wash (literally '<u>to wash oneself</u>'). You can use them in <u>any tense</u> as well — they take the <u>same endings</u> as their non-reflexive forms.

I have a wash	me lavo	nos lavamos	we have a wash
you (inf., sing.) have a wash	te lavas	os laváis	you (inf., pl.) have a wash
he/she/it/you (form., sing.) has/have a wash	se lava	se lavan	they/you (form., pl.) have a wash

   ¿**Te** sientes mal?   *Do you (inf., sing.) feel ill?*   **Me** llevo bien con él.   *I get on well with him.*

2) There are lots of these verbs, but here are the ones you really <u>should know</u>:

despertarse	*to wake up*	ponerse	*to get, become (+ adjective)*
levantarse	*to get up*	vestirse	*to get dressed*
sentirse	*to feel*	acostarse	*to go to bed*
llamarse	*to be called*		

'despertarse', 'sentirse', 'vestirse' and 'acostarse' are all stem-changing verbs (see p.176).

   Se puso nerviosa.   *She became nervous.*   **Me** despierto tarde.   *I wake up late.*

Grammar Questions

Write these reflexive verbs in the present tense. The subject has been given to you in brackets.

  1. llamarse (yo)   **3.** sentirse (él)   **5.** ponerse (vosotros)   **7.** vestirse (nosotros)

  2. llevarse (tú)   **4.** despertarse (usted)   **6.** levantarse (ellos)   **8.** acostarse (yo)

Make sure you know all the reflexive verbs on this page...

...because they'll be really handy in the exam. Just remember to put the reflexive pronoun in the right place.

Verbs with '-ing' and 'Just Done'

The continuous tenses help you specify that something is ongoing at a particular moment.

Use the present continuous for what's happening right now

1) <u>Most</u> of the time you'd translate 'I am doing' with the <u>present tense</u>, e.g. 'hago'.

2) If you want <u>to stress</u> that something <u>is happening</u> at the moment, you use the <u>present continuous</u>.

Estoy cenando.   *I'm having dinner.*

3) To form the present continuous, you need the correct part of '<u>estar</u>' (*to be*) in the <u>present</u> tense...

estar — to be	
I am	estoy
you (inf., sing.) are	estás
he/she/it is you (form., sing.) are	está
we are	estamos
you (inf., pl.) are	estáis
they/you (form., pl.) are	están

4) ...and the '<u>-ing</u>' part — also called the <u>present participle</u> or <u>gerund</u>.

5) It's made up of the <u>stem</u> of the verb (p.175), plus the correct <u>ending</u>.

   a) If it's an <u>-ar</u> verb, add '<u>-ando</u>'.

$$\underset{\textit{present of 'estar'}}{\text{estoy}} + \underset{\textit{'hablar' stem}}{\text{habl-}} + \underset{\textit{-ar ending}}{\text{-ando}} = \underset{\textit{I am speaking}}{\text{estoy hablando}}$$

   b) If it's an <u>-er</u> or <u>-ir</u> verb, add '<u>-iendo</u>'.

$$\underset{\textit{present of 'estar'}}{\text{estás}} + \underset{\textit{'comer' stem}}{\text{com-}} + \underset{\textit{-er ending}}{\text{-iendo}} = \underset{\textit{you (inf., sing.) are eating}}{\text{estás comiendo}}$$

6) There are a few <u>stem-changing</u> present participles. For example, in verbs like '<u>pedir</u>', the '<u>e</u>' changes to '<u>i</u>'.

pedir (*to ask for*) ⟶ *pidiendo*   decir (*to say*) ⟶ *diciendo*

The '<u>o</u>' changes to '<u>u</u>' in the <u>stem</u> of verbs like '<u>dormir</u>'.

dormir (*to sleep*) ⟶ *durmiendo*   morir (*to die*) ⟶ *muriendo*

If the verb's stem ends in a <u>vowel</u>, you add '<u>-yendo</u>' instead of '-iendo'.

leer (*to read*) ⟶ *leyendo*   construir (*to build*) ⟶ *construyendo*

The imperfect continuous is for saying what was happening

1) If you want <u>to stress</u> that something <u>was happening</u> in the past, use the <u>imperfect continuous</u>.

2) The imperfect continuous is <u>similar</u> to the present continuous, except '<u>estar</u>' has to be in the <u>imperfect</u> tense.

See p.180 for more on the imperfect tense.

$$\underset{\textit{imperfect of 'estar'}}{\text{estaba}} + \underset{\textit{'hablar' stem}}{\text{habl-}} + \underset{\textit{-ar ending}}{\text{-ando}} = \underset{\textit{I was speaking}}{\text{estaba hablando}}$$

Estaba buscando mis llaves.   *I was looking for my keys.*

Se estaba cayendo, pero lo cogí.   *It was falling, but I caught it.*

Estaba durmiendo cuando llegaron.
He was sleeping when they arrived.

The preterite tense is used here to show that a sudden action — the people arriving — interrupted an ongoing action in the imperfect continuous — i.e. the person sleeping.

Pavel wasn't letting a falling *manzana* spoil his *mañana*.

There are a few other ways to say '-ing'

Higher

1) If you want to say you <u>continue to do</u> something or you'll <u>still be doing</u> something, you can use the <u>present tense</u> of the verb '<u>seguir</u>' with a <u>present participle</u>.

Ron and Sue should have checked the forecast...

sigo *present of 'seguir'*	**+**	**habl-** *'hablar' stem*	**+**	**-ando** *-ar ending*	**=**	**sigo hablando** *I am still speaking*

Siguen andando. *They continue to walk.*   Sigue lloviendo. *It's still raining.*

2) To say you <u>have been doing</u> something <u>for a certain amount of time</u>, you can use the <u>present tense</u> of the verb '<u>llevar</u>', followed by a <u>time period</u> and a <u>present participle</u>.

llevo *present of 'llevar'*   **+**   **dos horas** *time period*   **+**   **escribiendo** *present participle*   **=**   **Llevo dos horas escribiendo.** *I have been writing for two hours.*

Lleva treinta minutos ordenando su habitación.   *He's been tidying his bedroom for thirty minutes.*

Llevamos casi cinco horas repasando.   *We've been revising for almost five hours.*

3) You can also use the <u>present tense</u> with '<u>desde hace</u>' to say <u>how long</u> you've been doing something.

Toco la guitarra desde hace cuatro años.   *I've been playing the guitar for four years.*

'Acabar de' — to say that something's just happened

Higher

To say what's <u>just</u> happened, use the present tense of '<u>acabar</u>', followed by '<u>de</u>' and a verb in the <u>infinitive</u>.

'Acabar' is a regular '-ar' verb.

acabar de... — to have just...	
I have just...	acabo de...
you (inf., sing.) have just...	acabas de...
he/she/it/you (form., sing.) has/have just...	acaba de...
we have just...	acabamos de...
you (inf., pl.) have just...	acabáis de...
they/you (form., pl.) have just...	acaban de...

Acabo de llegar.   *I have just arrived.*

Acaba de salir.   *She has just left.*

Acabamos de verla.   *We have just seen her.*

Grammar Questions

Put these verbs into the present continuous. The subject has been given to you in brackets.

1. traer (tú)   **3.** decir (ellos)   **5.** bailar (nosotros)   **7.** servir (ustedes)

2. abrir (usted)   **4.** correr (vosotros)   **6.** leer (yo)   **8.** seguir (ella)

Translate these sentences into **Spanish**.

9. He was asking for an orange.   **11.** The cat was sleeping.   **13.** They have just seen the film.

10. I was studying in my room.   **12.** She was working well.   **14.** We have just had breakfast.

The present continuous stresses what's going on at the moment...

Careful, though — it isn't used as much in Spanish as it is in English, so don't be tempted to put it everywhere. You'll need the present tense in most cases, so only use the present continuous for emphasis.

Negative Forms

No, I won't write anything here about negatives. Nothing at all... except that they're pretty useful.

'No' in front of the verb means 'not'

1) To change a sentence to mean the <u>opposite</u> in Spanish, you have to put 'no' in front of the <u>verb</u>:

Hablo español. *I speak Spanish.* → No hablo español. *I don't speak Spanish.*

2) You can do the <u>same</u> with <u>all the tenses</u>:

No fui al parque. *I didn't go to the park.*

3) Sometimes you have to say 'no' <u>twice</u>. This is because 'no' in Spanish means both '<u>no</u>' and '<u>not</u>'.

No, no quiero paella, gracias.
No, I don't want paella, thanks.

4) You can also put '<u>nada</u>' (*not anything, nothing*), '<u>nunca</u>' (*never*) or '<u>nadie</u>' (*nobody, no one*) <u>before</u> a verb to make it <u>negative</u>.

Nunca canta. *She never sings.*

5) These words can be used with 'no' too. The 'no' goes <u>before</u> the verb and the other negative word goes <u>after</u> it.

No vi a nadie. *I didn't see anybody.*

'nadie' can also mean 'anybody' or 'anyone' after a negative verb.

There are some tricky negatives to learn too

There are more negatives you need to <u>understand</u> — for top marks you should use them too.

(no) ... ningún / ninguna	*no, not ... any (pre-noun)*
(no) ... ninguno / ninguna	*no one, none, one (after a negative verb), anyone (after a negative verb)*
(no) ... ni ... (ni ...)	*nor, or (after a negative verb), neither ... nor ...*
(no) ... tampoco	*neither, either (after a negative verb)*
ya no	*no longer, no more*

Higher

See p.166 for more information on 'ningún'.

No hay ningún tomate. *There aren't any tomatoes.*

No queda ninguno. *There are none left.*

No van ni a Londres ni a Madrid ni a Barcelona.
They go to neither London, nor Madrid nor Barcelona.

In <u>negative lists</u>, you need a 'ni' <u>before</u> each item.

Tampoco hay uvas. *Neither are there grapes.*

No me gusta tampoco. *I don't like it either.*

Ya no voy a Sevilla. *I no longer go to Seville.*

Higher

Grammar Questions

Translate these sentences into **Spanish** using negative forms.
1. We didn't go to the library.
2. They don't have any apples.
3. There's nothing here.
4. Nobody is in the car.
5. It's neither red nor green.
6. We no longer go to the gym.

Remember — 'no' in Spanish means 'no' <u>and</u> 'not'...

Sometimes you'll need to say 'no' twice, especially if you're answering a question. In some cases, you don't need 'no' at all — you just have to put the negative word before the verb to make the sentence negative.

Impersonal Verbs and the Passive

Impersonal verbs and the passive come up occasionally, so it's important that you know about them.

Impersonal verbs use a generic subject

> You can make any Spanish verb impersonal by using its 'he/she/it' form and adding 'se' before it.

1) Impersonal verbs <u>don't</u> have a <u>specific subject</u> — they use a <u>general</u> one like 'it' or 'one'.

2) You can use '<u>se puede</u>' to say '<u>you (general) / one can</u>' and '<u>se necesita</u>' to say '<u>you (general) / one needs to</u>'.

Se puede comer. *You (general) can eat.*

¿Se necesita salir? *Does one need to leave?*

3) Use 'hace' and a noun to talk about the weather. See p.131 for more.

Hace calor. It is hot.

4) Here are some more important <u>impersonal verbs</u> you need to know:

Impersonal verb	Meaning	Example sentence
hay	there is / there are	Hay libros en esta caja. (*There are books in this box.*)
hay que	you (general) / one must	Hay que hacer la tarea. (*One must do the task.*)

Higher

Impersonal verb	Meaning	Example sentence
parece	it seems	Parece un poco raro. (*It seems a little strange.*)
basta + infinitive	you (general) only have to (+ verb)	Basta hacerlo una vez. (*You only have to do it once.*)
falta (+ infinitive)	it's/is still to be (+ past participle)	Falta investigarlo. (*It's still to be investigated.*)
hace falta (+ infinitive)	it's necessary (+ verb)	Hace falta trabajar. (*It's necessary to work.*)
vale la pena + infinitive	it's worth -ing	Vale la pena esperar. (*It's worth waiting.*)

There are two forms of the passive

> For the passive voice, past participles must agree with the subject. So 'escrita' is used because 'la carta' is feminine.

1) In an <u>active</u> sentence, the <u>subject does</u> something. In the <u>passive</u> voice, something is <u>done to</u> the <u>subject</u>.

Escribió la carta. *He wrote the letter.*

Fue escrita por él. *It was written by him.*

2) The passive is formed using '<u>ser</u>' (*to be*), a <u>past participle</u> (see p.181) and '<u>por</u>' (*by*).

fueron + limpiado + por = Las mesas fueron limpiadas por ellos.
they were *cleaned* *by* *The tables were cleaned by them.*

This part changes depending on the <u>tense</u> and <u>subject</u>. | <u>past participle</u> of the verb '<u>limpiar</u>' | A sentence in the <u>passive</u> voice. The past participle has to <u>agree</u> with the subject.

3) You can also form the passive with '<u>se</u>' and the <u>third-person forms</u> of any verb.
Use the '<u>he/she/it</u>' form for a single subject, and the '<u>they</u>' form for a plural subject:

El arroz se cocina por diez minutos.
The rice is cooked for ten minutes.

Las puertas se abren a las nueve.
The doors are opened at nine.

Grammar Questions

Translate these sentences into **Spanish** using impersonal verbs.

1. You can relax now.
2. One must do exercise.
3. You need to go to class.
4. There are many festivals.
5. It's worth learning this content. **H**
6. It seems like a marvellous idea. **H**

One has to learn this — it's nothing personal...

Impersonal verbs might seem tricky, but you just need to remember to use the 'he/she/it' form of the verb.

The Subjunctive

Now it's time to find out when you need to use the subjunctive and how to form it for five key verbs.

Forming the present subjunctive

1) Sometimes, the <u>present subjunctive</u> is needed <u>instead</u> of the <u>normal present</u> tense.

2) To <u>form</u> the present subjunctive of '<u>hacer</u>', '<u>tener</u>' and '<u>venir</u>', take the <u>stem</u> from the '<u>I</u>' form of the normal <u>present tense</u> and <u>add</u> the '<u>-ar</u>' verb <u>endings</u>.

hago → hag- + -a = hag**a**

You only need to know the singular forms of these verbs in the present subjunctive.

Verb	I	you (inf., sing.)	he/she/it/ you (form., sing.)
hacer (*to do, make*)	haga	hagas	haga
tener (*to have*)	tenga	tengas	tenga
venir (*to come*)	venga	vengas	venga
ir (*to go*)	vaya	vayas	vaya
ser (*to be*)	sea	seas	sea

3) You'll need to learn the subjunctive forms for '<u>ir</u>' and '<u>ser</u>' by heart — they are <u>completely irregular</u>.

Use the present subjunctive...

1) ...after '<u>cuando</u>' (*when*) when talking about the future:

Cuando sea mayor, viviré en Italia.   *When I am older, I will live in Italy.*

2) ...to <u>request</u> or <u>command</u> someone else does something:

Vyvan quiere que yo haga la cena.   *Vyvan wants me to make dinner.*

It looks like Vyvan and Greg will be having a takeaway...

3) ...to express a <u>wish</u> or <u>desire</u>:

Espero que Noor tenga los billetes.   *I hope that Noor has the tickets.*

You normally only use the subjunctive when there's a different person doing the second verb.

4) ...after expressing an <u>emotion</u>:

Es triste que no vayas de vacaciones.   *It's sad that you (inf., sing.) don't go on holiday.*

5) ...after '<u>para que</u>' (*so that*) to express purpose:

Mejoramos la app para que sea más fácil usarla.   *We're improving the app so that it's easier to use it.*

6) ...after '<u>que</u>' (*that*) to express <u>possibility</u> or <u>necessity</u>:

Es posible que venga a la fiesta.
It's possible that he'll come to the party.

Es importante que hagas los ejercicios.
It's important that you (inf., sing.) do the exercises.

Grammar Questions

Decide whether you need the present subjunctive or normal present tense in each of these sentences.

1. Piensan que Charvi _____ a su boda. (venir)

2. Lo explico para que _____ más claro. (ser)

3. Ya sé que ella _____ más hijos que yo. (tener)

4. Me preocupa que el libro no _____ bueno. (ser)

5. Llamo a mi novio cuando él _____ al café. (ir)

6. Es necesario que yo _____ mis deberes. (hacer)

Don't confuse the present tense with the present subjunctive...

The subjunctive can be a pretty tricky topic, even for people who have been learning Spanish for ages. Take all the time you need with the points on this page — you can always revisit them if you're feeling unsure.

The Imperative

Imperatives are words that give a command. They change depending on whether you're talking to one person or a group. So learn what's on this page and you'll be giving out orders in no time...

Singular informal commands

1) To form a <u>singular informal</u> command, take the '<u>tú</u>' part of the <u>present tense</u> verb and <u>take off</u> the '<u>s</u>'.

> escribes   *you write* ⟶ ¡Escribe!   *Write!*   escuchas   *you listen* ⟶ ¡Escucha!   *Listen!*

2) With commands, <u>pronouns</u> (e.g. me, them, it) are placed at the <u>end</u> of the word and you need to <u>add</u> an <u>accent</u> to show where the <u>stress</u> is.

> ¡Cómelo!   *Eat it!*   ¡Llámame!   *Call me!*

3) There are a few common <u>irregular imperatives</u> you <u>need to know</u>.

> ¡Ven aquí, por favor!   *Come here, please!*
>
> ¡Dime!   *Tell me!*   ¡Hazlo!   *Do it!*

You don't need an accent when you use pronouns with the irregular imperatives.

Infinitive	Informal singular
ser (*to be*)	¡Sé!
ir (*to go*)	¡Ve!
tener (*to have*)	¡Ten!
venir (*to come*)	¡Ven!
hacer (*to do, make*)	¡Haz!
decir (*to say, tell*)	¡Di!
poner (*to put (on)*)	¡Pon!
salir (*to go out, leave*)	¡Sal!

Plural informal commands

Higher

1) To tell <u>two or more people</u> what to do in an <u>informal</u> way, take the <u>infinitive</u> and <u>change</u> the final '<u>r</u>' to '<u>d</u>'.

> hablar (*to speak, talk*) ⟶ ¡Hablad!   *Speak!*   conducir (*to drive*) ⟶ ¡Conducid!   *Drive!*
>
> mirar (*to look, watch*) ⟶ ¡Mirad!   *Look!*   leer (*to read*) ⟶ ¡Leed!   *Read!*

2) The verbs that are <u>irregular</u> in <u>singular informal commands</u> follow the <u>same</u> rules as <u>regular</u> verbs in the <u>you (inf., pl.) form</u>.

> salir (*to go out*) ⟶ ¡Salid!   *Go out!*   ir (*to go*) ⟶ ¡Id!   *Go!*
>
> poner (*to put (on)*) ⟶ ¡Poned la caja allí!   *Put the box there!*

Laura was sure she could make space for more boxes...

Grammar Questions

Translate these sentences into **Spanish** using informal singular commands.

1. Sing this song!
2. Go to your room!
3. Write two sentences!
4. Take it!
5. Say something!
6. Drink the water!

Translate these sentences into **Spanish** using informal plural commands.

7. Learn these words!   **H**
8. Sign this document!
9. Wait here, please!
10. Buy that now!
11. Make your beds!   **H**
12. Cross the street!

Learn how to use the imperative... Go on...

The examiner will use the imperative in your speaking exam to give you instructions, so it's worth learning this page well. Commands are also handy if you want to tell someone who's annoying you to go away...

Verbs and Tenses — Grammar List

Regular Verbs

All regular verbs that end in '-ar', '-er' or '-ir' can be conjugated like these three examples.

-ar verbs, e.g. hablar (to speak, talk)

Subject	Present	Preterite	Imperfect	Proper Future	Conditional
yo	hablo	hablé	hablaba	hablaré	hablaría
tú	hablas	hablaste	hablabas	hablarás	hablarías
él / ella / usted	habla	habló	hablaba	hablará	hablaría
nosotros/as	hablamos	hablamos	hablábamos	hablaremos	hablaríamos
vosotros/as	habláis	hablasteis	hablabais	hablaréis	hablaríais
ellos / ellas / ustedes	hablan	hablaron	hablaban	hablarán	hablarían

-er verbs, e.g. comer (to eat)

Subject	Present	Preterite	Imperfect	Proper Future	Conditional
yo	como	comí	comía	comeré	comería
tú	comes	comiste	comías	comerás	comerías
él / ella / usted	come	comió	comía	comerá	comería
nosotros/as	comemos	comimos	comíamos	comeremos	comeríamos
vosotros/as	coméis	comisteis	comíais	comeréis	comeríais
ellos / ellas / ustedes	comen	comieron	comían	comerán	comerían

-ir verbs, e.g. vivir (to live)

Subject	Present	Preterite	Imperfect	Proper Future	Conditional
yo	vivo	viví	vivía	viviré	viviría
tú	vives	viviste	vivías	vivirás	vivirías
él / ella / usted	vive	vivió	vivía	vivirá	viviría
nosotros/as	vivimos	vivimos	vivíamos	viviremos	viviríamos
vosotros/as	vivís	vivisteis	vivíais	viviréis	viviríais
ellos / ellas / ustedes	viven	vivieron	vivían	vivirán	vivirían

Important Irregular Verbs

You only need to know the subjunctive forms for ser, ir, tener, hacer and venir.

ser (to be)

Subject	Present	Preterite	Imperfect	Proper Future	Conditional	Subjunctive
yo	soy	fui	era	seré	sería	sea
tú	eres	fuiste	eras	serás	serías	seas
él / ella / usted	es	fue	era	será	sería	sea
nosotros/as	somos	fuimos	éramos	seremos	seríamos	
vosotros/as	sois	fuisteis	erais	seréis	seríais	**Imperative**
ellos / ellas / ustedes	son	fueron	eran	serán	serían	tú ¡Sé!

You need the present tense forms of 'ir' to make the immediate future tense (see p.182).

ir (to go)

Subject	Present	Preterite	Imperfect	Proper Future	Conditional	Subjunctive
yo	voy	fui	iba	iré	iría	vaya
tú	vas	fuiste	ibas	irás	irías	vayas
él / ella / usted	va	fue	iba	irá	iría	vaya
nosotros/as	vamos	fuimos	íbamos	iremos	iríamos	
vosotros/as	vais	fuisteis	ibais	iréis	iríais	**Imperative**
ellos / ellas / ustedes	van	fueron	iban	irán	irían	tú ¡Ve!

tener (to have)

Subject	Present	Preterite	Imperfect	Proper Future	Conditional	Subjunctive
yo	tengo	tuve	tenía	tendré	tendría	tenga
tú	tienes	tuviste	tenías	tendrás	tendrías	tengas
él / ella / usted	tiene	tuvo	tenía	tendrá	tendría	tenga
nosotros/as	tenemos	tuvimos	teníamos	tendremos	tendríamos	
vosotros/as	tenéis	tuvisteis	teníais	tendréis	tendríais	**Imperative**
ellos / ellas / ustedes	tienen	tuvieron	tenían	tendrán	tendrían	tú ¡Ten!

Only the irregular imperatives are included on these pages. You can find
out how to form regular imperatives in the 'tú' and 'vosotros' forms on p.191.

hacer (to do, make)

Subject	Present	Preterite	Imperfect	Proper Future	Conditional	Subjunctive
yo	hago	hice	hacía	haré	haría	haga
tú	haces	hiciste	hacías	harás	harías	hagas
él / ella / usted	hace	hizo	hacía	hará	haría	haga
nosotros/as	hacemos	hicimos	hacíamos	haremos	haríamos	
vosotros/as	hacéis	hicisteis	hacíais	haréis	haríais	**Imperative**
ellos / ellas / ustedes	hacen	hicieron	hacían	harán	harían	tú ¡Haz!

venir (to come)

Subject	Present	Preterite	Imperfect	Proper Future	Conditional	Subjunctive
yo	vengo	vine	venía	vendré	vendría	venga
tú	vienes	viniste	venías	vendrás	vendrías	vengas
él / ella / usted	viene	vino	venía	vendrá	vendría	venga
nosotros/as	venimos	vinimos	veníamos	vendremos	vendríamos	
vosotros/as	venís	vinisteis	veníais	vendréis	vendríais	**Imperative**
ellos / ellas / ustedes	vienen	vinieron	venían	vendrán	vendrían	tú ¡Ven!

poner (to put (on))

Subject	Present	Preterite	Imperfect	Proper Future	Conditional	Subjunctive
yo	pongo	puse	ponía	pondré	pondría	ponga
tú	pones	pusiste	ponías	pondrás	pondrías	pongas
él / ella / usted	pone	puso	ponía	pondrá	pondría	ponga
nosotros/as	ponemos	pusimos	poníamos	pondremos	pondríamos	
vosotros/as	ponéis	pusisteis	poníais	pondréis	pondríais	**Imperative**
ellos / ellas / ustedes	ponen	pusieron	ponían	pondrán	pondrían	tú ¡Pon!

You also need to know the future and conditional forms of 'estar', but they are
regular — you can use the '-ar verbs' table on the previous page to form them.

You need these forms
of 'haber' to form the
present perfect tense.

estar (to be)

Subject	Present	Preterite	Imperfect
yo	estoy	estuve	estaba
tú	estás	estuviste	estabas
él / ella / usted	está	estuvo	estaba
nosotros/as	estamos	estuvimos	estábamos
vosotros/as	estáis	estuvisteis	estabais
ellos / ellas / ustedes	están	estuvieron	estaban

haber (to have done something)

Subject	Present
yo	he
tú	has
él / ella / usted	ha
nosotros/as	hemos
vosotros/as	habéis
ellos / ellas / ustedes	han

Verbs and Tenses — Grammar List

Other Common Verbs

The stems of these verbs change their spellings in certain tenses. See p.176 for more on stem-changing verbs.

decir (to say, tell)

Subject	Present	Preterite	Future	Conditional
yo	digo	dije	diré	diría
tú	dices	dijiste	dirás	dirías
él / ella / usted	dice	dijo	dirá	diría
nosotros/as	decimos	dijimos	diremos	diríamos
vosotros/as	decís	dijisteis	diréis	diríais
ellos / ellas / ustedes	dicen	dijeron	dirán	dirían

Higher (Future), *Higher* (Conditional)

Imperative tú ¡Di!

You can find out how to conjugate the regular forms of these verbs by using the regular verb boxes on p.192.

dar (to give)

Subject	Present	Preterite
yo	doy	di
tú	das	diste
él / ella / usted	da	dio
nosotros/as	damos	dimos
vosotros/as	dais	disteis
ellos / ellas / ustedes	dan	dieron

salir (to go out)

Subject	Future	Conditional
yo	saldré	saldría
tú	saldrás	saldrías
él / ella / usted	saldrá	saldría
nosotros/as	saldremos	saldríamos
vosotros/as	saldréis	saldríais
ellos / ellas / ustedes	saldrán	saldrían

Higher (Future), *Higher* (Conditional)

Imperative tú ¡Sal!

In the present tense, 'salir' is only irregular in its 'yo' form ('salgo').

ver (to see, watch)

Subject	Present	Imperfect
yo	veo	veía
tú	ves	veías
él / ella / usted	ve	veía
nosotros/as	vemos	veíamos
vosotros/as	veis	veíais
ellos / ellas / ustedes	ven	veían

Hilde reckons she's nearly finished revising for her GCSE Spanish exams.

traer (to bring)

Subject	Present	Preterite
yo	traigo	traje
tú	traes	trajiste
él / ella / usted	trae	trajo
nosotros/as	traemos	trajimos
vosotros/as	traéis	trajisteis
ellos / ellas / ustedes	traen	trajeron

Reflexive Verbs and Pronouns

Reflexive verbs are useful for talking about things you do to yourself — they use reflexive pronouns.

Reflexive Pronoun		llamarse (to be called)
me	*myself*	me llamo
te	*yourself (inf., sing.)*	te llamas
se	*himself, herself, itself, oneself, yourself (form., sing.)*	se llama
nos	*ourselves*	nos llamamos
os	*yourselves (inf., pl.)*	os llamáis
se	*themselves, yourselves (form., pl.)*	se llaman

For more on reflexive pronouns and where to put them in a sentence, see p.185.

Impersonal Verbs

These are the impersonal forms of 'haber':

Present	hay	*there is / are*
Imperfect	había	*there was / were / used to be*
Proper Future	habrá	*there will be / is going to be*
Conditional	habría	*there would be*

se puede	*you (general) / one can*
se necesita	*you (general) / one needs to*
hace + weather noun	*it is...*
hay que	*you (general) / one must*
parece	*it seems*
basta + infinitive	*you (general) only have to (+ verb)*
falta + infinitive	*it's, is still to be (+ past participle)*
hace falta + infinitive	*it's necessary (+ verb)*
vale la pena + infinitive	*it's worth -ing*

Higher (parece...vale la pena)

Modal Verbs

See p.184 for more information about modal verbs.

querer (to want (to), love)

Subject	Present	Preterite	Imperfect	Proper Future	Conditional
yo	quiero	quise	quería	querré	querría
tú	quieres	quisiste	querías	querrás	querrías
él / ella / usted	quiere	quiso	quería	querrá	querría
nosotros/as	queremos	quisimos	queríamos	querremos	querríamos
vosotros/as	queréis	quisisteis	queríais	querréis	querríais
ellos / ellas / ustedes	quieren	quisieron	querían	querrán	querrían

poder (to be able to, can)

Subject	Present	Preterite	Imperfect	Proper Future	Conditional
yo	puedo	pude	podía	podré	podría
tú	puedes	pudiste	podías	podrás	podrías
él / ella / usted	puede	pudo	podía	podrá	podría
nosotros/as	podemos	pudimos	podíamos	podremos	podríamos
vosotros/as	podéis	pudisteis	podíais	podréis	podríais
ellos / ellas / ustedes	pueden	pudieron	podían	podrán	podrían

saber (to know (how to))

Subject	Present	Preterite	Imperfect	Proper Future	Conditional
yo	sé	supe	sabía	sabré	sabría
tú	sabes	supiste	sabías	sabrás	sabrías
él / ella / usted	sabe	supo	sabía	sabrá	sabría
nosotros/as	sabemos	supimos	sabíamos	sabremos	sabríamos
vosotros/as	sabéis	supisteis	sabíais	sabréis	sabríais
ellos / ellas / ustedes	saben	supieron	sabían	sabrán	sabrían

Past Participles

Use past participles with the verb 'haber' to form the perfect tense ('I have done').

Regular endings for past participles:

-ar verbs	-er / -ir verbs
-ado, e.g. habl**ado**	**-ido**, e.g. viv**ido**

These past participles are irregular:

Verb	Past participle	
abrir	abierto	*opened, unlocked*
decir	dicho	*said, told*
escribir	escrito	*written*
hacer	hecho	*done, made*
poner	puesto	*put*
ver	visto	*seen*
volver	vuelto	*returned*
cubrir	cubierto	*covered*

To say what's just happened use this phrase:

acabar de + infinitive	*to have just (+ past participle)*

Present Participles

Use present participles with the verb 'estar' to form the present and imperfect continuous ('I am/was doing').

Regular endings for present participles:

-ar verbs	-er / -ir verbs
-ando, e.g. habl**ando**	**-iendo**, e.g. viv**iendo**

These present participles change the spellings of their stems:

Verb	Present participle	
pedir	p**i**diendo	*asking for*
decir	d**i**ciendo	*saying, telling*
dormir	d**u**rmiendo	*sleeping*
morir	m**u**riendo	*dying*
leer	le**y**endo	*reading*
construir	constru**y**endo	*building*

Some set phrases in Spanish need a present participle:

seguir + present participle	*(to) continue to, still be + -ing*
llevar + time period + present participle	*(to) have been + -ing for X time*

Section Fifteen — Verbs and Tenses

Revision Summary Test for Section Fifteen

Here it is — the final revision summary. Test yourself if you dare. *Plays suspenseful music*

- Yep, these questions are **hard** — they'll really help you see **how well you know your stuff**.
- Tackle the **revision summary test** below, or scan the QR code to do it **online**.
  Use the CGP RevisionHub to **track your progress** and see **which areas need more work**.
- You can find **sample answers** here: www.cgpbooks.co.uk/MadridExtras

The Present Tense ☑

1) List all the present tense forms of these verbs: a) preparar   b) beber   c) recibir

2) Explain how the verb stem changes its spelling in the present tense for:
   a) jugar   b) servir   c) doler   d) preferir   e) repetir   f) conocer   g) salir   h) empezar

3) Give a sentence in the present tense using these verbs: a) hacer   b) ir   c) ser   d) estar   e) tener

The Preterite, Imperfect and Present Perfect Tenses ☑

4) List all the preterite tense endings for '-ar' verbs and '-er' and '-ir' verbs.

5) Give the 'I' form of the preterite tense for: a) ser   b) dar   c) traer   d) poner   e) querer   f) decir

6) List all the singular imperfect tense endings for regular '-ar' verbs and '-er' and '-ir' verbs.

7) Translate these sentences into Spanish: a) She has danced.   b) I have learnt.   c) They have left.

8) Explain when you'd use the preterite, imperfect and present perfect tenses.

H L 9) Give the correct imperfect tense form for each of the verbs below. The subject is given in brackets.
   a) ser (vosotros)   b) ir (nosotros)   c) ver (ustedes)   d) estar (ellos)   e) tener (Luisa y yo)

The Future Tenses and the Conditional ☑

10) Translate these sentences into Spanish using the immediate future tense:
    a) I am going to go to Spain.   b) We are going to arrive tonight.   c) He is not going to get lost.

11) Using the proper future tense, say that you will buy a present for your sister.

12) 'En un mundo ideal, comería patatas fritas todos los días.' Translate this sentence into English.

H L 13) Translate these sentences into Spanish, using the proper future tense or the conditional:
    a) I would come.   b) They will tell you.   c) She would know the answer.   d) We will go.

Modal Verbs, Reflexives and -ing Verbs ☑

14) List all the modal verbs and phrases in this section. There are 7 you need to know.

15) Translate these sentences into Spanish: a) She feels tired.   b) Are you (inf., sing.) staying here?

16) What are the present participles of these verbs? a) pasar   b) volver   c) pedir   d) dormir   e) caer

H 17) Describe two ways to say how long you 'have been doing' something. Give an example of each one.

L 18) 'We have just found your (inf., pl.) keys.' How would say this in Spanish?

Negative Forms, Impersonal Verbs and the Passive ☑

19) Write a sentence using each of these negatives: a) (no) nunca   b) (no) nada   c) (no) nadie

20) List all the impersonal verbs in this section. There are 5 you need to know (plus 5 for Higher tier).

H 21) Say these sentences in Spanish: a) I no longer live there.   b) I wear neither skirts nor dresses.

L 22) Give a sentence using the passive voice with: a) 'ser' + past participle   b) 'se' + a third-person form

The Subjunctive and the Imperative ☑

23) What are the singular informal imperatives for these verbs? a) correr   b) decir   c) salir   d) tomar

24) In Spanish, use an imperative to tell two of your friends to open the door.

Higher 25) Translate this sentence into Spanish: 'I hope that Dídac comes to my party.'

26) List all the singular forms of the present subjunctive for: a) hacer   b) tener   c) ir   d) ser

Spelling and Pronunciation

Spanish pronunciation can be tricky, so use this page to help if you're unsure how to pronounce a word. You can scan the QR code to hear the sounds and words in the tables spoken aloud. →

Listening Track 44

Spanish pronunciation is quite different to English

The table below shows some of the main ways of spelling common sounds in Spanish.

Listen to the audio and practise pronouncing each sound out loud as you hear it.

Spelling	Example 1	Example 2
a	antiguo	abrir
o	copa	perro
e	esquina	viejo
i	ideal	instituto
u	comunidad	usar
ll	llevar	apellido
ch	noche	mucho
ca	campo	chica
co	comer	corazón
cu	discutir	excursión
cu + vowel	cuando	cuenta
ce	excelente	dulce
ci	estación	medicina
z	zapato	confianza
que	aunque	quedar
qui	quisiera	equipo
ga	lugar	gafas
go	luego	negocio
gu	gustar	segundo
ge	genial	argentino
gi	página	religión
gue	hamburguesa	juguete (Higher only)
gui	alguien	siguiente
j	jugar	bajo
ñ	sueño	compañero
v	varios	ver
-r-, -r	camarero	pasar
rr, r-, -r-	error	repetir
silent h	hermano	hora

In some Spanish-speaking countries, these → sound more like 's' than 'th' in English. (pointing to ce, ci, z)

In Spanish, you don't pronounce the 'h' at the beginning of words. →

Some Spanish words have an accent to show you which vowel you need to stress when you say them.

It's useful to know how accents change the pronunciation of a word, but you'll only be tested on these if you're taking Higher tier.

á	pájaro	práctico
é	éxito	francés
í	increíble	típico
ó	montón	avión
ú	autobús	útil

The Listening Exam

These pages are crammed full of advice to help you tackle your exams head on, so listen up.

There are four exams for GCSE Spanish

1) Your AQA Spanish GCSE is assessed by four separate exams — Listening, Speaking, Reading and Writing.

2) Each exam is worth 25% of your final mark. You'll get a grade between 1 and 9 (9 being the highest).

3) You won't sit all of the papers at the same time — you'll probably have
your speaking exam a couple of weeks before the rest of your exams.

Doug had found the best
listening practice for his GCSE
exam — his Spanish neighbours.

The listening exam has two sections

1) For the listening paper, you'll listen to various
recordings of people speaking in Spanish.

2) The paper is 45 minutes long for Higher-tier students and 35 minutes
long for Foundation-tier students. It's split into Section A and Section B:

Section A is the longer section — it's worth 40 marks at Higher tier and 32 marks at Foundation tier. It contains comprehension questions in English, and you'll write your answers in English.

Section B is a shorter dictation section — it's worth 10 marks at Higher tier and 8 marks at Foundation tier. You'll hear some short sentences and write them down in Spanish.

Read through the paper carefully at the start of the test

1) Before the recording begins, you'll be given five minutes to read through the paper.

2) In particular, look at the questions in Section A. Use this time to read each
question carefully. Some are multiple choice, and others require you to write
some short answers — make sure you know what each one is asking you to do.

3) Reading the question titles, and the questions themselves, will give you a good idea of
the topics you'll be asked about. This should help you predict what to listen out for.

4) You can write on the exam paper, so scribble down anything that might be useful.

5) You'll be given 2 minutes at the end of the recording to check your work.

Make notes while listening to the recordings

1) For Section A you'll hear each audio track twice, and then
there'll be a pause for you to write down your answer.

- While you're listening, it's a good idea to jot down a few details — e.g. dates, times, names
or key words. But make sure you keep listening while you're writing down any notes.

- Listen right to the end, even if you think you've got the answer — sometimes
the person will change their mind or add an important detail at the end.

- Don't worry if you can't understand every word that's being said — just listen carefully
both times and try to pick out the vocabulary you need to answer the question.

2) For Section B you will hear each sentence three times — first as a full sentence, then in short
sections and then again as a full sentence. Keep in mind that you'll be marked for accurate spelling.

Don't worry if you didn't quite catch the answer...

If you're still not sure of the answer after hearing the track, scribble one down anyway — it's worth a shot.

The Speaking Exam

The important thing to remember for the speaking exam is that no one is trying to catch you out.

The speaking exam has three parts

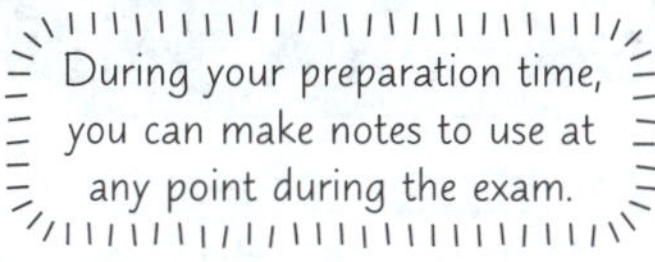

1) Your <u>speaking exam</u> will be conducted and recorded by your <u>teacher</u>.

2) The exam is in <u>three parts</u>. Before you start, you'll get <u>15 minutes</u> of <u>preparation time</u>. The time allowed for the exam is <u>10-12 minutes</u> at Higher tier and <u>7-9 minutes</u> at Foundation tier.

① Role-play	② Reading aloud task	③ Photo card discussion
You'll get a <u>card</u> with a <u>scenario</u> on it. It'll have <u>five tasks</u> — <u>four</u> will be <u>notes</u> on what you should talk about. The '<u>?</u>' shows you have to ask a question about the words next to it. See p.214 for an example.	You'll get a <u>card</u> with <u>several sentences</u> on it, in Spanish. You'll <u>read</u> the sentences <u>out loud</u>, then your teacher will ask you <u>four questions</u> in Spanish related to the topic of the sentences. See p.215 for an example.	Before the exam, you'll receive a <u>card</u> with <u>two photos on it</u> (look at the example on p.216). Your teacher will ask you to <u>talk about the photos</u> and then ask you <u>questions</u> related to the same theme.

Try to be imaginative with your answers

You need to find ways to <u>show off</u> the full extent of your <u>Spanish knowledge</u>. You should try to:

1) Use a <u>range of tenses</u> — e.g. for a question on daily routine, think of when <u>something different</u> happens.

> Pero mañana **será** diferente porque **jugaré** al fútbol después del instituto.
> *But tomorrow it will be different because I will play football after school.*

2) Talk about <u>other people</u>, as well as yourself — it's fine to <u>make people up</u> if that helps.

> Me gusta el rugby, pero **mi primo lo odia**. *I like rugby, but my cousin hates it.*

3) Give loads of <u>opinions</u> and <u>reasons</u> for your opinions.

> En mi opinión, debemos reciclar más porque producimos demasiada basura.
> *In my opinion, we must do more recycling because we produce too much rubbish.*

If you're really struggling, ask for help in Spanish

1) If you get <u>really stuck</u> trying to think of a word or phrase, you can <u>ask for help</u> — as long as it's <u>in Spanish</u>.

2) For example, if you <u>can't remember</u> how to say 'homework' in Spanish, <u>ask</u> your teacher. You <u>won't</u> get any marks for <u>vocabulary</u> your teacher's <u>given</u> you though.

> ¿Qué es 'homework' en español? *What is 'homework' in Spanish?*

3) If you <u>don't hear something clearly</u>, just ask:

> ¿Puedes repetir, por favor? *Can you repeat, please?*

Making mistakes isn't the end of the world...

Don't panic if you make a mistake in the speaking exam — what's important is how you deal with it. You won't lose marks for correcting yourself, so show the examiner that you know where you went wrong.

The Reading Exam

The reading exam is split into two parts, so make sure you know what to do for each section.

In Section A, you'll answer questions about texts

1) The <u>Higher-tier</u> reading paper is <u>1 hour long</u>, and the <u>Foundation-tier</u> paper is <u>45 minutes</u>. Both are worth <u>50 marks</u> and have <u>two sections</u>.

2) In <u>Section A</u>, you'll be given a <u>variety of Spanish texts</u> and then asked <u>questions</u> about them. The texts could include things like blog posts, emails, newspaper reports and adverts. The questions and answers will be <u>in English</u>.

3) <u>Scan through each text</u> first to <u>get an idea</u> of what it's about. Then read the <u>questions</u> that go with it carefully, making sure you understand <u>what information</u> you should be looking out for.

4) Next, <u>go back through the text</u>. You're not expected to understand every word, so don't get distracted by trying to work out what everything means — <u>focus</u> on finding the <u>information you need</u>. If you're having trouble with a particular question, you might want to <u>move on</u> and <u>come back to it later</u>.

Don't give up if you don't understand something

1) Use the <u>context</u> of the text to help you understand what it might be saying. You might be able to find some clues in the <u>title of the text</u> or the <u>type of text</u>.

2) Knowing how to spot <u>different word types</u> (e.g. nouns, verbs) can help you work out what's happening in a sentence. See the <u>grammar sections</u> (p.151-196) for more.

3) Make sure you put an answer down for <u>every question</u> — some of the questions are multiple choice, so even if you can't work out the answer, it's always worth putting down one of the options.

4) You can <u>guess</u> some Spanish words that look or sound the <u>same as English</u> words, e.g. el problema (*problem*), la música (*music*), el color (*colour*).

5) Be careful though — you might come across some '<u>false friends</u>'. These are Spanish words that look like an English word, but have a <u>completely different meaning</u>:

el pie	*foot*	la ropa	*clothes*	actual	*current*	grabar	*to record*
el éxito	*success*	largo/a	*long*	el instituto	*secondary school*	el pan	*bread*

In Section B, you'll translate from Spanish to English

1) <u>Section B</u> will ask you to translate several <u>short Spanish sentences</u> (between 35-50 words in total) <u>into English</u>. The sentences will be on <u>topics you've studied</u>, so the vocabulary should be familiar.

2) Here are some <u>top tips</u> for doing your translations:

- Translate <u>a whole sentence at a time</u>, rather than word by word — this will avoid any of the Spanish word order being carried into the English.

- Keep an eye out for different <u>tenses</u> — there will be a variety throughout the sentences.

- <u>Read through</u> your translations to make sure they sound <u>natural</u>. Some words and phrases don't translate literally, so you'll need to make sure that your sentences sound like normal English.

Familiarise yourself with the structure of the exam...

It's good to be prepared and know what you'll be facing in the exam, so remember that Section A is reading Spanish texts and Section B is translating sentences. Have a look at the Practice Papers for an example.

The Writing Exam

The writing exam is a great way of showing off what you can do — try to use varied vocabulary, include a range of tenses, and pack in any clever expressions that you've learnt over the years. You've got this.

There are various types of questions in the writing exam

1) The <u>Higher-tier</u> writing paper is <u>1 hour and 15 minutes long</u> and the <u>Foundation-tier</u> paper is <u>1 hour and 10 minutes long</u>. Some tasks are only for one tier, but others appear in both — these are explained below.

2) Each task is worth a <u>different number of marks</u>, so you should spend more time on the higher-mark tasks.

Foundation

Photo Response Task (10 marks)
You'll be asked to write <u>five short sentences</u> in Spanish to describe a black and white photo.

Translation Task (10 marks)
You'll translate sentences from English <u>into Spanish</u>. The sentences could be on <u>any topic</u> you've studied. See p.200 for some top tips for translation tasks.

Grammar Task (5 marks)
You'll need to complete <u>five</u> short sentences by choosing the <u>correct option</u>, using your <u>grammar</u> knowledge.

90-word Writing Task (15 marks)
You'll be asked to write <u>about 90 words</u> in response to <u>three bullet points</u>. You'll have a <u>choice between two questions</u>. Make sure you write about each bullet point.

50-word Writing Task (10 marks)
You'll be asked to produce a <u>short piece of writing</u> in response to <u>five bullet points</u>. You'll be expected to write <u>about 50 words</u> in total. Remember to write about each bullet point.

Higher

150-word Writing Task (25 marks)
You'll need to write <u>about 150 words</u> in Spanish, based on <u>two bullet points</u>. There will be <u>two questions</u> to choose from. This task is more creative — so don't forget to include some <u>opinions</u> with <u>reasons</u>.

Plan out your answers and carefully check them

1) In the writing paper, you'll have to translate <u>English sentences into Spanish</u>. <u>Read each sentence fully</u> before you start. Don't worry — the translation will only include the vocab and grammar you've <u>learnt</u>.

2) For the longer writing tasks, spend a few minutes for each question <u>planning out</u> your answer. Decide <u>how</u> you're going to <u>cover every bullet point</u> and <u>in what order</u> you're going to write things.

3) Write the <u>best answers</u> you can, using the Spanish <u>that you know</u> — it doesn't matter if it's not true. It's your chance to <u>show off</u> your Spanish knowledge.

4) Once you've got something that you're happy with, go back through and <u>check your answer</u>. Here's a checklist of useful things to look out for:

Remember — you can use non-binary or gender-neutral pronouns in the exam (see p.199).

- Are all the <u>verbs</u> in the <u>right tense</u> and do they have the <u>correct endings</u>?
- Do your <u>adjectives agree</u> with their nouns and are they in the <u>right place</u>?
- Is your <u>word order</u> correct, including any <u>negative structures</u>?
- Have you <u>spelt</u> everything correctly, including using the right <u>accents</u>?

Make sure you cover every aspect of the tasks...

When you're nervous and stressed, it's easy to miss out something the question has asked you to do. For questions with bullet points, try to write about each point in order — tick them off as you go along.

GCSE Spanish
Higher Tier

Listening Paper

Centre name					
Centre number					
Candidate number					

Surname	
Other names	
Candidate signature	

Time allowed: 45 minutes approximately (including 5 minutes' reading time before the test and 2 minutes' checking time at the end of the test)

You will need no other materials.
The pauses are pre-recorded for this test.
Instructions
- You must **not** use a dictionary.
- Use black ink or black ball-point pen.
- Fill in the box at the top of this page.

This is what you should do for each item.
- After the question number is announced, there will be a pause to allow you to read the instructions and questions.
- Listen carefully to the recording and read the questions again.
- Listen to the recording again, and then answer the questions.
- When the next question is about to start you will hear a bleep.
- You may write at any time during the test.
- At the end of the test you will have two minutes in which to check your work.
- In **Section A**, answer the questions in **English**. In **Section B**, which is the dictation, write in **Spanish**.
- You must answer **all** the questions in the spaces provided.
- Write neatly and put down **all** the information you are asked to give.
- Once you start the recording, you will have five minutes to read through the question paper before the first question begins. You may make notes during this time.

Information
- The marks for questions are shown in brackets.
- The maximum mark for this paper is 50.

Section A

Listening comprehension

Social media

Antonio and Diego are discussing their views on social media.

What do they say about social media?

Write **A** if only statement **A** is correct.
B if only statement **B** is correct.
A + **B** if both statements **A** and **B** are correct.

1   Antonio says that social media...

A	connects us with the rest of society.
B	is a quick way to communicate with people.

[1 mark]

2   Diego thinks the increased use of social media has...

A	replaced face-to-face communication.
B	made us less effective at communicating.

[1 mark]

3   According to Antonio, businesses look for people who...

A	are confident speaking to people without devices.
B	know how to use social media.

[1 mark]

4   Diego agrees that knowledge of the digital world is necessary for...

A	companies that only do business online.
B	anyone who works in social media.

[1 mark]

Celebrity culture

Dolores is talking about her life as a popular influencer.

Complete the sentences in **English**.
Write **one** word in each space.

Example   Dolores is very ....*famous*........ for her ....*paintings*........ .

5   Dolores loves having the opportunity to share her ....

with a large audience and gifting her art to her ....   *[2 marks]*

6   However, she likes neither the .... nor the responsibility

of having so much ....   *[2 marks]*

School pressures

Julia and Sofía are talking about their friend, Lola.
Answer the questions in **English**.

7   What happened to Lola last year?

....   *[1 mark]*

8   What was the consequence for Lola?

....   *[1 mark]*

9   What did Lola's teachers suggest she could do?

....   *[1 mark]*

10   What are Lola's friends going to do?

....   *[1 mark]*

Healthy living

You are listening to a personal trainer giving health advice.

Complete the sentences.

Choose the correct answer and write the letter in each box.

Answer both parts of question 11.

11.1 The personal trainer advises people to...

A	take their health seriously.
B	stop smoking.
C	look after their bodies.

[1 mark]

11.2 According to the personal trainer, frequent exercise...

A	decreases your energy.
B	helps you feel more healthy.
C	will protect your heart.

[1 mark]

Answer both parts of question 12.

12.1 The personal trainer also advises people to...

A	avoid really sweet food.
B	eat less junk food.
C	avoid drinks with lots of sugar.

[1 mark]

12.2 The personal trainer says people who don't do this can struggle with...

A	excess weight.
B	serious health problems.
C	being underweight.

[1 mark]

School subjects

You are listening to a student talking about the subjects she studies at school.

What is her opinion of the following subjects?

Write **P** for a **positive** opinion.
    N for a **negative** opinion.
    P + N for a **positive** and **negative** opinion.

Answer both parts of question 13.

13.1   Maths

[1 mark]

13.2   Geography

[1 mark]

Answer both parts of question 14.

14.1   History

[1 mark]

14.2   Science

[1 mark]

Eating out

Marcos is talking to his friend Andrea.
Answer the questions in **English**.

15   Where is the restaurant that Andrea went to?

....   *[1 mark]*

16   What did Andrea order at the restaurant?

....   *[1 mark]*

17   What did Andrea dislike about her boyfriend's food?

....   *[1 mark]*

18   Why does Andrea think it would be better to go to the restaurant later?

....   *[1 mark]*

Where people live

You are listening to a local guide talking about changes in their town.

Write the correct **number** of the feature they mention.
Write the correct **letter** for when it takes place.

Feature

1	Shops
2	Green spaces
3	Important buildings
4	Houses

When

P	Past
N	Now
F	Future

19   **Feature**   **When**

[2 marks]

20   **Feature**   **When**

[2 marks]

Future plans

A headteacher is giving advice to students about careers.

What does she say?

Choose the correct answer and write the letter in each box.

21 The headteacher says that choosing a career...

A	takes a long time.
B	is difficult for many people.
C	should be done after finishing school.

[1 mark]

22 She suggests that young people talk to...

A	their school friends.
B	their teachers.
C	adults they know.

[1 mark]

23 On Wednesday evening, students will be able to...

A	ask the headteacher questions.
B	talk to some local people about their careers.
C	talk to their teachers about their careers.

[1 mark]

24 According to the headteacher, the most important thing is to...

A	choose something you're good at.
B	think carefully about choosing your career.
C	choose a career you think you will enjoy.

[1 mark]

  Turn over

Travel

Leya is talking to Javier about a recent holiday.

What did she think about the following aspects?

A	awful
B	enjoyable
C	wonderful
D	calm
E	busy
F	free

Write the correct letter in each box.

Answer both parts of question 25.

25.1   Easter Week

[1 mark]

25.2   The campsite

[1 mark]

Answer both parts of question 26.

26.1   The activities

[1 mark]

26.2   The food

[1 mark]

Social issues

You are listening to a news report on a Spanish radio station about a crime.

Choose the correct answer and write the letter in each box.

Answer both parts of question 27.

27.1 The crime took place...

A	this afternoon.
B	several days ago.
C	last Monday.

[1 mark]

27.2 The man who stole the painting...

A	handed himself in to the police.
B	hid in the museum.
C	was found in a building far away.

[1 mark]

Answer both parts of question 28.

28.1 The man was going to...

A	sell the painting abroad.
B	hide the painting abroad.
C	steal another painting abroad.

[1 mark]

28.2 The painting has...

A	been badly damaged.
B	suffered no damage.
C	already been returned to the museum.

[1 mark]

Turn over

Section B

Dictation

You will now hear 5 short sentences.

Listen carefully and using your knowledge of Spanish sounds, write down in **Spanish** exactly what you hear for each sentence.

You will hear each sentence **three** times: the first time as a full sentence, the second time in short sections and the third time again as a full sentence.

Use your knowledge of Spanish sounds and grammar to make sure that what you have written makes sense. Check carefully that your spelling is accurate.

[10 marks]

Sentence 1

....

....

Sentence 2

....

....

Sentence 3

....

....

Sentence 4

....

....

Sentence 5

....

....

YOU NOW HAVE TWO MINUTES TO CHECK YOUR WORK

END OF QUESTIONS

GCSE Spanish
Higher Tier

Speaking Paper

Time Allowed: 10-12 minutes (+ 15 minutes' supervised preparation time)

Instructions to candidates
- Find a friend or parent to read the teacher's part for you.
- During the preparation time, you are required to prepare
  one Role-play card, **one** Reading aloud task and **one** Photo card.
- You may make notes during the preparation time for use during
  the test and you may use these notes at any time during the test.

Instructions to teachers
- You are expected to give candidates the opportunity to respond fully to all tasks,
  being aware of the recommended length of each task (as specified below) to
  ensure that they are able to access the maximum number of marks available.
- Timing of the test will start when you begin the Role-play using the introductory
  text in the Teacher's role. Timing of the test will end when the maximum time
  allowed is reached (**twelve** minutes for the whole test).

Information
The test consists of three parts:

- **Part 1**: a Role-play card (recommended to last around one and a half minutes).
- **Part 2**: a Reading aloud text and short conversation based on the topic of the text
  (recommended to last between three and three and a half minutes in total).
- **Part 3**: discussion of a Photo card containing two photos
  (recommended to last between six and seven minutes in total).

Candidates must **not** use a dictionary at any time during this test. This includes the preparation time.

ROLE-PLAY
CANDIDATE'S ROLE

Instructions to candidates

- You are talking to your Argentinian friend.

- Your teacher will play the part of your friend and will speak first.

- You should address your friend as *tú*.

- When you see this – **?** – you will have to ask a question.

In order to score full marks, you must include at least one verb in your response to each task.

    1. Describe a typical morning at your school. (Give **two** details).

    2. Say what you did in your Spanish class last week. (Give **one** detail.)

    3. Say what your favourite school subject is and why. (Give **one** subject and **one** reason.)

    4. Describe one school rule that you don't like and why. (Give **one** rule and **one** reason.)

?   **5.** Ask your friend a question about school.

READING ALOUD TASK
CANDIDATE'S CARD

Instructions to candidates

When your teacher asks you, read aloud the following text **in Spanish**.

Mis amigos y yo vamos al gimnasio a entrenar dos veces a la semana.

Antes no participaba en muchas actividades físicas.

Además, comía mucha comida basura y no me gustaba ni la fruta ni las verduras.

Hice unos cambios en mi vida y ahora me siento mucho mejor.

Ahora trato de mantener una dieta equilibrada.

La semana que viene cocinaré una paella para mi familia.

You will then be asked four questions **in Spanish** that relate to the topic of **Healthy living and lifestyle.**

In order to score the highest marks, you must try to **answer all four questions as fully as you can**.

PHOTO CARD
CANDIDATE'S MATERIAL

Instructions to candidates

- During your preparation time, look at the two photos. You may make as many notes as you wish on a separate sheet of paper and use these notes during the test.

- Your teacher will ask you to talk about the content of these photos. The recommended time is approximately **one and a half minutes**. **You must say at least one thing about each photo**.

- After you have spoken about the content of the photos, your teacher will then ask you questions related to **any** of the topics within the theme of **Popular culture.**

Photo 1

Photo 2

ROLE-PLAY
TEACHER'S ROLE

- You begin the role-play.

- You should address the candidate as *tú*.

- You must read out the teacher's role shown below in italics **without any changes**.

You must begin the role-play by using the introductory text below.

Introductory text: *Estás hablando con tu amigo argentino/tu amiga argentina.*
Yo soy tu amigo/tu amiga.

1		Ask the candidate to describe a typical morning at their school. *¿Cómo es una mañana típica en tu colegio?* Allow the candidate to give **two** details about a typical morning at their school.
2		Ask the candidate what they did in their Spanish class last week. *¿Qué hiciste en tu clase de español la semana pasada?* Allow the candidate to give **one** detail about what they did in their Spanish class last week.
3		Ask the candidate what their favourite school subject is and why. *¿Cuál es tu asignatura favorita? ... ¿Por qué?* Allow the candidate to say what their favourite school subject is and to give **one** reason why.
4		Ask the candidate to describe a school rule they don't like. *¿Qué regla en tu colegio no te gusta? ... ¿Por qué?* Allow the candidate to say which rule they dislike and to give **one** reason why.
5	**?**	*Muy bien.* Allow the candidate to ask you a question about school. *(Give an appropriate response.)*

READING ALOUD TASK
TEACHER'S ROLE

This part of the test is recommended to last between **three and three and a half minutes**. This includes the reading aloud of the text and the four questions below.

After the role-play is finished, ask the candidate to read the text, by saying *Lee el texto*.

Allow the candidate to read aloud the text and then ask the following four questions. You must ask the candidate these questions as they are printed here **without any changes**.

- ¿Qué tipo de comida te gusta preparar en casa?

- ¿Qué haces para mantenerte en forma?

- ¿Por qué es importante cuidar tu salud mental?

- ¿Cuál es tu opinión sobre el alcohol?

PHOTO CARD
TEACHER'S NOTES

Theme: Popular culture

The candidate is given a card containing two photos from the same topic and makes notes on them in the preparation period.

You ask the candidate to talk about the photos. At Higher tier, the recommended time is approximately **one and a half minutes**. The candidate must say at least one thing about each photo. You then have an unprepared conversation which is recommended to last between **four and a half and five and a half minutes**.

Candidates may use any notes they have made during the preparation time.

You begin by asking the candidate to tell you about the photos.

• Háblame de las fotos.

When the candidate has finished talking about the photos for approximately one and a half minutes, you have a conversation within the theme of **Popular culture**. This can include **any or all** of the prescribed topics:

• Free-time activities

• Customs, festivals and celebrations

• Celebrity culture

You may wish to use the list of sample questions below, but this list is not exhaustive.

1. Háblame de tu celebración favorita.

2. ¿Qué te gusta hacer cuando sales con tus amigos?

3. ¿Cómo celebraste tu último cumpleaños?

4. ¿Cuáles son las ventajas de ser famoso?

5. ¿Cómo prefieres pasar tu tiempo libre?

6. ¿Por qué te gusta tu famoso favorito?

This part of the test is recommended to last in total **between six and seven minutes**.
This includes the description of the photos and the unprepared conversation.

GCSE Spanish
Higher Tier

Reading Paper

Centre name				
Centre number				
Candidate number				

| Surname |
| Other names |
| Candidate signature |

Time Allowed: 1 hour

You will need no other materials.

Instructions
- You must **not** use a dictionary.
- Use black ink or black ball-point pen.
- Fill in the boxes at the top of this page.
- Answer **all** questions.
  You must answer all the questions in the spaces provided.
- In **Section A**, answer the questions in **English**.
  In **Section B**, translate the sentences into **English**.
- Do all rough work in this answer book. Cross through any work you do not want to be marked.

Information
- The marks for questions are shown in brackets.
- The maximum mark for this paper is 50.

Section A

Reading Comprehension

Newspaper headlines

You see some headlines in a Spanish newspaper.

A	**Una especie rara de pájaro regresa al parque nacional.**
B	**Los profesores universitarios siguen estando en huelga.**
C	**Un estudio reciente dice que pasear cada día mejora la salud mental.**
D	**El turismo ha aumentado aun más en los dos últimos años.**
E	**Un incendio destruye la nueva exposición en el museo de cultura.**

Which headline matches each description?

Write the correct letter in each box.

1   A local disaster

[1 mark]

2   A new research publication

[1 mark]

3   A protest

[1 mark]

Directions

Your Spanish friend, Marta, has sent you directions to the youth club in the town centre.

Read her message and answer the questions in **English**.

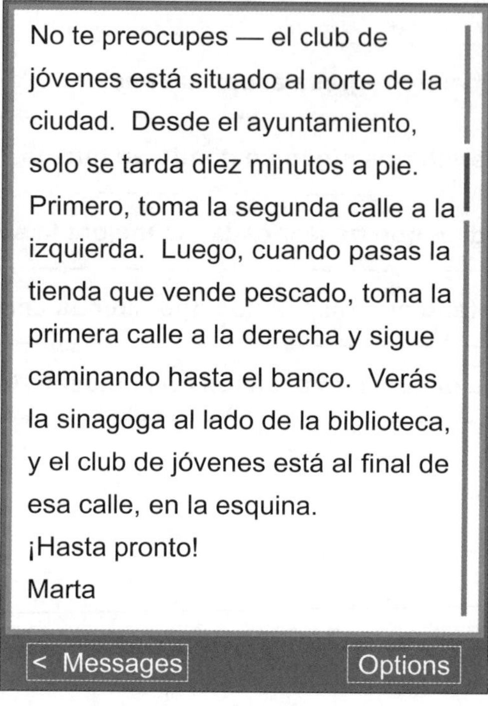

4 How long does it take to get to the youth club using the route Marta has suggested?

.... *[1 mark]*

5 When should you turn right?

.... *[1 mark]*

6 Name **two** other buildings which are on the same street as the youth club.

1. ....

2. .... *[2 marks]*

The life of a celebrity

You visit a website where some Spanish influencers are talking about their lives as celebrities.

> **Luisa:** Me encanta ser famosa y subir vídeos a las redes sociales. Me hace feliz leer los comentarios donde las personas explican la influencia positiva que he tenido en sus vidas.
>
> **Jalil:** Desde el momento en que me hice famoso, mi vida ha estado llena de estrés. Si no sigo la moda, el público me criticará. Por eso, no recomendaría la vida de un influencer a los jóvenes.
>
> **Hugo:** Mi familia es lo más importante en mi vida y preferiría pasar más tiempo con ella. Sin embargo, resulta difícil porque mi trabajo suele llevarme lejos de casa.
>
> **Andrea:** Además de ser influencer, soy música. Me da la oportunidad de viajar por todo el mundo y conectarme directamente con mis seguidores.

Match the correct person with each of the following questions.

Write **L** for **Luisa**

   J for **Jalil**

   H for **Hugo**

   A for **Andrea**.

Write the correct letter in each box.

7   Who wishes they could spend more time at home?

[1 mark]

8   Who meets people all over the world?

[1 mark]

9   Who regrets becoming an influencer?

[1 mark]

10   Who loves to hear what their fans think of them?

[1 mark]

A festival in Spain

You read this article about a festival in Valencia, a city in Spain.

Durante diecinueve días en marzo, los habitantes de Valencia salen a la calle para celebrar Las Fallas. Esta fiesta es distinta a otras que hay en España por las estatuas* de madera enormes que se ven por las calles. Son construidas y luego quemadas por los ciudadanos. Es un espectáculo increíble.

Las celebraciones incluyen conciertos donde se puede escuchar música de varios géneros y desfiles en los cuales los habitantes llevan el traje tradicional. La tradición de celebrar Las Fallas en Valencia no es nada nueva. La gente celebra la llegada de la primavera de esta manera desde hace más o menos seiscientos años. Esta fiesta tiene un ambiente de alegría y un carácter único. Todos deberían verla por lo menos una vez.

estatuas = statues

Complete these sentences. Write the letter for the correct option in each box.

11 Las Fallas is celebrated...

A	for almost twenty days in spring.
B	over nineteen days in summer.
C	every year in autumn.

[1 mark]

12 The festival is unique because of...

A	where it takes place.
B	the wooden statues.
C	its amazing shows.

[1 mark]

13 People celebrate by...

A	painting statues and playing traditional music.
B	burning buildings and partying in the streets.
C	listening to music and attending parades.

[1 mark]

14 The festival has been celebrated for...

A	nearly 60 years.
B	almost 6,000 years.
C	around 600 years.

[1 mark]

15 According to the article, Las Fallas is...

A	a festival that has a strange atmosphere.
B	something everyone should see at least once.
C	an old tradition that should be stopped.

[1 mark]

Healthy living

You read this magazine article about healthy lifestyle choices.

Aquí hay unas medidas que podrías tomar para mejorar tu vida.

En primer lugar, está el ejercicio. Practicar un deporte tiene muchos beneficios para el cuerpo. No solo contribuye a la buena salud física, sino también a la buena salud mental. Además, es una manera de luchar contra el estrés diario.

Segundo, está el sueño. Es muy importante dormir bastante y bien. Por eso, deberías dejar los dispositivos electrónicos fuera del dormitorio. También deberías dejar de ver la tele una hora antes de acostarte.

Y en último lugar, no se puede olvidar una dieta equilibrada. Deberías incluir en ella alimentos con alto contenido en fibra*, como **las lentejas**. Es importantísimo también beber bastante agua y reducir el consumo de bebidas que contienen mucho azúcar.

fibra = fibre

16 According to the article, why is it beneficial to do more exercise? Give **two** details.

1...

2.. *[2 marks]*

17 What **two** pieces of advice does the article give to improve your sleep?

1...

2.. *[2 marks]*

18 Read the last paragraph again. What should you do with **las lentejas**?

A	Drink them.
B	Eat them.
C	Wash them.

[1 mark]

The latest technology

Read Miguel's email.

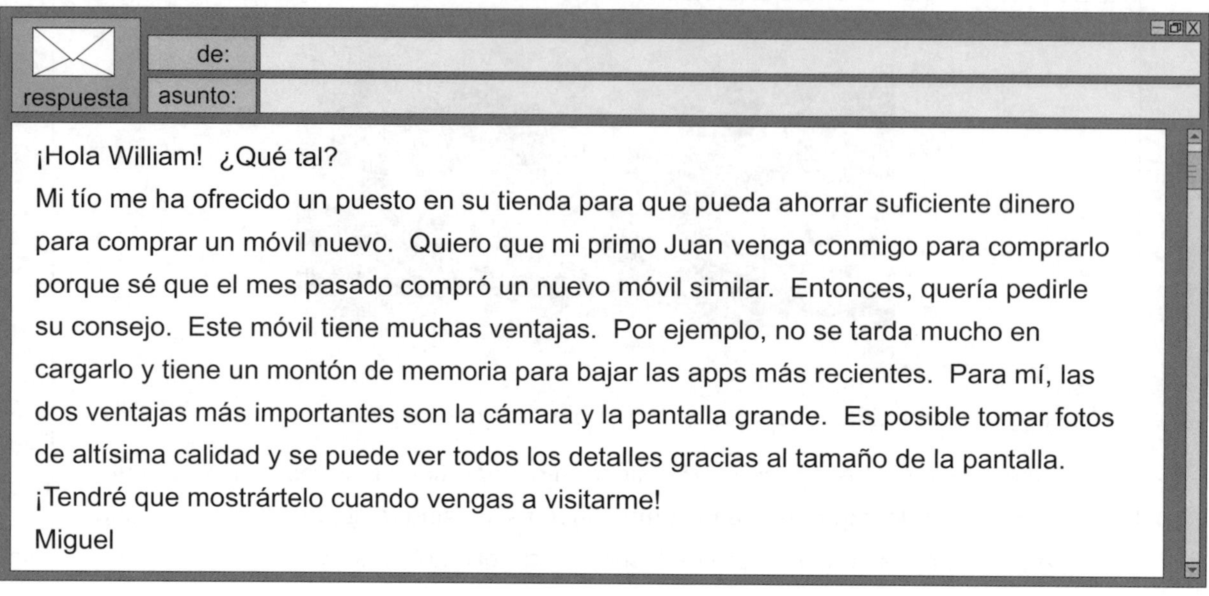

19 How does Miguel plan to get enough money to buy the new phone?

.... *[1 mark]*

20 Why does Miguel want Juan to come with him when he buys the phone?

.... *[1 mark]*

21 According to Miguel, what are the **two** most important advantages of the new phone?

1...

2... *[2 marks]*

22 What does Miguel want to do when William comes to visit him?

.... *[1 mark]*

Future study and work

You see this article about study and work options available to students.

Después de terminar sus exámenes finales, la mayoría de los alumnos no saben cuál será el próximo paso. En el pasado, mucha gente entraba directamente en el mundo laboral. Pocas personas iban a la universidad, pero ahora es mucho más común tomar esta opción. Hoy hay muchas carreras universitarias que puedes eligir y es más sencillo encontrar una que te interesa. O si no quieres continuar con la educación formal, puedes hacer la formación profesional. Así consigues otro tipo de calificación* con la cual podrás solicitar puestos de trabajo en varias empresas. Otra opción sería buscar un trabajo y ganar un salario desde el momento en que terminas la escuela.

calificación = qualification

23 According to the article, what problem do students often face after their final exams?

.... *[1 mark]*

24 What did most people used to do after leaving school?

.... *[1 mark]*

25 What are students more likely to do nowadays?

.... *[1 mark]*

26 What does the article say is easier to do now?

.... *[1 mark]*

27 What other options for post-16 education does the article list? Give **two** details.

1...

2... *[2 marks]*

Film reviews

While on holiday in Spain, you decide to go to the cinema.

You read these film reviews in a magazine.

El castillo	Generalmente, me gustan las películas de terror. Sin embargo, encontré esta película muy aburrida. Era demasiada larga y no había bastante acción para mantener mi interés.
Los soldados perdidos	Para las personas que les gustan las películas históricas, les recomiendo esta obra maravillosa. La actuación crea un ambiente increíble. ¡No hay otra película igual!
Hay un caballo en mi jardín	Tenía muchas ganas de ver esta película, pero es decepcionante. Mis amigos me dijeron que era graciosa, pero había algunos aspectos muy tristes, lo que me molestó.
Ahora sin ti	Esta película cuenta la historia de un anciano que debe acostumbrarse a la vida sin su mujer. Aunque está escrita muy bien, no menciona ningún detalle sobre los eventos pasados. Eso me pareció extraño.

What opinion do they express about each film?
Write **P** for a **positive** opinion
    N for a **negative** opinion
    P + N for a **positive** and **negative** opinion.

Write the correct letter in each box.

28   El castillo

[1 mark]

29   Los soldados perdidos

[1 mark]

30   Hay un caballo en mi jardín

[1 mark]

31   Ahora sin ti

[1 mark]

Travel and society

Two people have written blog posts about how they contribute to society.

Carmen

Cuando viajé a España, intenté coger el autobús o el tren en lugar de alquilar un coche porque el transporte público produce menos contaminación. Siempre intento ser consciente del medio ambiente cuando voy de vacaciones porque a mí me importa muchísimo protegerlo. Unos dicen que es responsabilidad de los gobiernos, pero en realidad todos deberíamos ayudar a salvar la Tierra.

Nico

El año pasado fui de vacaciones a Sudamérica con mi novio. Esperábamos el autobús cuando unos chicos nos robaron. La única persona que nos ayudó fue un hombre que vivía en la calle. Mientras hablábamos con él, descubrimos lo difícil que es vivir así. Ahora ayudamos a las personas sin hogar lo máximo posible. Por ejemplo, preparamos comida para ellos y les damos ropa.

Answer these questions by writing the correct letter in each box.

32 How did Carmen make her trip to Spain more eco-friendly?

A	She hired a car.
B	She took public transport.
C	She protected local trees.

[1 mark]

33 Who does Carmen think is responsible for saving the planet?

A	Governments
B	Other people
C	Everyone

[1 mark]

34 What happened to Nico on his trip to South America?

A	He learnt about the lives of homeless people.
B	He was robbed by a homeless person.
C	He got stopped as he tried to take the bus.

[1 mark]

35 What has Nico done since he returned home?

A	Given clothes to his friends.
B	Cooked for homeless people.
C	Donated money to charity.

[1 mark]

Section B

Translation into English

---

36 Translate the following sentences into **English**.

Mi novia y yo nos prometimos mientras estábamos de vacaciones.

....

.... *[2 marks]*

Acabo de ver un documental interesante sobre el medio ambiente.

....

.... *[2 marks]*

Mis padres asistirán a la reunión con mis profesores.

....

.... *[2 marks]*

La banda ofrecía entradas gratis para sus conciertos.

....

.... *[2 marks]*

Si hay un descuento en ese portátil, lo compraré.

....

.... *[2 marks]*

END OF QUESTIONS

GCSE Spanish
Higher Tier

Centre name					
Centre number					
Candidate number					

Surname	
Other names	
Candidate signature	

Writing Paper

Time Allowed: 1 hour 15 minutes

Materials
* You will need no other materials.

Instructions
* Use black ink or black ball-point pen.
* Fill in the boxes at the top of this page.
* You must answer **three** questions.
* In **Section A**, you must answer Question 1.
* In **Section B**, you must answer **either** Question 2.1 **or** Question 2.2.
  You must only answer **one** of these questions.
* In **Section C**, you must answer **either** Question 3.1 **or** Question 3.2.
  You must only answer **one** of these questions.
* Answer all questions in **Spanish**.

Information
* The marks for questions are shown in brackets.
* The maximum mark for this paper is 50.
* You must **not** use a dictionary during the test.
* In order to score the highest marks for Question 2.1 / Question 2.2,
  you must write something about each bullet point.
* In order to score the highest marks in Question 3.1 / Question 3.2,
  you must write something about both bullet points.

Section A

Translation into Spanish

1 Translate the following sentences into **Spanish**.   *[10 marks]*

1.1 My brother and I no longer fight like before.

1.2 It's worth doing relaxing activities because they reduce stress.

1.3 Last summer my region held three festivals.

1.4 Next month my family will come to a concert at my school.

1.5 I wanted to visit the new café, but I couldn't follow the directions.

Section B

Answer **either** Question 2.1 **or** Question 2.2
You must only answer **one** of these questions.

2.1   You are writing an email to your friend about work experience.

      Write approximately **90** words in **Spanish**.

      You must write something about each bullet point.

      Mention:

- what you did on a recent work experience placement
- how you discovered the job
- what you would like to do for a job in the future.

[15 marks]

2.2   You are writing a blog post about holidays.

      Write approximately **90** words in **Spanish**.

      You must write something about each bullet point.

      Mention:

- your opinion on the best time of year to go on holiday
- what you did on your most recent holiday
- what your perfect holiday would be like.

[15 marks]

Section C

Answer **either** Question 3.1 **or** Question 3.2
You must only answer **one** of these questions.

3.1   You are writing a post on social media about technology usage.

      Write approximately **150** words in **Spanish**.

      You must write something about both bullet points.

      Mention:

- what you have used technology for recently
- how you think technology will change in the future.

[25 marks]

3.2   You are writing an article about social problems for your school's magazine.

      Write approximately **150** words in **Spanish**.

      You must write something about both bullet points.

      Mention:

- a social problem that affects people in your local area
- what you will do to help your local community.

[25 marks]

       End of test

Answers

The answers to the translation questions are sample answers only, just to give you an idea of one way to translate them. There may be different ways to translate these sentences that are also correct.

For dictation and translation questions, this symbol (|) shows where to divide the marks. There is 1 mark awarded for the first part of the text, and 1 mark awarded for the second.

Section One — General Stuff

Page 5: Numbers and Times
1) a) 17   b) 88   c) the second street on the right
2) a) A+B   b) B   c) B

Page 7: Times and Dates
2) a) yesterday   b) Bath   c) on Friday

Page 9: Questions
2) a) ¿Cuál portátil | debería comprar?
   b) ¿Con quién | bailabas?
   c) ¿Cuántos | canales de televisión hay?
   d) ¿De qué | hablas?

Page 13: Opinions
1) a) watching films at home
   b) They seem boring to him.
   c) They are sometimes silly.
2) a) i) P   ii) P+N
   b) i) N   ii) P

Page 14: Listening Questions
1) a) P+N   b) N   c) N   d) P   e) P
2) a) His friend is ill.
   b) There are no tickets left for the next flight.
   c) 4:45 pm
   d) 132 euros

Page 16: Reading Questions
1) a) A   b) B   c) A
2) a) on the second floor   b) It's easier to listen to the teacher.

Page 17: Writing Questions
1) a) media   b) es
2) a) Necesitan comprar | la comida para la fiesta.
   b) Debe responder | a mi madre hoy.
   c) ¿A qué hora deberíamos salir | para la fiesta?
   d) Acabo de organizar un evento | para el doce de diciembre.

Section Two — Identity and Relationships with Others

Page 25: My Family and Friends
2) a) three
   b) They enjoy the same activities.
   c) her dad, his wife and her stepbrother
   d) They're the same age and have the same birthday.

Page 27: Describing People
1) a) B   b) A   c) C   d) D

Page 29: Relationships and Partnerships
1) a) A   b) B
2) a) C   b) C

Page 30: Listening Questions
1) a) B   b) A   c) C
2) a) A   b) A + B   c) B

Page 32: Reading Questions
1) a) 18 years old   b) Alejandro   c) his parents
2) a) Luisa is very good-looking. | She has blue eyes.
   b) I get on better with my younger brother | than my older sister.
   c) We will be happy if our parents | allow us to have a pet.
   d) Before getting married, | my grandparents didn't live together.
   e) When I am an adult, | I will be tolerant and understanding.

Page 33: Writing Questions
1) a) es   b) serios
3) a) Tiene dos hermanos | y una hermana.
   b) Tengo un abuelo inglés | y una abuela francesa.
   c) Mis amigos y yo nos animamos | y nos apoyamos.
   d) Siempre se sentirá orgulloso | de ser transgénero.
   e) Practicábamos el español | con nuestros familiares argentinos.

Section Three — Healthy Living and Lifestyle

Page 37: Food
1) a) fat or sugar
   b) vegetables
   c) There aren't many dishes without meat at restaurants.

Page 39: Healthy and Unhealthy Living
2) a) It's as dangerous as taking drugs.
   b) not knowing where you are
      not knowing how much you've drunk
   c) They drank too much and had to go to hospital.

Page 41: Illnesses and Treatments
2) a) Water got into his tent on a camping trip.
   b) If he feels worse than when he returned home.
   c) He feels very cold.
   d) Any two from:
      Drink hot drinks.
      Try to relax.
      Wear more clothes if you're cold.
      When you go to bed, try to breathe slowly and deeply.

Page 42: Listening Questions
1) a) C, 2   b) A, 3
2) a) B   b) C   c) B

Page 44: Reading Questions
1) a) B   b) C   c) E
2) a) A vast number of people struggle with excess weight.
   b) Any two from:
      consumption of alcohol
      a lack of knowledge about healthy food
      a tendency to do little exercise
   c) Encourage the government to take measures to help people change bad habits.

Page 45: Writing Questions
2) a) Quiero ser vegetariano/a | en el futuro.
   b) Prepara un bocadillo | con jamón y tomate.
   c) Mis amigos dicen que | el ejercicio es relajante.
   d) Cuando mi padre estaba enfermo, | perdió mucho peso.
   e) No tomaría drogas nunca | porque hay demasiados riesgos.

Section Four — Education

Page 51: School Life
1) a) 9:20   b) 10:30   c) 13:30
2) a) 800
   b) You can find everything you need there.
   c) enormous
   d) It's very dirty.

Page 53: School Pressures and Difficulties
2) a) C & D   b) B & C

Page 54: Listening Questions
1) a) La informática | es práctica.
   b) Me gusta estudiar | esa asignatura.
   c) Ayer estudié | una selección de literatura.
   d) Siempre intento | prestar atención en el aula.
2) a) Not a problem: D   Needs to improve: E
   b) Not a problem: C   Needs to improve: B
   c) Not a problem: F   Needs to improve: A

Page 56: Reading Questions
1) a) A   b) C   c) A
2) a) N   b) P+N   c) N   d) P+N

Page 57: Writing Questions

2) a) El director era | muy serio.
   b) Repasamos | en la biblioteca.
   c) Debo estudiar el inglés | porque es obligatorio.
   d) Mi amiga va a estudiar | en un instituto privado.
   e) Estudiaba | muchos idiomas diferentes.

Section Five — Future Study and Work

Page 63: Career Choices and Ambitions

2) a) M   b) H   c) P

Page 64: Listening Questions

1) a) N   b) P+N   c) P   d) P+N
2) a) A   b) B   c) A

Page 66: Reading Questions

1) a) They could continue their studies.
   b) Someone who prefers practical subjects.
   c) They would spend more time in the workplace than at school.
2) a) D   b) A   c) B

Page 67: Writing Questions

1) Here are some examples of sentences you could have written:
   Es un hospital.
   Hay un grupo de médicos.
   Una médica está hablando.
2) a) Quiero estudiar | español.
   b) Llevó un traje | a la oficina ayer.
   c) Quisiera solicitar | el puesto de periodista.
   d) Mi hermana montó un negocio | porque es empresaria.
   e) Ayudaban a su padre | en su tienda de flores.

Section Six — Free-time Activities

Page 71: Cinema and TV

1) a) No le gusta nada | el cine.
   b) Recomiendo muchas películas | a mis amigos.
   c) Dijo que los personajes | hicieron cosas tontas.
   d) La escena al final de la película | era muy triste.
2) a) A   b) B

Page 72: Music

1) a) It's very quick to download songs. / It costs less than buying music
      in a shop.
   b) Live music is always wonderful.
   c) Travelling around the world to give concerts.

Page 75: Going Out and Other Hobbies

1) a) The menu has a lot of variety. | I want to try a Chinese dish.
   b) The admission tickets are free | for small children.
   c) Reading newspapers is boring | and the articles can be very strange.

Page 76: Listening Questions

1) a) F   b) A   c) D
2) a) reading
   b) drawing
   c) Free time is for doing nothing.
   d) It allows them to exercise and enjoy themselves too.
   e) Play in an orchestra.

Page 78: Reading Questions

1) a) I can't stand basketball | because it is boring.
   b) Some activities can be | difficult and dangerous.
   c) Our school won | the football tournament.
   d) Three of my friends are going to be | part of the swimming team.
2) a) B   b) A   c) A+B

Page 79: Writing Questions

2) a) Me encantan los concursos | porque son divertidos.
   b) Le gusta cantar | mientras pinta.
   c) Quisiera pagar | la cuenta, por favor.
   d) En mi opinión, | la obra era fatal.
   e) La selección jugará | su primer partido mañana.

Section Seven — Customs, Festivals and Celebrations

Page 85: Customs and Festivals

2) a) la Tomatina, event
   b) spring, parades / processions

Page 86: Listening Questions

1) a) A   b) C   c) Spending time with her family
2) a) A + B   b) A   c) A + B   d) A

Page 88: Reading Questions

1) a) P   b) P   c) N   d) P
2) a) I love fireworks | even though they make a lot of noise.
   b) My brother tricks me all the time, | even on my birthday.
   c) We will not invite | many people to our wedding.
   d) The locals have been celebrating | this tradition for three centuries.

Page 89: Writing Questions

1) Here are some examples of sentences you could have written:
   Es una plaza de toros.
   La gente mira la corrida.
   El toro corre.
3) a) ¿Con quién | vas a pasar la Navidad?
   b) Acabo de ver | un espectáculo en Las Fallas.
   c) El año pasado pasamos | la Nochevieja en España.
   d) Cada diciembre mis amigos vienen conmigo | a un evento
      de la Nochebuena.

Section Eight — Celebrity Culture

Page 93: Favourite Celebrities

1) a) He loves cinema and how movies are made.
   b) The director is also a musician. /
      The director writes the songs for her films.
   c) She always wears unique clothing. /
      She has long hair. /
      She has blue hair. /
      She has brown eyes.
   d) She went back to her neighbourhood to help collect rubbish
      from the streets.

Page 95: Celebrity Life

2) a) B   b) A   c) A

Page 96: Listening Questions

1) a) P   b) P + N   c) N   d) P
2) a) El modelo es | bastante popular.
   b) Esa influencer gana | mucho dinero.
   c) El público los criticó | por su comportamiento.
   d) Mañana emitirán una entrevista | con el deportista.

Page 98: Reading Questions

1) a) A (Álex)   b) E (Elena)   c) D (David)
2) a) N   b) P   c) F   d) F

Page 99: Writing Questions

1) a) sigo   b) rico   c) ha
3) a) Sigo a mi autor favorito | desde hace dos años.
   b) Cuando éramos más jóvenes, | queríamos formar una banda.
   c) Lo mejor de ser una estrella | es tener muchos aficionados.
   d) En mi opinión, no vale la pena | ser famoso.

Section Nine — Travel and Tourism

Page 103: Where to Go

1) a) B   b) B   c) A

Page 105: Accommodation and Travel

1) a) by train
   b) It's cheaper than travelling by plane. /
      It's more comfortable than travelling by bus.
   c) a flat
   d) Any two from:
      It has a kitchen.
      It has a nice balcony.
      It's close to the station.
2) a) Nuestro hotel | no tiene ascensor.
   b) Los turistas tienen | dos maletas y una mochila.
   c) Una habitación de lujo | cuesta mucho dinero.
   d) Habrá muchos retrasos | en el aeropuerto.
   e) Espero que la vista | sea maravillosa.

Page 107: Getting Around and What to Do

2) a) in the north of Spain
   b) a beautiful cathedral
      various museums
   c) going for a stroll through the streets.

236

Page 108: Listening Questions

1) a) February
   b) because he has never done it before
   c) visit historic places
2) a) A + B   b) B   c) A   d) B

Page 110: Reading Questions

1) a) on the bus
   b) there was a lot of traffic
   c) because of bad weather
2) a) to the mountains
   b) riding a bike through the mountains
      swimming in natural lakes
   c) The sense of adventure that you feel from being outdoors all day.

Page 111: Writing Questions

2) a) Organiza un viaje | al extranjero.
   b) El viaje en metro | costó cinco euros.
   c) Mi tía alquiló un barco | para la excursión.
   d) Si regresas en tren, | habrá un retraso.
   e) Viajaríamos en coche, | pero tardaría mucho tiempo.

Section Ten — Media and Technology

Page 115: Technology

1) a) P + N   b) N   c) N   d) P

Page 117: The Internet

2) a) Spending time outside.
      Doing exercise.
   b) Being able to get information quickly
   c) Someone could steal your data.
   d) Some of them look real.

Page 119: Social Media

2) a) her parents
   b) To talk with her friends
   c) It annoys her having to wait a long time for a response.

Page 120: Listening Questions

1) a) Doing his homework / Buying games
   b) People can steal your information.
   c) Websites that communicate false information
   d) It makes it difficult to know what you should believe.
2) a) A, 4   b) D, 2   c) C, 1

Page 122: Reading Questions

1) a) They are really slow.
   b) to send homework to teachers
   c) to share school news (with parents)
2) a) P   b) N   c) N

Page 123: Writing Questions

2) a) Veo vídeos | en las redes sociales.
   b) Me gusta bajar música | en mi móvil.
   c) Deberían cambiar sus contraseñas | si no son seguras.
   d) Compré un dispositivo con mejor memoria | para guardar más fotos.
   e) Mi amigo no responde a los mensajes | hasta el día siguiente,
      lo cual me molesta.

Section Eleven — Where People Live

Page 127: At Home

2) a) B   b) A   c) B

Page 129: The Local Area

2) a) There isn't much to do in his region.
   b) They charge a lot for their products.
   c) There are some marvellous buildings. /
      The art museum in his town is very interesting.

Page 131: Directions and Weather

1) a) B   b) C   c) D   d) A
2) a) La casa de mi amigo no está | muy lejos de la mía.
   b) Preguntaremos por | el camino correcto.
   c) El otoño pasado | apenas llovió.
   d) Las temperaturas frías | son las mejores.

Page 132: Listening Questions

1) a) B   b) C   c) B
2) a) her parents
   b) Taking out the rubbish because it seems disgusting to her.
   c) tidy the living room / wash the dishes / clean the bathroom
   d) If chores are shared, both he and his mum have time to relax. /
      He's learnt a lot about adult life.

Page 134: Reading Questions

1) a) H   b) S   c) E
2) a) C   b) B   c) E

Page 135: Writing Questions

1) a) vive   b) cómodo   c) está
3) a) Siempre me visto | rápidamente.
   b) Mi casa ideal tendría | arte en cada cuarto.
   c) Anda hacia el banco y | luego cruza la calle.
   d) Lo peor de mi región es que | siempre hace mal tiempo.

Section Twelve — The Environment and Social Issues

Page 140: Environmental Impacts

1) a) Building more industrial zones | increases the use of energy.
   b) Air pollution can cause | serious illnesses.
   c) We have lost many species | due to the damage caused to forests.
   d) According to various recent studies, | the climate is changing.

Page 141: Protecting the Environment

1) a) i) Collect rubbish from the beach
      ii) It's important to protect the species of the sea.
   b) i) To walk or cycle to school
      ii) People should turn their lights off when they're not using them.

Page 143: Social Issues

2) a) poverty, initiatives
   b) discrimination, opportunities

Page 144: Listening Questions

1) a) increased, scientists
   b) against, factories
   c) crops, fires
2) a) The big difference between the rich and poor.
   b) The rich don't have to worry about money.
      The poor don't have enough money to buy food for their families.
   c) The prices of food and clothing should go down.
   d) The government should increase taxes for the very rich.

Page 146: Reading Questions

1) a) Pollution destroys | nature.
   b) You must pick up | and recycle your rubbish.
   c) I would like to do something | to reduce hunger in my country.
   d) We should act if we want | to develop a fairer society.
2) a) B   b) C   c) B

Page 147: Writing Questions

2) a) Podemos hacer cambios | para mejorar la sociedad.
   b) Cada mes ayudo a | limpiar las calles en mi pueblo.
   c) Muchas especies no sobrevivirán | si la contaminación aumenta.
   d) Vale la pena reducir la cantidad | de plástico y vidrio que utilizas.
   e) Para mí, la igualdad es | la preocupación social más importante.

Section Thirteen — Nouns, Articles and Linking Words

Page 151: Nouns

1) el zapato — los zapatos
2) la camisa — las camisas
3) la tradición — las tradiciones
4) el color — los colores
5) la vez — las veces
6) la mitad — las mitades
7) el monte — los montes
8) la dificultad — las dificultades
9) el ciudadano — los ciudadanos
10) la huelga — las huelgas
11) la impresión — las impresiones
12) el siglo — los siglos

Page 152: Forming Nouns
1) Me gusta comer la comida mexicana.
2) El francés es un idioma divertido.
3) Fumar está prohibido.
4) Los españoles son simpáticos.
5) No disfruto de ser famoso/a.
6) Alquilar un coche es caro.

Page 153: Articles
1) Comí un bocadillo de pollo.
2) El agua corre rápido.
3) Es profesora de inglés.
4) Quiere unas patatas fritas.
5) Juego al baloncesto los jueves.
6) Tardó unas horas.

Page 154: Subject Pronouns
1) ellos
2) ustedes
3) ellos
4) vosostros
5) él
6) nosotras
7) ella
8) él

Page 155: Object Pronouns
1) the window — la ventana   **La** rompe.
2) the water — el agua (f)   **La** bebo.
3) **Le** compró una falda.
4) **Les** enviaré un correo electrónico.
5) to you (inf., pl.) — os   **Os** di el gato.
6) to us — nos   **Nos** dijo el secreto.

Page 157: More Pronouns
1) What is your favourite colour?
2) the film that I saw yesterday
3) Have you eaten something?
4) That isn't true.
5) Yours is here.
6) I cooked for you.
7) They would go with you.
8) I will want that (thing).

Page 158: Prepositions
1) Hablamos sobre el tiempo.
2) El tren va hasta España.
3) Lo vi en la pared.
4) Son de Valencia.
5) El perro corrió hacia mí.
6) Vivo fuera de la ciudad.

Page 159: Prepositions with Verbs and Nouns
1) He/She organised a party without telling me.
2) They're doing the task again.
3) He/She has stopped smoking.
4) I play in order to win.
5) I will close the door before going out.
6) I'm trying to drink more water.

Page 160: 'Por', 'Para' and the Personal 'a'
1) The train for Paris is arriving now.
2) I'll do it for tomorrow.
3) The exit is around here.
4) I was walking through the countryside.
5) They were keeping it for their children.
6) They rarely used to go out because of the heat.
7) No, the personal 'a' isn't needed.
8) Yes, the personal 'a' is needed because there's a word for a human being ('gente') after the verb.
9) No, the personal 'a' isn't needed.
10) Yes, the personal 'a' is needed because there's a word for a human being ('abuelo') after the verb.
11) Yes, the personal 'a' is needed because there's a word for a pet ('las mascotas') after the verb.
12) No, the personal 'a' isn't needed.

Page 161: Conjunctions
1) La geografía es divertida, pero es dura.
2) Me gusta la historia porque es fácil.
3) Como estoy enfermo/a, me quedaré en casa.
4) Si hace calor, voy a la playa.
5) Hablo francés e italiano.
6) ¿Prefieres azul o verde?

Section Fourteen — Adjectives and Adverbs

Page 165: Adjectives
1) el perro feliz
2) una ensalada vegana
3) el coche azul
4) una botella reciclable
5) la hermana alemana
6) un problema evitable
7) El grupo está cansado.
8) ¿Ella está lista?

Page 167: More Adjectives
1) el primer día
2) pocos productos
3) cada familia
4) ningún plato
5) sus libros
6) esas películas
7) El bolígrafo es mío.
8) aquella manzana

Page 168: Comparative and Superlative Adjectives
1) Esta página es más fácil.
2) Soy tan alto como mi padre.
3) Faiza es mayor que Emilio.
4) Los libros son mejores que las películas.
5) Hoy es el peor día.
6) Ella es la menor.

Page 169: Adverbs
1) positivamente — positively
2) directamente — directly
3) socialmente — socially
4) diferentemente — differently
5) exactamente — exactly
6) perfectamente — perfectly
7) posiblemente — possibly
8) tradicionalmente — traditionally
9) evidentemente — evidently
10) estrictamente — strictly
11) nacionalmente — nationally
12) efectivamente — effectively

Page 170: Adverbs and Adverbial Phrases
1) Mis zapatos están aquí.
2) Quiero salir ahora.
3) A veces viajo.
4) Vivimos lejos.
5) Por fin puedo dormir.
6) La tienda está allí.

Page 171: Comparative and Superlative Adverbs
1) Wafa come más rápidamente que yo.
2) Yo pinto mejor que ella.
3) Luis baila tan bien como tú.
4) Alba es la que habla más tranquilamente.
5) Ellos son los que mejor conducen.
6) Inoke es el que peor corre.

Page 172: Quantifiers and Intensifiers
1) Hay demasiados gatos aquí.
2) Es bastante interesante.
3) Tengo muchos amigos.
4) Hablan tan rápidamente.
5) Es un libro muy bueno.
6) Hay una playa buenísima.

Section Fifteen — Verbs and Tenses

Page 175: Verbs in the Present Tense
1) bailo   3) discuten   5) aprende   7) escribes
2) bebemos   4) rompen   6) nadáis   8) visitan

Page 177: Irregular Verbs in the Present Tense
1) **Comienza** a las tres.
2) **Queremos** leche.
3) Yo **doy** el libro a Lola.
4) **Puedes** conducir.
5) **Repiten** las direcciones.
6) **Pienso** que es importante.
7) Vengo a la fiesta también.
8) Vamos allí mañana.
9) Me visto rápidamente.
10) No tengo bolígrafo.
11) Los estudiantes tienen hambre.
12) La reconozco de la película.

Page 178: 'Ser' and 'Estar' in the Present Tense
1) **Está** muy enojado hoy.
2) Siempre **es** trabajador.
3) **Somos** de Hull.
4) **Estoy** en Bradford.
5) **Es** mi hermano.
6) Mi padre **es** médico.

Page 179: The Preterite Tense
1) viniste   3) di   5) pidió
2) cenaron   4) fue   6) jugué

Page 180: The Imperfect Tense
1) cantabas   3) aprendía   5) estaba   7) volvían   9) éramos
2) decía   4) nadaba   6) tenías   8) seguíais   10) iban

Page 181: Using the Past Tenses
1) Ha viajado a España.
2) Ha corrido quinientos metros.
3) Han terminado la prueba.
4) ¿Has comido ya?
5) Hemos escrito una carta.
6) Han vuelto a casa.

Page 182: The Future Tenses
1) vas a hacer, harás
2) va a tener, tendrá
3) va a bailar, bailará
4) voy a dar, daré
5) vas a poder, podrás
6) voy a jugar, jugaré
7) van a poner, pondrán
8) vamos a venir, vendremos
9) vamos a querer, querremos
10) vais a vivir, viviréis
11) va a decir, dirá
12) vais a saber, sabréis

Page 183: The Conditional
1) iría   4) hablaría   7) diríais   10) sabrían
2) cantaría   5) haría   8) vendríamos
3) pondrías   6) pediría   9) querrían

Page 184: Modal Verbs
1) You have to revise for the test.
2) Juanjo doesn't know how to speak Spanish.
3) Can they / you come to the wedding?
4) We have to listen well.
5) I don't want to return home.
6) I would like to pay the bill.

Page 185: Reflexive Verbs and Pronouns
1) me llamo   3) se siente   5) os ponéis   7) nos vestimos
2) te llevas   4) se despierta   6) se levantan   8) me acuesto

Page 187: Verbs with '-ing' and 'Just Done'
1) estás trayendo
2) está abriendo
3) están diciendo
4) estáis corriendo
5) estamos bailando
6) estoy leyendo
7) están sirviendo
8) está siguiendo
9) Estaba pidiendo una naranja.
10) Estaba estudiando en mi habitación.
11) El gato estaba durmiendo.
12) Estaba trabajando bien.
13) Acaban de ver la película.
14) Acabamos de comer el desayuno.

Page 188: Negative Forms
1) No fuimos a la biblioteca.
2) No tienen ninguna manzana. / No tienen ningunas manzanas.
3) No hay nada aquí.
4) Nadie está en el coche. / No está nadie en el coche.
5) No es ni rojo ni verde.
6) Ya no vamos al gimnasio.

Page 189: Impersonal Verbs and the Passive
1) Se puede descansar ahora.
2) Hay que hacer ejercicio.
3) Se necesita ir a clase.
4) Hay muchas fiestas.
5) Vale la pena aprender este contenido.
6) Parece una idea maravillosa.

Page 190: The Subjunctive
1) You need the normal present tense 'viene'.
2) You need the present subjunctive 'sea' — it follows 'para que', which is used to express purpose.
3) You need the normal present tense 'tiene'.
4) You need the present subjunctive 'sea' — it follows a phrase that expresses an emotion.
5) You need the normal present tense 'va'.
6) You need the present subjunctive 'haga' — it follows a phrase that expresses necessity.

Page 191: The Imperative
1) ¡Canta esta canción!
2) ¡Ve a tu habitación!
3) ¡Escribe dos frases!
4) ¡Tómalo!
5) ¡Di algo!
6) ¡Bebe el agua!
7) ¡Aprended estas palabras!
8) ¡Firmad este documento!
9) ¡Esperad aquí, por favor!
10) ¡Comprad eso ahora!
11) ¡Haced vuestras camas!
12) ¡Cruzad la calle!

Practice Exam — Higher Listening Paper

Section A (Listening comprehension) — Mark Scheme

Question Number	Answer	Marks
1	A	[1 mark]
2	B	[1 mark]
3	A + B	[1 mark]
4	A	[1 mark]
5	talent, followers	[2 marks]
6	pressure, influence	[2 marks]
7	Her parents separated.	[1 mark]
8	She didn't have enough time to revise.	[1 mark]
9	Revise in their classrooms after class.	[1 mark]
10	Call her and ask if they can help her.	[1 mark]
11.1	B	[1 mark]
11.2	C	[1 mark]
12.1	C	[1 mark]
12.2	A	[1 mark]
13.1	P	[1 mark]
13.2	N	[1 mark]
14.1	P	[1 mark]
14.2	P + N	[1 mark]
15	In the main square	[1 mark]
16	The chicken and orange salad	[1 mark]
17	It smelt like the sea.	[1 mark]
18	There would be a more relaxing atmosphere.	[1 mark]
19	4 and P	[2 marks]
20	2 and F	[2 marks]
21	B	[1 mark]
22	C	[1 mark]
23	B	[1 mark]
24	C	[1 mark]
25.1	E	[1 mark]
25.2	D	[1 mark]
26.1	B	[1 mark]
26.2	F	[1 mark]
27.1	C	[1 mark]
27.2	A	[1 mark]
28.1	A	[1 mark]
28.2	B	[1 mark]

Section B (Dictation) — Mark Scheme

The dictation section of the Listening Exam is assessed based on two criteria — 'Communication of meaning' (5 marks) and 'Transcription and grammatical accuracy' (5 marks). The maximum mark for Section B is 10. Using the mark schemes below, consider the 5 dictation sentences as a whole and award a mark out of 5 for 'Communication of meaning' and a mark out of 5 for 'Transcription and grammatical accuracy', to give an overall mark out of 10.

- A mark of zero for 'Communication of meaning' automatically results in a mark of zero for 'Transcription and grammatical accuracy', but apart from that, the two marks are not related.
- Occasional minor errors in transcription do not stop you from getting a top level mark for 'Transcription and grammatical accuracy'; perfection is not required.

Marks	Communication of meaning
5	The meaning of the spoken extracts is communicated very clearly throughout.
4	The meaning of the spoken extracts is almost always communicated clearly.
3	The meaning of the spoken extracts is mostly communicated.
2	The meaning of the spoken extracts is sometimes communicated.
1	The meaning of the spoken extracts is rarely communicated.
0	The meaning of the spoken extracts is not communicated.

Marks	Transcription and grammatical accuracy
5	Words are always or nearly always transcribed correctly with a very high level of grammatical accuracy.
4	Words are frequently transcribed correctly with a good level of grammatical accuracy.
3	Words are generally transcribed correctly with a reasonable level of grammatical accuracy.
2	Words are occasionally transcribed correctly with a limited level of grammatical accuracy.
1	Words are very rarely transcribed correctly with a very limited level of grammatical accuracy.
0	Words are not transcribed correctly and there is almost no grammatical accuracy.

Below are the dictation sentences for this exam:

Sentence 1 Nos reunimos | para celebrar | la Tomatina.
Sentence 2 Recibiste | muchas tarjetas | para tu cumpleaños.
Sentence 3 Mi hermana | me perdonó | por molestarla.
Sentence 4 Destruir los bosques | pone varias especies | en peligro.
Sentence 5 Las iniciativas | protegerán los derechos | de la población. *[10 marks]*

Total marks for Listening Paper: 50

You'll find mark schemes for the Speaking and Writing papers on p.242 and p.243.

Practice Exam — Higher Speaking Paper

Role-play sample answer

1) Tenemos tres clases por la mañana y el recreo empieza a las once.

2) En mi clase de español de la semana pasada aprendimos sobre los festivales españoles, incluso las Fallas en Valencia.

3) Mi asignatura favorita son las matemáticas porque es divertido trabajar con los números.

4) En mi colegio está prohibido beber zumo en clase. Esta regla me molesta porque no me gusta el agua.

5) ¿Qué piensas sobre llevar uniforme en el colegio?

Reading aloud task sample answer

1) En casa prefiero preparar comida china. El plato favorito de mis padres y mío es el pollo a la naranja que servimos con arroz. También es divertido hacer caramelos, pero intento no hacerlos con mucha frecuencia porque no son muy saludables.

2) Para mantenerme en forma, los sábados voy a clases de natación con mis hermanos. Cuando hace buen tiempo camino al colegio. Además, me gusta pasear al perro y hago yoga en el jardín.

3) Sin buena salud mental, puedes sufrir mucho en la vida diaria. El estrés puede afectar a tus emociones, tu confianza e incluso a tus relaciones con los demás. Por eso, es importantísimo buscar ayuda si la necesitas.

4) En mi opinión, el alcohol es bastante peligroso porque puede causar problemas de salud graves. Conozco a un amigo de mi familia que tuvo que ir al hospital porque bebía demasiado. Estaba muy enfermo. Debido a esto, creo que cuando sea mayor no beberé alcohol. No vale la pena probarlo.

Photo card sample answer

Photo 1: En la primera foto, un grupo de personas celebra una boda. Puedes ver al novio y a la novia. La novia lleva un vestido y flores. Todos los hombres visten trajes y un hombre camina con la novia.

Photo 2: La segunda foto muestra una fiesta de cumpleaños. El grupo celebra la fiesta en casa. Un hombre da un regalo a una mujer que está sentada. Hay platos y bebidas en la mesa y el grupo ha comido.

1) La celebración que más me gusta es la Nochevieja porque me encanta ver los fuegos artificiales. Los veo cada año con mis amigos. Siempre organizamos una fiesta y nos divertimos mucho.

2) Cuando salgo con mis amigos, me gusta ir al cine. Lo mejor de ir al cine es poder charlar juntos sobre una película después de verla. También me encanta visitar tiendas de ropa para ver artículos nuevos.

3) Para mi último cumpleaños, mis amigos me organizaron una fiesta sorpresa. Nos reunimos en el jardín de mi amigo para comer y luego me regalaron una camiseta bonita y un libro. Después, jugamos a mi videojuego favorito e hicimos karaoke. Lo pasé bien.

4) Una ventaja de ser famoso es conseguir muchos premios por tu trabajo. Sin embargo, la mejor ventaja es poder utilizar tu influencia para cambiar vidas y animar a otras personas a ser buenos ciudadanos.

5) En mi tiempo libre me gusta ver documentales y escuchar música. Voy a conciertos con mis amigos varias veces al año. Además, cuando hace buen tiempo, me encanta ir de camping con mi padre.

6) Mi famosa favorita es actriz. Es muy graciosa pero también destaca en papeles serios. Recientemente ha organizado varias campañas para salvar los teatros públicos, lo que me parece estupendo. Gracias a ella, me gustaría ser actriz después de terminar mis estudios.

Practice Exam — Higher Writing Paper

Section A — Sample answers

1.1 Mi hermano y yo ya no peleamos como antes.

1.2 Vale la pena hacer actividades relajantes porque reducen el estrés.

1.3 El verano pasado mi región celebró tres fiestas.

1.4 El mes que viene mi familia vendrá a un concierto en mi colegio.

1.5 Quería visitar el nuevo café, pero no podía seguir las direcciones.

Section B

Q2.1 — Sample answer

Acabo de terminar una experiencia laboral de dos semanas en una empresa de tecnología. Tuve la oportunidad de trabajar con equipos diferentes. Vi en qué consiste el papel de director y escuché las llamadas de los clientes. Además, pude probar dispositivos nuevos, lo que fue muy divertido. Descubrí el puesto porque mi tío trabaja para la misma empresa y me lo recomendó. Aunque esta experiencia laboral me permitió ganar muchos conocimientos nuevos, aprendí que no me gustaría trabajar en un ambiente de oficina. Mi plan para el futuro es ser artista.

Q2.2 — Sample answer

En mi opinión, la mejor época del año para ir de vacaciones es el verano porque suele hacer mejor tiempo. Puedes tomar el sol y puedes olvidarte del colegio y relajarte mucho. Recientemente fui de vacaciones con mi familia a Madrid. Nos quedamos en un hotel agradable. Vimos el Estadio Santiago Bernabéu y visitamos un parque temático que me encantó. Incluso probé el gazpacho, pero desafortunadamente pensé que era asqueroso. Para mí, las vacaciones perfectas serían en Australia. Visitaría el puente del puerto de Sídney y estaría en la playa todos los días.

Section C

Q3.1 — Sample answer

Recientemente, he usado mucho la tecnología en mi tiempo libre. Anoche vi una película de acción en mi tableta y luego jugué a videojuegos con mi hermano. La semana pasada, usé el móvil para llamar a mis amigos y colgar fotos en las redes sociales. Esta semana he utilizado mi portátil para hacer investigaciones para un proyecto y he enviado unos correos electrónicos a mi profesor. Pienso que en el futuro veremos grandes cambios de tecnología. La inteligencia artificial es una parte de la tecnología que ya ha crecido rápidamente y me parece que tendrá una mayor influencia en la sociedad. Además, creo que aparecerán dispositivos nuevos para hacer la vida diaria más fácil, sobre todo en el entorno laboral. Por ejemplo, las empresas podrían utilizar la tecnología para hacer las tareas aburridas que a los empleados no les gustan. En mi opinión el mundo digital se mezclará más con el mundo real.

Q3.2 — Sample answer

Un problema social que afecta a la gente de mi barrio, sobre todo a los ancianos, es la soledad. En este momento muchas personas mayores viven solas y algunas no tienen familiares o amigos para ayudarles con las tareas diarias. Les resulta difícil salir solos, y por eso eligen quedarse en casa. Como consecuencia, pueden sufrir una gran soledad. Para apoyar a la comunidad local, querría ayudar a una organización que lucha contra la soledad. Organiza actividades en grupo en las que los ancianos pueden reunirse y conocer a otra gente. Además, el próximo mes voy a comenzar un trabajo en un banco de alimentos local los fines de semana. Espero ayudar a más personas que necesitan apoyo para obtener los alimentos básicos. Finalmente, como hay un problema de contaminación en mi barrio, ayudaré a limpiarlo recogiendo basura de las calles. Me gustaría tener un impacto positivo en la comunidad.

<u>Practice Exam — Higher Reading Paper</u>

Section A (Reading comprehension) — Mark Scheme

Question Number	Answer	Marks
1	E	*[1 mark]*
2	C	*[1 mark]*
3	B	*[1 mark]*
4	10 minutes	*[1 mark]*
5	when you pass the shop that sells fish	*[1 mark]*
6	Any two from: the bank; the synagogue; the library	*[2 marks]*
7	H	*[1 mark]*
8	A	*[1 mark]*
9	J	*[1 mark]*
10	L	*[1 mark]*
11	A	*[1 mark]*
12	B	*[1 mark]*
13	C	*[1 mark]*
14	C	*[1 mark]*
15	B	*[1 mark]*
16	Any two from: It contributes to good physical health. It contributes to good mental health. It's a way to fight against stress.	*[2 marks]*
17	**1.** Leave electronic devices outside the bedroom. **2.** Stop watching TV an hour before going to bed.	*[2 marks]*
18	B	*[1 mark]*
19	working in his uncle's shop	*[1 mark]*
20	Any one from: because he bought a similar phone last month, because he wants to ask for his advice.	*[1 mark]*
21	**1.** the camera **2.** the screen size	*[2 marks]*
22	show him his new phone	*[1 mark]*
23	They don't know what their next step will be.	*[1 mark]*
24	They went straight into the working world.	*[1 mark]*
25	go to university	*[1 mark]*
26	find a degree course that interests you	*[1 mark]*
27	**1.** Doing more professional training. **2.** Looking for a job right after finishing school.	*[2 marks]*
28	N	*[1 mark]*
29	P	*[1 mark]*
30	N	*[1 mark]*
31	P + N	*[1 mark]*
32	B	*[1 mark]*
33	C	*[1 mark]*
34	A	*[1 mark]*
35	B	*[1 mark]*

Section B (Translation into English) — Mark Scheme

The answers below are sample answers only, just to give you an idea of the way to translate them.

There may be different ways to translate these sentences that are also correct.

This symbol (|) denotes where to divide the marks.

There is 1 mark awarded for the first portion of the sentence, and 1 mark awarded for the second.

Below are the translation sentences for this exam:

Sentence 1 My girlfriend and I got engaged | while we were on holiday.

Sentence 2 I have just watched | an interesting documentary about the environment.

Sentence 3 My parents will attend | the meeting with my teachers.

Sentence 4 The band were offering | free admission tickets for their concerts.

Sentence 5 If there is a discount on that laptop, | I will buy it.   *[10 marks]*

Total marks for Reading Paper: 50

Higher Speaking Paper — Mark Scheme

It's very difficult to mark the practice Speaking Exam yourself because there isn't one 'right' answer for most questions. To make it easier to mark, record the exam and use a dictionary, or get someone who's really good at Spanish, to mark how well you did. Use the mark schemes below to help you, but bear in mind that they're only a rough guide. Ideally, you need a Spanish teacher who knows the AQA mark schemes well to mark it properly.

Role-play (10 marks)

In the Role-play, you'll be marked on how accurately you respond to spoken language. There are 2 marks available for each of the five questions (tasks) in the Role-play (10 marks in total). Where students are required to give two responses or details in one task, failure to convey an unambiguous message in reply to one of them means that the message is partially conveyed and one mark is awarded.

Marks	Role-play Task
2	You convey your message without ambiguity.
1	You partially convey your message with some ambiguity.
0	None of your message is conveyed.

Reading Aloud Task (15 marks)

The Reading Aloud task is divided into two parts. There are 5 marks available for reading aloud a text, and then 10 marks are available for answering four compulsory questions.

Marks	Reading the Text
5	Your pronunciation is always or nearly always accurate but there may be an occasional minor error.
4	Your pronunciation contains a few minor errors.
3	Your pronunciation contains some minor errors and very occasional major errors.
2	Your pronunciation contains minor errors and a few major errors.
1	Your pronunciation contains regular minor and some major errors.
0	Does not meet the standard required for 1 mark.

Marks	Responding to the Questions
9-10	You answer all questions clearly. At least two answers have an extended response and at least one other is developed well.
7-8	You answer at least three questions clearly. One answer has an extended response and at least one other is developed well.
5-6	You answer at least two questions clearly. One answer is developed well and at least one other is developed minimally.
3-4	You answer at least two questions understandably. One answer is developed minimally.
1-2	You answer at least one question understandably. The answer(s) may be a very limited response.
0	Does not meet the standard required for 1 mark.

Photo card (25 marks)

For the Photo Card, you're marked on three separate criteria. 5 marks are available for your response to the content of the photos on the card, whilst 20 marks are available for the unprepared conversation — 15 marks for 'communication' and 5 marks for 'grammar and vocabulary'.

Marks	Describing the Photos
5	You convey a lot of information. Information is always conveyed clearly.
4	You convey a lot of information. Information is nearly always conveyed clearly.
3	You convey quite a lot of information. Information is nearly always conveyed clearly.
2	You convey quite a lot of information. Information may lack clarity from time to time.
1	You convey some information. Information may lack clarity from time to time.
0	Does not meet the standard required for 1 mark.

Marks	Unprepared Conversation — Communication
13-15	You convey a lot of information with consistent good development and regular extended responses. Information is always or nearly always conveyed clearly.
10-12	You convey a lot of information with consistent good development and some extended responses. Information is conveyed clearly, with occasional lapses.
7-9	You convey quite a lot of information with consistent good development and occasional extended responses. Information is generally conveyed clearly.
4-6	You convey quite a lot of information with regular good development of responses. Information may lack clarity from time to time.
1-3	You convey some information with good development and regular minimal development of responses. Information may lack clarity from time to time.
0	Does not meet the standard required for 1 mark.

Marks	Unprepared Conversation — Grammar and Vocabulary
5	You use a wide variety of vocabulary and structures. You make a few minor errors but few or no major errors when you attempt more complex language.
4	You use a very good variety of vocabulary and structures. You make some minor errors and some major errors when you attempt more complex language.
3	You use a good variety of vocabulary and structures with occasional repetition. You make quite a lot of minor errors and occasional major errors, not only in attempts at more complex language.
2	You use a good variety of vocabulary and structures with some repetition. You make frequent minor errors and some major errors, even with basic language.
1	You use some variety of vocabulary and structures with regular repetition. You make frequent minor errors and some major errors in most responses to questions.
0	Does not meet the standard required for 1 mark.

Higher Writing Paper — Mark Scheme

Section A — Q1 (10 marks)

For this question, there are five sentences that you have to translate into Spanish. There are 5 marks available for 'Rendering of the original meaning' of each sentence and 5 marks for 'Grammar and vocabulary' across the five sentences as a whole.

Marks	Rendering of the original meaning	Marks	Grammar and vocabulary
5	You sufficiently render the meanings of all or nearly all of the English.	5	You show very good knowledge of vocabulary with few errors. Grammar is highly accurate and any errors that occur are only minor.
4	You sufficiently render most elements of the English.	4	You show good knowledge of vocabulary with some inappropriate or omitted items. Grammar is generally accurate but with regular minor errors.
3	You sufficiently render some elements of the English.	3	You show satisfactory knowledge of vocabulary with regular inappropriate or omitted items. Grammar is more accurate than inaccurate but with regular major and minor errors.
2	You sufficiently render the meanings of few elements of the English.	2	You show limited knowledge of vocabulary with many inappropriate or omitted items. Grammar is generally inaccurate with many major and minor errors.
1	You sufficiently render the meanings of very few elements of the English.	1	You show very limited knowledge of vocabulary with few appropriate items. Grammar is highly inaccurate with major or minor errors in all or almost all sentences.
0	You don't convey any meanings of the English.	0	Does not meet the standard required for 1 mark.

Section B — Q2 (15 marks)

For this question, there are three compulsory bullet points that you must cover — you don't need to cover the bullet points equally. There are 10 marks available for 'Communication' and 5 marks for 'Grammar and vocabulary'.

Marks	Communication	Marks	Grammar and vocabulary
9-10	You cover all three bullet points and communicate clearly. Your ideas are developed and you convey a lot of information.	5	You use a good variety of vocabulary with complex language and structures. You use all three time frames and any errors are mainly minor.
7-8	You cover all three bullet points and mostly communicate clearly. Your ideas are often developed and you convey quite a lot of information.	4	You use a variety of vocabulary and attempt to use complex language and structures. You use at least two time frames and errors are mainly minor.
5-6	You cover at least two bullet points and generally communicate clearly. You develop a few ideas and convey some information.	3	You use some variety of vocabulary and occasionally attempt complex language and structures. You try to use at least two time frames. There are regular minor errors and may be some major errors.
3-4	You cover at least one bullet point and sometimes communicate clearly. You convey little information.	2	You use a limited variety of vocabulary and use mainly simple language. You might fail to use different time frames and make regular errors.
1-2	You cover at least one bullet point. Your communication is often unclear and you convey very little information.	1	Your vocabulary is narrow and/or repetitive. You use simple language and structures. You fail to use different time frames and make frequent errors.
0	Does not meet the standard required for 1 mark.	0	Does not meet the standard required for 1 mark.

Section C — Q3 (25 marks)

For this question, there are two compulsory bullet points that you must cover — you don't need to cover the bullet points equally. There are 15 marks available for 'Communication', 5 marks for 'Range of language' and 5 marks for 'Accuracy of language'.

Marks	Communication
13-15	You convey a lot of information with very few or no lapses in clarity. Your ideas are regularly developed.
10-12	You convey quite a lot of information, and communication is mostly clear with occasional lapses in clarity. Your ideas are often developed.
7-9	You convey an adequate amount of information, and communication is usually clear with some lapses in clarity. A few of your ideas may be developed.
4-6	You convey some information, but communication is sometimes unclear with regular lapses in clarity. There is only a little development of your ideas.
1-3	You convey a limited amount of information, and communication is unclear with frequent lapses in clarity. There is very limited development of ideas.
0	Does not meet the standard required for 1 mark.

Marks	Range of language
5	You use a very good variety of appropriate vocabulary and grammatical structures with regular successful attempts at complex language.
4	You use a good variety of appropriate vocabulary and grammatical structures with regular, generally successful attempts at complex language.
3	You use some variety of appropriate vocabulary and grammatical structures with occasional, sometimes successful attempts at complex language.
2	You use a limited variety of vocabulary and grammatical structures. You often use short and simple structures but also regularly use longer sentences.
1	You use a very limited variety of appropriate vocabulary. You mainly use short and simple structures.
0	Does not meet the standard required for 1 mark.

Marks	Accuracy of language
5	Your response is usually accurate, with occasional errors in attempts at more complex structures. Your verb and tense formations are secure.
4	Your response is generally accurate, with several errors in attempts at more complex structures. Your verb and tense formations are generally correct.
3	Your response is reasonably accurate, with errors in both simple and complex structures. Your verb and tense formations are sometimes correct.
2	Your response is more inaccurate than accurate. There are frequent errors. Your verb and tense formations are often incorrect.
1	Your response is mostly inaccurate and there are errors in all sentences. Your verb and tense formations are nearly always incorrect.
0	Does not meet the standard required for 1 mark.

Index